mosaic

A Journey Across the Church of God

Books by Patrick Nachtigall
Available from Warner Press

Passport of Faith
Faith in the Future
Mosaic

mosaic
A Journey Across the Church of God

BY PATRICK NACHTIGALL

Warner Press
Anderson, Indiana

Coordinator of Publishing & Creative Services
Church of God Ministries, Inc.
PO Box 2420
Anderson, IN 46018-2420
800-848-2464
www.chog.org

To purchase additional copies of this book, to inquire about distribution, and for all other sales-related matters, please contact:

Warner Press, Inc.
PO Box 2499
Anderson, IN 46018-2499
800-741-7721
www.warnerpress.org

All Scripture quotations, unless otherwise indicated, are taken from New American Standard Bible, © Copyright 1960, 1962, 1963, 1968, 1971, 1972, 1973, 1975, 1977, 1995 by the Lockman Foundation. Used by permission.

Cover & Text design by Carolyn Frost.
Edited by Joseph D. Allison and Stephen R. Lewis.

ISBN-13: 978-1-59317-513-9

Library of Congress Cataloging-in-Publication Data

Nachtigall, Patrick, 1970-
    Mosaic : a journey across the Church of God / by Patrick Nachtigall.
        p.   cm.
    ISBN 978-1-59317-513-9 (pbk.)
    1. Church of God (Anderson, Ind.) I. Title.
    BX7026.N33 2010
    289.9--dc22   2010016638

Printed in the United States of America.

10 11 12 13 14 15 16 / EP / 10 9 8 7 6 5 4 3 2

this book is dedicated to:

Abraham Nachtigall (1868–1951)
Samuel Nachtigall (1902–1986)
Harry Nachtigall and
Marco Nachtigall

contents

acknowledgements

It is a sign of General Director Ronald Duncan's faith in God and in the people of our movement that when Joe Allison and I proposed the idea for this book, he agreed. He encouraged us to do a book that would require speaking to many people with opposing views, that would mean digging deeply into organizational and theological issues, and that would be brutally honest about the challenges we face. We proposed to go anywhere and talk to anyone—even people outside our movement. Few leaders facing the challenges that Dr. Duncan faces on a daily basis would be so gracious as to endorse this kind of study, since the results are far too unpredictable. However, Dr. Duncan is a man of integrity who firmly believes in God's call upon this movement and trusts the Holy Spirit to be our guide. During the past few years, Dr. Duncan has been constantly traveling on his own listening tour as well. So on behalf of all of us: "Thank you, Dr. Duncan."

Dr. Robert Edwards, the coordinator of Global Missions, was completely supportive of this project and allowed me to research and write this book for two years while working in China. I thank him for giving me this great opportunity from which we can all benefit.

I never intended to write a book on the Church of God, knowing full well that there are plenty of people with far greater expertise. But I am grateful that Joe Allison suggested the idea to me and then allowed me to address the issues in a unique way. Stephen Lewis and Joe were my partners through this, and the book was greatly enhanced by their insights and wisdom. I especially appreciate Stephen's friendship, which kept me sane in what ended up being a very exhausting project.

Around the world, people opened up their homes, their churches, and their lives to me. National leaders, regional administrators, pastors, and church members were candid and cooperative. I will be eternally grateful for this and am both humbled and awed by the trust they put in me. I sincerely ask for forgiveness if I have not lived up to expectations. There are so many people in the Church of God who contributed to this book that they are too numerous to mention. I will have to trust that the Lord will bless all of those who contributed to this book and made generous sacrifices.

A few people outside of the Church of God also encouraged me in this project. Dr. David Roozen and Dr. Adair Lummis at the Institute for Religious Research at Hartford Seminary listened to my reports and contributed great insight and advice. Dr. Sheldon Sorge at the Louisville Institute was very supportive as well, and Dr. Steven Lewis at the Northwest House of Theological Studies provided outsider-insider knowledge of the Church of God that was invaluable.

Presentations on the book's findings were made in Berlin, Germany, and at the Oregon State-SW Washington Campmeeting. I would like to thank Dr. Bob Edwards, Rev. Don Deena Johnson, and Rev. Doug Biesley for arranging those opportunities.

I would like to thank my son, Marco Nachtigall. I missed many boys' nights at our then-home in Hong Kong while writing this book, but my six-year-old son was very patient and understanding and made great sacrifices for this project. I am so very proud of him. Sometimes when we played football together and I seemed distracted, he would say, "Dad, stop thinking about your book." I owe him a great apology for those moments when the less important job distracted from the more important one.

Finally, I want to thank my beautiful wife, Jamie Nachtigall, who had to manage an ever-inquisitive six-year-old, all the finances and paperwork for our ministry in China and for this book, as well as taking care of everything else while I was often away from home. My wife Jamie knows more about the Church of God than I do, so her insightful comments and editing where invaluable. Never once did she complain about this project that so dominated our lives for two years. As far as I am concerned, this book is hers as much as it is mine. All the slings and arrows, however, should be directed only at me.

introduction

Is the Church of God reformation movement finished? The question is disturbing, and it is not one anyone wants to ask aloud. Nevertheless, there is great concern and even resignation in many corners of the Church of God as people ponder the future of our movement. Ever since its establishment in the late nineteenth century, the Church of God has grown throughout the world and been a force for the expansion of the kingdom of God. We produced classic hymns, talented musicians, significant radio programs, colleges that have educated tens of thousands, and churches that excelled at making people feel welcome. We have a rich Wesleyan-Holiness heritage that was expounded on by many great thinkers. Furthermore, many of us can say that our connection to the Church of God (Anderson, Indiana) spans generations. Nevertheless, our history, our heritage, and even our growth have been challenged by new forces in the global religious scene.

The truth is that for a long time in the Church of God we have known that something is wrong. A holy pride in our unique heritage has given way to indifference with some arguing that the change in our sense of identity is simply the reality of living in a post-denominational age and others suggesting that we have been theologically lax and incoherent.

As we've felt the sands shift, there have been a number of brave Church of God voices through the years willing to ask the difficult questions that needed to be asked. Most recently, historian Merle Strege has chronicled our past and challenged us about where we are headed. Dr. Gilbert Stafford has helped to articulate our theological beliefs and explore our heritage and traditions in an effort to help us see what should unite us at the crossroads where we now find ourselves. Dr. Barry Callen has recently compiled an extremely helpful book that articulates Church of God beliefs and practices in a number of key areas. Dr. Jerry Hickson has asked us to reevaluate our place within the broader evangelical movement. They and many others before them over a period of decades have covered key areas that need to be addressed by the Church of God. These have all been important pieces of the puzzle. All of them have made valuable contributions to the discussion and many of their efforts will be revisited throughout this book.[1]

I do not possess the expertise of these many fine theologians, pastors, and historians who have written extensively on the movement. I do, however, have a unique vantage point from which to see the movement, having been able to travel to a great many Church of God congregations throughout the United States and on six continents. As I have traveled and worshiped with my brothers and sisters around the world over the past three decades, I am struck by three things regarding our current situation:

1. Most people in the Church of God movement are not aware of how diverse the movement is at this point in history—this includes those in leadership throughout the world.

2. In most regions around the world, the identity *of* and the identification *with* the Church of God movement is under considerable strain.

3. The movement is filled with many wonderful ministries that are succeeding, as well as great opportunities, but most people remain unaware of this fact because of our lack of familiarity with each other and our failure to communicate and cooperate.

Objectives of the Book

What I am setting out to do in this book is to help everyone in the Church of God see the movement anew. If the Church of God movement is in decline, what does that decline look like? *Who* are we in the Church of God, and *what* are we actually doing? Perhaps if we use a bigger lens, it would help us to identify the numerous areas where we need to ask questions, not only on a local level, but on a global level. We may also find that there are many

---

1. See John W. V. Smith and Merle D. Strege, *The Quest for Holiness and Unity* 2nd ed. (Anderson, IN: Warner Press, 1980/2009); Gilbert W. Stafford, *Church of God at the Crossroads* (Anderson, IN: Warner Press, 2000); Gilbert W. Stafford, *Vision for the Church of God at the Crossroads* (Anderson, IN: Warner Press, 2002); Barry L. Callen, comp. and ed., *Following Our Lord* (Anderson, IN: Warner Press, 2008); Jerry A. Hickson, *Are You Sure You're Right?* (Anderson, IN: Warner Press, 2006).

reasons for hope instead of despair. Once we have taken a more expansive view of the movement (the challenges we face and the people dealing with these difficult realities), we can begin a more productive dialogue with each other, return to the expertise of those theologians, historians, and leaders in our movement, as well as listen to many new voices to help us put the pieces of the puzzle together. But first we must familiarize ourselves with the various pieces.

This book aims to do four things:

- Take the reader on a journey around the world to see what the Church of God actually looks like at the dawn of the twenty-first century.

- Identify the key challenges that are threatening to pull the movement apart.

- Identify leaders and ministries that are engaging these challenges and learn about the realities of doing ministry in the twenty-first century.

- Set the stage for a new era of dialogue and communication about our Church of God identity and purpose. I am not proposing what that identity and purpose should be, but rather setting up a platform from which we can seek God's will for our future together.

One of the sad ironies of the Church of God is that despite our movement's emphasis on unity, we are a strikingly fragmented community. My sense is that we need to get to know each other all over again. The issues that are keeping us apart are more complex than the trend for churches to drop the name "Church of God" from their signs. They go beyond the smaller attendance at camp meetings or the decision by some congregations to put away the Church of God hymnal in favor of praise choruses. These are merely symptoms of the underlying issues. In order to truly see the scope of the problem, we must look at the various theological, generational, liturgical, organizational, geographical, multicultural, and spiritual challenges from a variety of angles up close and in person. My aim is not only to identify the issues but to put faces on the Church of God people dealing with these issues. After all, these are our brothers and sisters whom we are talking about, not just some faceless entity known as the Church of God.

To give voice to the diversity of the movement and its people at the grassroots level, I have deliberately chosen not to include any interviews with or commentary by movement leaders in Anderson, Indiana, apart from my interview with David Sebastian. But in presenting a snapshot of the movement in all of our diversity, this book sets the stage for movement leaders to discuss the issues facing the Church of God reformation movement in public forums. It is my sincere hope that this book stimulates thoughtful dialogue throughout the movement, at all levels.

Method of Approach

I decided the best way to understand the issues and to humanize the people involved would be to travel around the Church of God and talk to the people of the movement firsthand. When assessing our challenges as a movement, it has become too easy to generalize. "Those people in Anderson," "those missionaries," "those Fellowship Pastors," "those academics" is a refrain that I've heard too often in my Church of God experience. We need to get to know other Christians on their terms and understand their complexity and the challenging environments where they are working to expand the kingdom of God.

I have always loved to travel, and one of the things I love most about it is the way that it forces you to challenge your own assumptions, broaden your own worldview, and get into the heads of people very different from yourself. And best of all, it often leads to friendship. In this book, I am inviting you, the reader, to lace up your shoes, put on your backpack, grab your cup of coffee, and open your mind as we go deep into the Church of God as it exists around the world at the dawn of the twenty-first century. I can assure you that you will struggle with homesickness, culture shock, and a desire to run back to familiarity, but I urge you to press on in this journey. By the end of this book, you will walk away with many more friends than you have now—this is your family.

The Church of God exists in nearly ninety countries around the world and includes more than 1.1 million believers and more than 7,000 churches (2,192 in the United States and Canada).[2] Needless to say, I was not able to

---

2. *2010 Yearbook of the Church of God* (Anderson, IN: Warner Press, 2010).

visit every country, every church, and every person (although I would love to do so one day). However, I traveled to as many locations as I could and spoke to people who are facing the various aforementioned challenges. I am sorry that I could not recognize every country or hear the experience of every pastor. It is important to note that I was on a tight budget, which meant I could not just go anywhere at any time. I also wrote this book from Hong Kong which made access to some parts of the world more difficult. In addition, I had a regular full-time job and needed to make sure that I was home enough to be a good father and husband, which is always my top priority. I covered as much ground in two years as I could given these considerable limitations; and in the end, it is just one person's journey.

Hopefully, those places that are included in this book will be able to help us identify the pieces of the puzzle. Success, size, and reputation did not play a role in my selection of the ministries that appear in this book. Some of these ministries may have changed since the book was published. Some might be doing better; others, worse. What was important to me was that this book be filled with a wide variety of people who are grappling with the kinds of issues that churches all over our movement are facing. Ultimately, this book is about the challenges facing Christianity in the twenty-first century as reflected by one movement's experience. Of course the choosing and categorizing is my responsibility as a writer, and if I have failed to paint the picture accurately, I ask for your forgiveness and grace. I don't consider this an academic work (although I spent a lot of time examining scholarship on denominational issues in preparation to write this book), and I do not anticipate writing any further books on the Church of God. I do hope, however, that this book generates further dialogue and scholarship on the movement—even if they are critical of this work. This book aims to be catalytic, not prescriptive.

As we go on this journey together, there will be two big questions looming over us: *How do we keep an aging, autonomous-spirited movement together in an era of decentralization and denominational decline?* is the first question. But on the deeper level is this question: *Is God finished with the Church of God reformation movement, or is there more for us to do?*

Perhaps at times on the journey we will feel that the answer is within our grasp. At other times, the solutions to our problems may seem frighteningly far from us. In those times let us depend on the peace of God, which surpasses all understanding and will guard our hearts and minds in Christ Jesus (Phil 4:7) for "God is not a God of Confusion but of peace" (1 Cor 14:33 NASB).

Can the forces of disintegration and decline be overcome? Is our tradition so unique that it deserves to be preserved? How and why did it all begin? Let us find out together as we search out the puzzle pieces. The puzzle is just a part of a much larger painting, and my hope is that you will see an informative and thoughtful portrait emerge of a movement filled with holiness but which also deals with the reality that our unity is more precarious than ever. It is also an imperfect mosaic of a beautifully, diverse church that we may not want to lose. "*This* is our story, *this* is our song…"

the beginning or the end?

Surveying the Tough Road Ahead
South Dakota

I am standing on a windswept hill in South Dakota looking at a tombstone with my name on it. It is a perfectly sunny day with a blue-domed sky surrounding thousands of acres of highly fertile farmland. These are the flatlands of the Great Plains of America, but there are occasional green rises on the horizon. The temperature is in the nineties, but it is a dry heat and the day feels fresh. It is the kind of day that makes you feel good to be alive as the sun warms you and the wind cools you off. But on this particular day, I am not thinking about life but rather contemplating death—my own death and the death of the Church of God reformation movement that I love.

On the ground beneath my feet is a cemetery, but it is no ordinary final resting place. It is a Church of God cemetery, and under the earth are the remains of my ancestors. Carved into the granite tombstone are the letters N-A-C-H-T-I-G-A-L-L, and as I look at it, I suddenly get a strong sense of my own mortality. It is the first time I have ever seen our family name on a tombstone, and it is a bit jarring. Most all of my relatives, including my grandparents, were either cremated or buried in places that I have never been able to visit. Now for the first time in my life, I am seeing a tombstone with my name on it. And here I am able to see where it all began for our family more than a century ago—in Marion, South Dakota, with the grand spiritual patriarch of our family, my great-grandfather Abraham Nachtigall.

1

Great-Grandfather Abraham was the son of an immigrant who settled his family in this land of fertile soil—his own private Canaan. Abraham begat Samuel, who begat Harry, who—well, there it gets a bit complicated because I am adopted.[1] Abe Nachtigall lived in Marion, South Dakota, and joined the Church of God. They worshiped in the small white wooden church with a classic steeple next to the cemetery grounds. Interestingly, the town of Marion and the Church of God movement were both founded in the year 1881, thirteen years after Abe's birth in 1868. As Abe's town grew, so did the Church of God reformation movement.

Marion, South Dakota, was first called Turner Junction before becoming Marion Junction and then simply Marion. Originally there were two parts to the town: Yankee town and Russian town. Marion had English, Scottish, and Irish settlers, but the outer areas had many German-speaking Mennonites. The First Church of God was opened in 1896.[2] That is where Abe worshiped with his German-speaking clan.

One of his sons, Samuel, my grandfather, became a Church of God pastor and was a missionary to Canada. Samuel's son Harry became a Church of God missionary to Africa and Latin America and picked me up in Central America. I, in turn, became a pastor and a missionary for the Church of God in Asia.

Our family story very much mirrors the story of the Church of God. The church's origins ultimately go back to Europe—Germany to be precise—and what we can see and experience of our church family began on the wide open spaces of Middle America toward the end of the nineteenth century. After experiencing the Holy Spirit, this spiritual family quickly grew to cover America and almost immediately took the message to lands far away. Even those of different colors and ethnicity were quickly welcomed into the family, and that family's ministry continues until the present day. That's the story of the Nachtigalls, and it is the story of the Church of God movement we love. The Church of God cemetery in Marion is not only a testament to the origins of our family but also to a movement that grew

---

1. No one has claimed responsibility for begetting me, and I don't blame them, whoever they are. I am originally from Costa Rica, whereas the Nachtigalls are of Prussian (German) ancestry. They may have been ethnic Germans living in what today would be the Ukraine. *Nachtigall* means "Nightingale" in the German language. It has never mattered to me that I am not a Nachtigall by blood, and it never mattered to any of my relatives either. Our family story is not about blood but about spirituality.

2. City of Marion SD, 2004, "History of Marion," http://www.marionsd.com/History_of_Marion. htm

in the heartland of America and saw its vision of holiness and unity spread throughout the world.

Many in the Church of God have a similar story to mine. I don't have to look very far to be reminded of that. Standing in the cemetery with me are my wife Jamie and her mother Sharon, who belong to the Prussian Gossen clan. My mother-in-law Sharon grew up on a farm just down the road. I teasingly ask her if it was hard to hide from the dinosaurs in these wide-open spaces. I'm pretty sure she is not amused.

Like the Nachtigalls, the Gossens settled in this area near Marion, South Dakota, and attended the Church of God as well. The Gossens knew the Nachtigalls very well as they passed each other in their covered wagons.

"Abe was a righteous man," Grandma Gossen once told me, "but he tended to fall asleep in church." I finally understood where I get that from. Unlike old Abe, however, I'm the pastor, which is somewhat problematic.

Jamie is a Gossen and a Skaggs, and she too is the daughter and grand-daughter of Church of God missionaries and pastors. We are both third-generation missionaries for the Church of God. Even more amazing is the fact that we are technically related to each other. They say that there are only six degrees of separation, but in the Church of God there are only two. Suddenly, my lack of blood relation to old Abe seems like a blessing in disguise.

The spiritual blood of the Church of God runs strong in our family, as it does in so many other Church of God families who have seen generation after generation belong to this unique Wesleyan-Holiness movement. But as I watch my three-year-old son Marco running around the tombstones, I can't help but wonder where the movement will be when he is my age. He is the fifth generation of our family in the movement. Will his great-grandchildren be in the Church of God? Will they know what that is? Will it still exist? And considering our belief that we are not a denomination and that we are members of the universal Church of God, a more troubling question comes to mind as I think about our family's identity: Does any of this matter?

A Time for Answers

Those are the questions I seek to answer, and I am not the only person in the Church of God asking these important and at times frightening ques-tions. It is apparent to many that the Church of God is changing and that many issues regarding the future of our movement remain unresolved. Differences of opinion abound about what all of this means. More and more there are just big differences in general: differences of opinion about worship styles, differences about how our organization and its ministries should be structured, differences in ordination standards, differences in theology, and differences in culture and ethnicity. There are also geographical and generational divides within our movement as well as philosophical and technological shifts that make it challenging for any movement or denomination to maintain its unique identity in today's world of globalization. Furthermore, there are demographical challenges, with our aging population and a lack of people entering into ministry in many regions of the movement. And then there are those Church of God congregations that proudly display the name of the movement and those that have dropped the name altogether. As I survey the road ahead for the Church of God, it seems considerably more rocky and challenging than the gentle green plains surrounding the Marion cemetery.

There have been cultural shifts within Christianity that have greatly complicated the picture as well. Churches like Willow Creek and Saddleback possess an influence on American Christians whose affinity used to be reserved for denominations. Baby Boomers, upon reaching positions of leadership, deemphasized denominationalism in an effort to appeal to non-Christians. Then there is the fact that in a world of *hyper*-globalization, there is a massive decentralizing effect taking place that makes any kind of centralization difficult to maintain—thus affecting any one location's ability to serve as the recognized center of a denomination or movement. Another challenge is that our history and heritage, which in some ways fit the post-denominational, postmodern environment very well, also make us vulnerable to disintegration. Since we were born as a movement not concerned with forming creeds, organizations, and becoming a denomination, it is hard to make the case that we should do so now or even that we should centralize to any significant extent. As is so often the case, our greatest strengths can be our greatest weaknesses as well.

Our greatest strengths can be our greatest weaknesses as well.

Things have changed dramatically in the past twenty years. Clearly, "this is not your father's Church of God." As I survey the landscape, I wonder, "What can be done to address the variety of challenges facing our movement?" Furthermore, "how do we keep an aging, autonomous-spirited movement together in an era of decentralization and declining denominationalism?" These are the questions I ask myself as my three-year-old son plays amid the tombstones, oblivious to my existential queries.

Behind these important yet theoretical questions that need to be asked are real people, and perhaps therein lies the key to finding a solution to the situation we now face. As a missionary I am often on the road traveling across America or throughout the world sharing about our ministry. It is for this purpose that I am now in South Dakota, visiting the good people of Rustic Hills Community Church in Sioux Falls. Since we have more than fifty churches supporting us in twenty-five states, I have seen many different faces of the Church of God. Prior to writing this book, I also had the good fortune to travel to over fifty countries and experience the Church of God outside of North America. What I have found over the years of visiting churches and talking to pastors is that our movement is shockingly diverse, both in North America and throughout the world.

The things I have seen have often been inspiring, sometimes confusing, and occasionally disturbing. In the Great Plains there are Church of God pastors in churches that are struggling to stay open. In Anderson there are administrators facing daunting social and economic challenges as they try to preserve a movement that they feel God is not finished with yet. A thousand miles away in New England there are Hispanic brothers and sisters accepting Christ for the first time and proudly joining "La Iglesia de Dios." On the other coast is a pastor disconnecting from the movement because he feels too far removed geographically and culturally from the Church of God as it has been traditionally understood.

Meanwhile internationally, in Uganda, a church is exploding with new converts, while in Brazil a Church of God pastor is struggling with the phenomenal growth of Pentecostalism occurring in his neighborhood. In the South, a Baby Boomer pastor is deciding to send out his own missionaries directly from his church, while in India, a pastor contemplates planting a church in China.

Back on American shores, in the Pacific Northwest, two college students graduate from Warner Pacific: one chooses to go into ministry with the

Church of God; the other does not. One Church of God woman struggles to find a place for ministry in the twenty-first century, while another attending the North American Convention wears a bonnet and dresses as if it is the nineteenth century. A Church of God professor chooses a text on feminist issues in order to prepare his Church of God students for ministry in the twenty-first century, while a pastor in Kentucky feels that the movement has gotten too liberal and joins a more conservative fellowship within the Church of God.

In Europe, one pastor preaches the rapture, while another preaches Calvinism. A graduate of a Church of God Bible college in the Caribbean assumes the pastorate of a church in London, while another European pastor relies on the Alpha course for church growth and education instead of Church of God curricula.

Who are these people? Who makes up the Church of God at the dawn of the twenty-first century, and what can they tell us about our past, our present, and our future?

My suspicion is that we will not be able to move forward in unity until we have a better grasp of the variety within the Church of God and meet the faces behind the various positions, divisions, and communities. In meeting the people, we will inevitably discover that there are many cultural, theological, historical, political, geographical, demographical, and sociological factors pulling on this movement—a movement which was once much smaller, more defined, and more contained.

So I decide to set out on a journey, a journey across the Church of God at the dawn of the twenty-first century to find out who we are as we begin our second century as a movement. These are my brothers and sisters whom I am looking for, and I want to hear their stories and understand the realities that they face. I am not the expert; I am the student. They will be my teachers.

I want to visit a congregation in one of the wealthiest cities in the world as well as one of the poorest. I want to speak to the underpaid administrator and the church without a pastor. I want to meet with our African-American brothers and sisters as well as our African brothers and sisters. I want to talk to the Gen-Y youth pastor and the veteran missionary. I want to walk the halls of our hallowed educational institutions and the country roads surrounding most of our churches. I want to visit the new church plant in

Indiana and then return to the Church of God graveyard in South Dakota where my great-great-grandparents are buried and tell them what I saw.

I know I will find a lot of holiness, but will I find enough unity to keep us together? The only way to find out is to proceed forward from this grave-yard, armed with many questions, and a desire to learn more about this special, yet fragile movement known as the Church of God reformation movement. Before the journey across the Church of God can begin however, it's important to get a handle on where we've come from and why we are here.

We Are Not Alone: Denominations in Crisis

Since we started as a movement with a strong anti-institutional bias and no intention of turning into a denomination, Who are we? and Where are we going? are two questions that have been difficult for the Church of God to answer for much of our history. In more recent years, some, but not all of us, are concerned about the future of the Church of God. Each decade sees the number of people who are concerned about the movement's future decline. For those who are worried, let me start by putting you somewhat at ease before our journey begins by giving you a bit of good news.

First of all, we are a pretty good-sized movement—larger than most of us think. The Church of God is listed as the second largest Wesleyan church group in the United States (not counting the United Methodist Church), and it is present in eighty-eight countries around the world. [3] Although it is true that we are not growing significantly in numbers in Europe and North America, many other parts of the world are seeing significant growth.

Second, we are not the only ones struggling to grow as we once did. Movements and mainstream denominations overall are in decline. Mainline denominations have seen their numbers go down since at least the mid-1960s, and those on the more liberal end of the spectrum have seen dramatic drop-offs in countries where they were once a considerable presence. Furthermore, denominations used to hold a lot more sway in the national culture and in local communities in the United States than they do now.

---

3. This rank is based on statistics reported in Eileen W. Lindner, ed., *Yearbook of American and Canadian Churches* (Nashville, TN: Abingdon Press, 2006). The five largest Wesleyan church groups are Church of the Nazarene, Church of God (Anderson), Wesleyan Church, Salvation Army, and Free Methodist Church.

The bad news is that we have now reached a point where even well-known, large conservative denominations like the Southern Baptist Church are seeing rapid decline in membership and baptisms.[4] The SBC, with sixteen million members, has long been respected and admired for the loyalty and strong identity that it has been able to maintain over the decades. But if current numbers hold, it is projected that half of the SBC congregations will close by 2030.[5] The United Methodists are in decline as well with a split having opened up between the traditionalists and the modernists. In 2004, the movement of eight million declined by eight hundred thousand.[6] The Presbyterian Church (PCUSA) lost 2.5 percent of its membership in 2007. Nearly sixty thousand people left the denomination that year, the steepest percentage loss since 1974.[7]

The decline is not always a global issue. Some denominations, such as the Anglican Church, are seeing significant growth among the church in the non-Western world; but are experiencing a steep decline "at home" in the West where they originated. This has led to a new divide as the larger more conservative non-Western church is often at odds with the theological liberalism espoused by the Western leadership.

Within the United States, the growth of megachurches and now emerging churches have fostered new networks that provide resources and direction to many churches including those within denominations. Church of God pastors may take more inspiration from Willow Creek or Saddleback than they do from their own particular tradition.

The decline is also about the fact that the culture within denominations is disappearing. People no longer know the songs, traditions, and theologies that birthed their particular denominations and that provided them with their identity for much of the past centuries. The church person in the pew is not there because they identify with the overall identity of the denomination, but rather because they like a particular church, pastor, or particular program that just happens to be a part of a denomination. In the old days, to say one was Southern Baptist, United Methodist, or Church of God used to mean something. It said a lot about what your core values and

4. "SBC Reports Baptism Rate Lowest in a Decade," *Christian Century*, June 3, 2008, 19.
5. Christine Wicker, "The Great Evangelical Decline," *Dallas Morning News*, June 1, 2008, http://www.dallasnews.com/sharedcontent/dws/dn/opinion/points/stories/DN-wicker_01edi.ART1.State.Edition1.46dace2.html.
6. *The United Methodist:The Weekly Newsletter for United Methodist Leaders*, August 5, 2005.
7. *The Washington Post*, religion section, June 28, 2008.

beliefs were within the greater body of Protestant Christianity. My friends from other denominations even made jokes about it.

There were jokes about the Southern Baptists. You know you are Southern Baptist when:

- you clap in church and feel guilty about it.

- you wake up in the middle of the night and crave fried chicken and interpret that as a call to preach.

- you think that someone who said "Amen" during the sermon might be charismatic.

- you judge the quality of the sermon by the amount of sweat the preacher puts out.

These jokes pointed toward a truth about Southern Baptist culture. The Southern Baptists were known to place a high value on preaching, they were a clear product of Southern culture, they were not charismatic, and so forth.

There were also jokes about United Methodists:

- You know you are a United Methodist pastor when you get a Christmas card each year from United Van Lines.

- What's the difference between a Methodist and a Baptist? The Methodist will wave to you from the liquor store.

- What's the difference between a Methodist and a Baptist? A Methodist is a Baptist who can read.

- Name the three sacraments of Methodism: baptism, holy Communion, and potluck suppers.

Having worked in a United Methodist church for a time, I've experienced the culture that the jokes describe—a culture of intellectualism, comfort with alcohol, a love of evening gatherings, and a system of rotating pastors. All of those cultural and theological traits define the United Methodist Church.

What is the Church of God culture? Growing up, I understood it to be our belief that we were not a denomination but rather a movement. It was an important distinction that we all knew about. We were proud to have avoided the unnecessary sectarianism unleashed by denominations and their need to separate themselves from the greater body of Christ. We viewed ourselves as very open-minded Protestants, ready to call anyone who believed in Jesus Christ as their Savior part of the Church of God. "Experience makes you a member," we would say about our belief that official church membership was unnecessary and that faith in Christ was an experiential matter as opposed to being simply about right doctrine and rational knowledge.

As a child, I also understood that we truly considered each other family and that we would often use the words *brother* and *sister* before people's proper names. I grew up around Brother Barge, Sister Heines, Hermano Cajina, and Hermana Monge. We took the idea of being a part of the family of God as a very important component to our relationships as Church of God Christians.

As far as our practices went, we sang Church of God hymns, and we were proud of the many beautiful songs composed by Church of God writers. Our services were restrained, but not really liturgical like the Anglicans and Lutherans. We were excitable, but not prone to extreme displays of emotion during worship. And my personal favorite Church of God distinction was the fact that footwashing was an ordinance that we would practice on the Thursday before Easter Sunday (Maundy Thursday). It was and still is a unique, beautiful, and highly meaningful tradition. Oh, and everything came in and out of Anderson, Indiana, which was the center of all Christianity, don't you know—even though we didn't have a headquarters, because it was in heaven.[8]

We didn't have a headquarters, because it was in heaven.

---

8. I'm somewhat embarrassed to admit that at the tender age of seventeen, on my first visit since childhood to Anderson I was absolutely stunned to find out that not everyone in Anderson, Indiana, was part of the Church of God and that—indeed, there are other churches (of various denominations no less) scattered throughout the city. On this journey I have met Church of God people much older than I, however, who were under the same impression when they first visited Anderson. For those who did not grow up in an era of denominational/movement loyalty, it is easy to underestimate how the spiritual ties to the group can form an important, pride-filled, and deeply personal part of one's spiritual identity. Even in a movement as nonhierarchical as ours, the location of the headquarters can take on a subtle sacredness. We underestimate this at our peril.

Those were some of the aspects of our Church of God culture that I remember fondly from my youth. There was more, of course, but I knew enough to understand our unique culture. Were there jokes about us CHOGers as there were about Southern Baptists and Methodists? Probably not nearly as many since we have always been a small movement compared to those larger denominations. There is one joke though that points to a particular aspect of Church of God culture—its lack of official creeds and theological statements:

- Ask a theological question of seven Church of God pastors and you'll get seven different answers.

The joke is funny, but it points to a problem that is resulting in fewer and fewer Church of God parishioners and pastors being familiar with the particular theology and culture of the Church of God. Without a demand for firm theological statements or an expectation that traditions will be carried on, Church of God particulars can easily disappear as the movement ages. That seems to be what is happening.

It is probably safe to say that the average CHOGer under the age of forty (certainly under thirty) is unfamiliar with the unique history of the Church of God as well as its place within the spectrum of Protestant theology. While there have always been many in the church pews not particularly interested or well-informed about the specifics of denominations or movements, today the problem is more severe as the denominational culture itself is being lost.

- How many people in the Church of God are familiar with the teachings of early Church of God reformers and how those teachings were challenged or expounded upon over the years?

- How many could name the three ordinances of the Church of God (or could offer a description of what an ordinance is)?[9]

- How many congregations still regularly use the Church of God hymnbook, and within those congregations, are members able to identify the Church of God writers and the Church of God theology found in those hymns?

---

9. The three are baptism by immersion, communion, and foot-washing.

- How many people in Church of God churches regularly (if ever) hear sermons on the doctrine of sanctification? Can they explain this key doctrine?

As with other denominations and movements, fewer and fewer people in the Church of God are familiar with what makes us distinctive and why those distinctions might be important. The question even lingers particularly in this postmodern age: Is any of that important anymore? After all, we started out as a movement that strived for unity among all believers. Should we not celebrate the fact that many Church of God people today simply view themselves as Christian instead of as members of a particular movement within the Wesleyan-Holiness tradition? Perhaps to answer that question, it would be important to go back to the beginning and find out how all of those core Church of God beliefs arose in the first place.

The Wild, Wild Theological West: How It All Began

Americans tend to think that there was a day and age when Christianity ruled this country peacefully and churches were harmonious houses of worship filled with gentlemen who tipped their hats and women who dressed modestly. My image of nineteenth-century American Christianity was formed by the TV show *Little House on the Prairie*. When Pa and Laura Ingalls went to church, the only thing unseemly in church was the scowl on Nellie's face and Mrs. Olson's propensity for gossip. In other words, I grew up thinking that America had been a place filled with happy and peaceful churches until secular humanism messed it up for everyone. Well, nothing could be further from the truth. From the beginning, there was a lot of variety, volatility, and divisiveness in American Christianity. Our images are that the Wild West was full of gunslingers but the churches were filled with pious settlers. But the church during this time was filled with theological gunslingers aiming their spiritual condemnations at each other, competing for converts as much as they competed for land and financial prosperity. "This church ain't big enough for both of us" could have been American Christianity's motto in the nineteenth century.

The period following the Civil War was a turbulent era of rampant denominationalism, sects, schisms, moral decline, and competition. Denominations and movements such as the Methodists, the Baptists, the Presbyterians, the Disciples of Christ, and the Congregationalists were growing, but the challenge of secular ideas (particularly Darwin's *Origin of Species* in 1859) and low spiritual expectations of members were perceived to be weakening Christianity in America. The rapid urbanization was also creating a divide between the more secular city and the more traditional rural towns. It was amid this spiritual atmosphere that numerous protests groups and sects were formed, including the Church of God reformation.[10]

As secularism grew and competition between Christian denominations destroyed the Christian witness, there was a need for churches to represent holiness and Christian unity. The National Association for the Promotion of Holiness (organized in New Jersey in 1867) was an attempt to restore piety to American Christianity.[11] By holding regular campmeetings and distributing literature, people from various denominations came together to preach an experiential faith rooted in the belief that people needed to experience a dramatic work of the Holy Spirit to clean their hearts of sin. Members of the Holiness Movement increasingly separated themselves from the established "respectable" denominations, which they viewed as being spiritually lax. The more liberal denominations were made up of a wealthier, urban class. But even other more conservative denominations such as the Baptists and Presbyterians were often better off than Holiness believers, who often consisted of people from a lower socioeconomic class.[12] The demands of wealthier denominations were significantly less than those put upon the lower socioeconomic class of Holiness believers. It is often the case that wealth decreases spiritual dynamism in religious groups and the willingness

---

10. The name Church of God was existent before the Church of God (Anderson, Indiana). There are, in fact, more than twenty denominations or movements with the name Church of God. There may be two hundred groups or more that have used a variation of this name. In the Church of God reformation movement, the name signifies that the Church is *of* God and belongs only *to* God. D. S. Warner, an early pioneer, also felt it important that the name be from the Bible. Some places around the world use a different name in their own language to distinguish themselves from other Church of God congregations. The Church of God in the Dominican Republic, for instance, goes by the name Accíon Misionera.

11. The Holiness Movement can be said to have begun with the teachings of Wesley's doctrine of perfection and continued by the mainstream Methodist movement as well as through the preaching of Phoebe Palmer, Charles Finney, Dwight Moody, and many others. Methodists were not always happy with the sects that emerged from the movement. Out of the Holiness Movement emerged not just the Church of God (Anderson, Indiana) but many other groups, such as the Wesleyan Church, the Free Methodists, Church of the Nazarene, Church of Christ (Holiness) USA, Salvation Army, and Church of God (Cleveland, Tennessee).

12. Interestingly though, quite a few of the first generation of leaders in the Church of God were well-educated, and significant land-owners. However in comparison to the atmosphere of intellectualism and wealth that had formed in the East, the Midwest and West were considerably more provincial and disenfranchised.

13

to sacrifice.[13] The lower-income Holiness faith called people to renounce the world and make great sacrifices, which was in contrast to the large denominations, which placed significantly less demands on their people as they increased in wealth, power, and perceived accommodation to the world. The same thing would eventually happen to the Church of God as its people ascended from the lower ranks to the middle class. In the early days (which they believed to be "the Last Days"), however, the Church of God was a small group of believers who made great sacrifices for each other and for the Lord and correspondingly saw miracles, rapid growth, and the birth of a new movement as they tried to unite the church before Christ's imminent return.

The people of the Church of God have always viewed our church as having been founded by Jesus Christ, since we do not think of ourselves as a denomination. However, when we talk about the beginning of the Church of God reformation movement, we are referring to the year 1881 when Daniel Sidney Warner and five others separated from the Northern Indiana Eldership of the Church of God at a meeting in Beaver Dam, Indiana.[14] D. S. Warner (1842–95) grew to be opposed to some of the teachings of the Winebrennarian Church of God.[15] For instance, Warner felt that the multiplicity of sects and their lack of unity was a work of Satan. He also believed,

---

13. It has often been noted by scholars that religious dynamism tends to decrease as religious adherents get wealthier. A recent Pew Survey found that even in emerging nations that have traditionally been very religious such as Poland, Egypt, Brazil, and India, as people enter the middle class, the level of religiosity declines. See http://pewglobal.org/commentary/pdf/1051.pdf. The United States is unusual in that it is a wealthy developed nation and still has a healthy religious scene. However, this is changing, and even within religious groups like the Church of God, it seems that the lower-income level people are more inclined to take risks and have a faith where the supernatural is a more prominent part of their life.

14. Even this date is problematic for our movement since the movement was not centered around any one person or any one event as it would for a new church being founded by a particular person in a particular place. Important events happened in the 1870s and some use the date 1880.

15. The Winebrennarian Church of God, officially known as the General Eldership of the Church of God of North America, had many similar beliefs to D. S. Warner's movement, but it differed in the fact that it had a presbyterial government, believed in premillenarianism, and was not linked to the Holiness Movement. But even before that, it can be said that the Winebrennarian Church of God as well as D. S. Warner's doctrine had been a product of the theology of the early church fathers (who articulated the doctrine of the Trinity, for instance, which helps us understand the nature of God), Luther's Protestant Reformation (with its emphasis on Scripture and the priesthood of all believers), the Anabaptist Reformation (with its baptism of adults and belief in pacifism), the Pietist Movement (with its preference of experiential knowledge over a rationalist approach to theology), and the Methodist Movement (with its low church liturgy and theological belief in every human being's need to exercise his own free will to be saved), and the Holiness Movement (with its emphasis on personal holiness and sanctification). Although we agree with many of the tenets of the evangelical movement, the Church of God is not technically a part of the evangelical movement.

in line with much of Holiness theology at the time, that for individuals entire sanctification through a second work of grace was possible after physical baptism through baptism in the Holy Spirit, which would then lead a person to be completely free of sinful thoughts, motives, and actions. [16]

"We're Not a Denomination!"

"We're not a denomination!" my mother would cry out when I used the dreaded "d" word. D. S. Warner and his bretheren started a movement. They did not start a denomination. It is hard to overstate how much contempt the Church of God reformers had for denominations (a.k.a., "Babylon, the whore"). The theological wild wild West had convinced them that de-nominations and sects were wrong because they encouraged division and competition in what is actually one holy church. This divisiveness was sinful. Increasingly, denominations cared about membership at the expense of expecting Christlike behavior from their people. In the eyes of the reformers, they were making a mockery of all things Christian. The reformers wanted to restore the whole Christian church—the bride of Christ—to unity so that all of us Christians would be ready for the bridegroom's imminent return. A denomination in their opinion was "human ecclesiasticism:" organizations that usurped the place of the Holy Spirit in favor of the rule of man. They sought to model a new way of being a church in which men and women would depend on the Holy Spirit to lead them. They believed the key to unity for the church was holiness. Being the church—living holy lives—was their pursuit, not forming a new denomination. Lastly, they believed that this particular last reformation was foretold in the Bible and would usher in the end of the world in a relatively short period of time. The biblical interpretation behind

> It is hard to overstate how much contempt the Church of God reformers had for denominations.

---

16. This differed from John Wesley's position. Wesley viewed salvation as consisting of two branches: justification and sanctification. Justification was the process by which God forgives us of our sin. It is God's action for us. Sanctification, however, is God's action in us in which we receive an infilling of the Holy Spirit that purifies our nature so that we can love God and others more fully. While Wesley's emphasis was on love, the emphasis of the Holiness Revival was on eradicating sin completely and thus being made sinless. For D. S. Warner, H. C. Wickersham, and other early Church of God leaders, Wesley did not go far enough. Over the years, the movement in general moved away from Warner's interpretation, although a significant number of people, including key leaders, still hold to it.

this apocalyptic belief was later challenged in the 1920s and ultimately abandoned.[17]

With these firm convictions, a movement was born. A movement seeks to usher in change or make a correction within the church, not to exist as a separate body or become a denomination. The early Church of God began urging people to "come out" of their sectarian churches and "see the church"—the one truly holy church. But the question was soon asked of them: "By starting a reformation and asking others to leave their sects (denominations) behind, is that not fostering division and creating a new sect?" Warner and others defended themselves from the charges, arguing that to create a sect would result in them becoming part of the sin. They understood themselves to be the "Evening light." They felt that the Spirit was calling them to be the first in what would become a large group of people that were living according to the Holy Spirit completely outside of the sect/denomination paradigm.[18]

The Church of God would forever be conscious of not appearing like a denomination as it grew organizationally. Of course none of the denominations that existed at the time or exist now came to be because people dreamed of creating Christian bureaucracies just for the sake of having them. What we don't often realize in the Church of God is that numerous other Christian movements went through the same exact phases that we have, including once believing that they were the last true church before Christ's return and that organization would not be needed.[19] It has probably

---

17. This happened to many other sects that emerged in this same time frame. The end did not come as expected, and as the church members became part of the middle class, the apocalyptic teachings waned.

18. Of course, the Church of God did become a sect and is historically classified as such. In a 1963 *Christian Century* article, Church of God scholar Valorous Clear suggested three reasons for the growth of sects: 1) Firm answers regarding the problems in the world. 2) A different world for individuals to be a part of is offered, which creates a new framework for processing reality. 3) The social psychology of their new world meets their physical and psychological needs. Val Clear argued that sects "are safety valves letting off the steam of over-institutionalism" and that when the church fails to produce sects, it will cease to be the vehicle of God's grace to all men ("Reflections of a Post-Sectarian," *Christian Century*, January 16, 1963, 72–75).

19. These movements are often referred to as primitivist, revivalist, or restorationist. They are generally formed as part of the periphery of a more established group. Usually, they form around a charismatic leader and accentuate a theological belief they fear is being lost. They appeal to their own interpretation of the Bible and view the established groups they are rejecting as apostate. In return, they are rejected by the majority, which only solidifies their identity. The movements usually teach that they are the new embodiment of the church found in Acts and often have an apocalyptic bent. There is often a disregard and/or lack of awareness of Christian history between the time of the Apostolic church and their own movement. In time, if the movement survives, it will become increasingly institutionalized out of necessity. Leland Jamison identified four particularly prominent emphases: 1) perfectionism—a

been very detrimental to our movement's ability to dialogue with itself that few have understood that the phases we have gone through mirror those of other groups. What happens, however, is that as more and more people coalesce toward a common set of beliefs and the movement grows, the need to organize, create guidelines, and clarify beliefs grows dramatically. Today, most outside the Church of God view us as a denomination, not a movement. We, on the other hand, are guilty of calling other movements like the Disciples of Christ, Churches of Christ, and Assemblies of God, denominations.

From the beginning, there were sincere attempts to not be organized around a particular person or the laws of man. The goal was to be a Spirit-directed apostolic church. Initially, the voice of the movement was not a person but a publication: *The Gospel Trumpet*. But as much as they tried to avoid it, the reality is that the Church of God reformation movement, like the church in Acts, felt the need to organize itself right out of the gate.[20] It began simply enough with a need to clarify specific theological points. There were soon theological factions, such as the anticleansers and the

---

doctrine of perfect sanctification; 2) millennialism—a doctrine of last things; 3) universalism—a doctrine of Christ's accomplished sacrifice and salvation open to all; and 4) illuminism—the claim that "new light" or further revelation had been given to man in these latter times. See A Leland Jamison, "Religions on the American Perimeter," in *Religion in America: The Shaping of American Religion*, ed. A Leland Jamison and James Ward Smith, 197–98 (Princeton, NJ: Princeton University Press, 1961). See also Sydney E. Ahlstrom, "Sectarian Heyday," ch. 29 in *A Religious History of the American People* (New Haven, CT: Yale University Press, 1972). Edith L. Blumhofer suggests that the following restorationism impulses propelled the rise of Pentecostalism: 1) a call for Christian perfection; 2) calling for unity by reminding Christians of their "fundamental oneness in Christ"; 3) viewing themselves as interpreters of the end times; and 4) antidenominationalism (Edith L. Blumhofer, *Restoring the Faith: The Assemblies of God, Pentecostalism, and American Culture* (Chicago: University of Illinois Press, 1993), 13.

20. This is what sociologist Max Weber described as the "routinization of charisma." A prophetic leader will begin a movement which attracts followers to his anti-traditional message through his personal "charisma." When the charismatic leader dies or leaves, the problem of succession arises. To keep a movement going after the death of the original founder, the charisma must be "routinized," in order to create structures that will keep the message alive. In the case of the Church of God, E. E. Byrum's assumption of the role of editor of the *Gospel Trumpet* ushered in that phase of routinization. (See Max Weber, *Economy and Society* [New York: Bedminster Press, 1968]). As movements become institutionalized, they are able to spread their teachings on a larger scale. The danger is always that they will over-institutionalize and preserve their traditions and institutions at the cost of their original message and spirit. "Charisma—elusive, fragile, affective, rather than rational—is particularly difficult to maintain in a modern and secular society," Margaret M. Poloma writes in regard to the struggle of the Assemblies of God with this issue. "Charismatic experiences and institutional controls often conflict" ("Charisma and Institution: The Assemblies of God," *The Christian Century*, October 17, 1990, 932–34).

antinecktie faction.[21] Then there were business decisions that needed to be made regarding the Gospel Trumpet Company. In time, the second editor, E. E. Byrum, produced a list of clergy, which helped those ministers get discounts on the railroads. The communal homes and transient nature of pastors morphed into more typical sedentary congregations with an assigned pastor, and a mission agency was eventually created to organize global outreach. The early leaders distinguished between organizing the church and the business of the church. But by the 1950s, the Church of God had many of the trappings of a denomination. Valorous Clear, a professor at Anderson College, wrote a thesis (followed by a book) chronicling the movement's path from reformation toward becoming a more established institutionalized body. Even Church of God architecture in the 1950s was a testimony to the fact that the movement on the margins now wanted to be a part of the respectable middle class that made up the Protestant mainstream.

Consistently throughout every era of the Church of God, there have been people who felt the movement was becoming too much like a denomination. Even today, in many quarters there remains unease about the role of the central offices in Anderson, Indiana. Ironically, the movement that didn't want to become a denomination began to look like a denomination just as North America entered into a post-denominational age.

A double irony is that now in an era in which few people are even conscious of denominational identity, those traditional Church of God people who long for a return to a cohesive sense of what the movement believes have to ask themselves how that movement can even be remembered without an organizational center to keep the connection to the tradition alive. Truly on many levels, the Church of God is a case study in irony. When a movement prides itself on a heritage of autonomy and anti-institutionalism, it's hard to cry foul when the movement's historical and theological heritage is forgotten by autonomous churches that don't respect institutions.

---

21. The Anticleansers were a faction in the Church of God that believed a doctrine called Zinzendorfism, which taught that entire sanctification occurred in one moment, as opposed to occurring through justification (God's reconciliation with the believer) and then followed by sanctification (the transformation of the believer's heart). The Antinecktie faction consisted of people who believed a holy life should be demonstrated by abstaining from tobacco, alcohol, caffeine, dancing, hats, jewelry, corsets, theatre, and, of course, the evil necktie. Although they didn't exist for long, they are fun to talk about.

Losing Our Identity

It seems clear that over time, like many denominations and movements, with each generation we are losing our sense of unique identity. But how can a denomination or movement preserve its unique identity over time? Are they all simply doomed to disintegrate as less committed generations replace the original founders?

A number of methods create identity and help a denomination or a movement retain its identity.[22] Some of these methods are:

- A recognized publication that is widely-read and widely-distributed, and that continually informs the readers about what is happening in the movement and where the movement stands on theological issues.

- Regular, well-attended regional, national, and international conferences that bring people together, that provide interaction that creates synergy, and that ultimately mobilize people for cooperative ministry within the movement.

- The use of a common curriculum from a denominational publishing house.

- The channeling of mission resources and activity through a mission agency.

- Seminaries, or Bible schools, that clearly teach the movement's theology and train its pastors.

- Consistent standards and theological expectations by ordination committees.

- A common musical heritage used consistently in congregations throughout the movement.

- A commitment to continue planting churches throughout the world.

---

22. These various means of creating, transmitting, and maintaining identity have been much studied by scholars. As in this book, scholars have examined what is sometimes referred to as the "ecology" of denominations, focusing their studies on these key areas of identity transmission and how and why they go into decline. The most extensive study I have found is The Presbyterian Presence, a seven-volume series that looks at issues surrounding ordination, hymnody, publishing houses, colleges and seminaries, and curricula and other key vehicles of identity transmission in the Presbyterian Church (PCUSA) that are in decline and under strain (Milton J. Coalter, John M. Mulder, Louis B. Weeks, eds. [Louisville, KY: Westminster/J. Knox Press, 1990–92]).

In the Church of God, we used to be strong in all of these areas. Camp meetings were an important part of our annual life and were well-attended by people of all ages. In addition to this, regional conferences and an international conference held on a different continent every four years enabled the movement to gather in large numbers. *The Gospel Trumpet*, which later became *Vital Christianity*, served as a unifying voice for the global movement and allowed difficult issues to be tackled and processed. As for curriculum, in previous decades, the curriculum and literature put out by Warner Press was commonly found in Church of God Sunday schools across the country and around the world. Our Church of God schools produced pastors well-schooled in Church of God history and theology. We also had many students leave our Bible colleges committed to a lifetime in ministry who then went out and started new congregations. In our Church of God mission efforts, we were supported by our congregations who viewed the Missionary Board as their sole connection to global engagement. Most impressive of all was the rich musical heritage of the Church of God, which produced many of gospel music's finest artists, including Bill and Gloria Gaither, Sandi Patty, Doug Oldham, and many others.

Today, however, many regions do not have regular meetings. In some countries, there are regions within countries that will not cooperate with each other to even have meetings or, more tragically, ministry. While the annual North American Convention in Anderson is still well-attended, the crowd is increasingly older and smaller as the years go by. *Vital Christianity's* final issue was in 1996 and has never been resurrected. A magazine entitled *ONEvoice!* was started up, but it never engendered the kind of interest or respect (nor did it seem to possess the same level of gravitas) of *Vital Christianity*. As for curriculum, many churches go to other organizations with pastors and leaders resourcing the work of John Maxwell, Willow Creek, and many other outside organizations. Ordination standards vary from state to state and region to region, while many ministerial candidates (and ordained pastors) are very unfamiliar with Church of God theology or not very committed to it. Our schools do not always expect faculty or students to adhere to any kind of specific Church of God orthodoxy. There has also been a dramatic decline in young people choosing to go into ministry, and church planting has been minimal. In regard to mission efforts, approximately 75 percent of Church of God congregations are not affiliated with the Living Link program connecting our missionaries to the local congregation and most churches give to mission organizations and projects outside of Global Missions. Finally, many of our churches now not only favor more contemporary music but have done away with the Church of God hymnal altogether. While not all of these trends can be labeled as bad things (for instance, it is good that churches give to a variety of global ministries), the collective weakening of these pillars and the lack of a strong concerted effort to restrengthen these pillars in new ways has put us in a precarious position.

So it can be said that the Church of God, on the whole, is not doing a good job of maintaining these key pillars that help to hold a denomination or movement together. The end result is that fewer and fewer of our people have spiritual, emotional, educational, ministerial, and theological ties to the Church of God movement as it has been understood for most of its history.

Why Have a Denomination or Movement?

The center of the movement is not holding. The Church of God's sense of identity and community as a distinct part of the greater Church of God is disappearing. Why should a movement or denomination even have a center? Traditionally it is important for a denomination or movement to have a center because this identity and central organization allows the church to do a variety of important things.

- Bring a common purpose and vision to a large number of churches.

- Mobilize for large global mission endeavors.

- Preserve, record, debate, and transmit theology for future generations.

- Hold property and manage funds.

- Give licenses to pastors and uphold ordination standards.

- Represent pastors and churches to local and foreign governments.

- Assist/mediate in conflict resolution between churches and/or pastors.

- Help with pastor placement.

- Provision of services through agencies, colleges, and other organizations.

- Help pastors/churches with tax and legal issues.

- Provide pension plans and insurance for pastors.

- Assist in church planting and the funding of buildings.

All of these things are very important and have the potential to benefit many churches in many nations. Denominations and movements like the Church of God grew as our societies became more bureaucratic and complex. Legal issues, needing the approval of foreign governments to send missionaries to foreign soil, and the expectation that people are entitled to a pension are just a few examples of the kind of complexities that arose in the twentieth century that demanded an organizational response from the Church of God. In the Church of God movement, we have never been comfortable with our central offices (in Anderson, Indiana), yet the movement needed those central offices to make it this far. Although we never reconciled ourselves with the role of the central office, it may be a moot point if current trends continue, as all denominational central offices are struggling to survive. We will explore this in chapter 4.

As competitive as the era of denominations was in the twentieth century, today it is even more competitive as a variety of large churches, movements, and Christian non-profits rise up often supplanting the work that was done by denominations. Most of the challenges central offices are facing are not of their own doing. There are many shifts that have taken place that have been out of the control of central administrators. Protestantism has been displaced by culture, so denominations do not have the same sway as they once did. The evangelical movement has become more unified, and being "born again" is more of an identification today than one's denomination or theological heritage. Brand loyalty in general has been in decline, and there has been a dramatic decrease in volunteer organizations (aimed at mobilizing for goals larger than the individual). The rise of the Christian marketplace has led to more competition among colleges, curricula, publishing, services, movements, and mission agencies.

Through the past half century, the educational level of the population has been rising as well, which erodes denominational loyalty. We've also seen a consumer mentality toward the church, wherein people choose their church based on the services it provides rather than for theological or denominational reasons. The 1970s also saw a push toward the laity and the local church and away from central organizations. The stunning rise in college tuition has led kids away from Christian schools, and high debts made low-paying ministry a less attractive option. These are just some of the greater trends that have challenged the administrators of denominations. All of this has led to a lot of confusion. People sense something is wrong but can't identify exactly what it is. Perhaps this is because it is not just one thing. It is many things.

So was the Church of God reformation movement only a moment in time, or does God still have a calling on us as a particular community within the greater universal church? Looking around the cemetery in South Dakota, the future seems frightening. But I also feel a sense of excitement, with the future possibilities as wide open as these Great Plains I am standing on. It is time to leave the tombstones of yesterday behind, and see the church as it exists today. It will be a challenging journey, but we will also have fun. I assure you. The journey across the Church of God begins now.

boomers, xers, and y
should i care?

The Generational Challenge
Seattle, San Antonio, Uganda, Dominican Republic

One of the biggest challenges facing the Church of God is that culturally, organizationally, and theologically, the Church of God is not being transmitted from one generation to another. The generational gap is also one of the biggest divides facing the movement. The Church of God reformation was a movement, which meant that it was never about creating a denomination and perpetuating its identity and institutions. Over time, however, a Church of God identity did emerge, and today its loss is being felt by many around the world.

In the cemetery in Marion, South Dakota, I wondered if the Church of God would still be around when my son is my age. To get a better sense of the situation, I wanted to find out how each generation alive right now perceives their Church of God experience. Doing so may help us to know what to expect in the future. The generation that seems to be feeling the most loss is the older generation, whose members have seen the Christian landscape change dramatically in their lifetimes and who often find themselves alone with their own generation on Sunday morning, in planning sessions, and at camp meetings. More than a few Church of God congregations around the world are made up of elderly people struggling to keep the church open; they wonder what has made today so different from yesterday.

The sad truth is that in the Church of God today, we are missing three generations. The first generation missing is today's youth (Millennials), who are increasingly disconnected from church in general and do not have much familiarity with the traditions and theology of the Church of God. Furthermore, they have a strong aversion to involvement in or loyalty to institutions that they view as inflexible and irrelevant. From Lebanon to Canada, it is difficult to keep young people in church, let alone keeping them invested in the Church of God movement. The second missing generation is known as Generation X in the United States. Its members were saddled by college debt and grew up cynical about the church. They avoided ministry in droves and remain mostly disengaged from Church of God leadership. In many countries throughout the Church of God world, even if this generation remains committed to the Church of God, they have not been allowed or sufficiently encouraged to assume positions of leadership. Across the world, few countries have done a good job of creating a talent pipeline that identifies and recruits the most talented youth and puts them into leadership. At this point in time, there should be quite a few leaders from this generation (forty- and thirty-year-olds), but they are largely absent.

But what about the Baby Boomers, many of whom are in leadership today? Why do I consider them a missing generation? While many Baby Boomers are involved in the Church of God and even in key positions of leadership, they were the first generation to migrate en masse to other movements, turn to non-Church of God resources for their ministries, and start up their own competing nonprofit organizations within the Church of God. That leaves only one generation—the "Greatest Generation."[1] Its members are the last truly loyal generation of the Church of God, and they are now retiring from leadership and dying.

---

1. I realize that the terms I'm using to refer to the different generations come from how we in the United States have decided to classify them. I also realize that many people have an aversion to classifying people by their generations. But for the purpose of this book, using these designations will be very helpful. Furthermore, I found that these generational patterns do bear out within the church around the world. Of course, there are always exceptions, but for the most part around the world, the Church of God has been sustained culturally, organizationally, and theologically by the older generation, has become negotiable for the Baby Boomer generation, and is mostly unknown by Gen-X and the Millennials.

The Road Map

Our journey examining the generational challenge begins in Seattle as we meet a group of senior citizens from the Greatest Generation reflecting on the days when the Church of God had a stronger cultural, theological, and organizational presence. Then we will go to the International Youth Convention in San Antonio to see how today's young people experience their faith. Then we will travel to Uganda to see how leadership is being passed down from one generation to another. We will then go to the Caribbean to see how the church in the Dominican Republic is successfully mentoring young people and using them to plant churches.

Seattle: Church of God Golden Girls

I thought a good place to start my journey across the Church of God would be in Seattle, one of my favorite cities in the world. Located alongside the waters of the Puget Sound with the Olympic Mountains on one side and fourteen-thousand-foot Mt. Rainer on the other, this city of hills, evergreen trees, and coffee houses is one of the most dynamic and beautiful places in the United States. In this beautiful setting, I sat down to interview four women with a lifetime of experience in the Church of God.

The Church of God has traditionally been strong in the Pacific Northwest. As I would hear many times on my trip, the first missionary for the Church of God movement was not a person but rather a periodical: *The Gospel Trumpet*. This publication, which emerged in 1881, spread across the country and the world, inspiring many to join the reformation. More than a century ago, readers in Washington State began writing to the editors to request that people be sent to continue sharing the unique message of holiness and unity. On August 12, 1893, four young people—F. N. and Susie Jacobson, C. H. Tubbs, and Mary Sowers—arrived in Spokane.[2] The first annual Western Washington Camp Meeting began in 1904 in Seattle, and the first Church of God congregation was built in 1906 for $5,000. [3]

Today in Washington, there are many Church of God congregations. I am not going to a church, however, but rather to Cristwood, an attractive multilevel building nestled in the woods of northern Seattle. Cristwood is part of the Crista senior residential community in the attractive suburb of

---

2. Donald Johnson "An Historical Survey of the Church of God in the Pacific Northwest" (master's thesis, Anderson School of Theology, 1955), 231.

3. Ibid., 301

Shoreline. It is here that I meet up with a special group of senior citizens, ladies who grew up in the Church of God and watched it expand around the world.

I invite the women to assemble in the apartment of my grandma, Evelyn Skaggs, who served as a missionary to Egypt (1945–57, 1989–92). Recorder in hand and laptop open, I sit surrounded by Evelyn's fellow Church of God friends: Violet Davis, Lavinia Worthen, Lee Maddox, Helen Flynt, and Cora Ashmore—all women who have served God for many years and who deeply love the Church of God reformation movement. I want to hear from these saints about what is being lost, where we have gone wrong, and why it matters. I want to hear from them about the old days, their love of the church, and their fears about its future. Surrounded by the Church of God Golden Girls, I get an earful.

I begin by asking if they distinctly remember being taught about Church of God theology in the church when they were young people.

Helen Flynt spoke up first: "I was very fortunate. From the time I was nine or ten years old, we had a pastor who very definitely taught us the basic premises of the Church of God. As we went into our teen years, he was very careful; every time we made any kind of decision, such as getting a job, he had a personal interview with us to explain what tithing was. He saw to it that we went to youth camp and state camp meetings. I was third-generation Church of God, and by the time I was in college, no one was going to deter me from going to a Church of God. And then I married a person who instilled that in me more. But today, the pastors are enamored with the megachurch idea."

The megachurch is something that troubles many from this generation. Many traditional churches have seen their size shrink dramatically after a megachurch develops nearby. For them, it's like the Walmart that comes to town and closes down the mom-and-pop stores.

All of the ladies agreed that in the old days, pastors taught about Church of God theology and people grew up understanding what makes the movement distinct. This contrasts with many churches today that no longer spend much time on talking about their denomination's theology.

I follow up by asking them in what ways the Church of God has changed over the course of their lifetimes.

Evelyn quickly spoke up: "Camp meetings are getting smaller, and perhaps there's less interest in them. We have fewer evangelists. Many Church of God congregations don't have a Church of God name. Fewer people are called into the Church of God, and we don't hear much about VBS. Also, *Vital Christianity* is no more."

Evelyn hits on many of the key pieces that have helped the Church of God to stay united and that defined our particular identity. The loss of our flagship publication, *Vital Christianity*, the successor to the *Gospel Trumpet*, is something that hit this generation particularly hard.

"Of course nowadays a lot of information from the Church of God is transmitted through the Internet," I interject.

"Only two of us in this room are on the Internet," Evelyn responds, shooting me down like a World War I fighter over lower Saxony.

She continues: "We don't hear about doctrine very much. We don't have Wednesday night meetings anymore. But some churches have dinner and group meetings on Wednesday night. It seems like we don't have very many revivals. I used to really enjoy the revivals we had every year, usually in the fall."

"We had revivals?" I think to myself. I don't remember ever having a revival meeting, and Wednesday nights were phased out in my mid-twenties.

"Missionary emphasis and support of missionaries has declined," Helen says. "But I have observed that the larger churches are the ones that are very missions-minded. They are compassionate about missions and passionate about missions. They are taught that, and the response is phenomenal. They are the growing churches."

So although Helen laments the infatuation with the church growth movement in the younger generations, she also observes that these larger churches are doing a good job of reaching out globally. Rick Warren comes to mind.

"The dress code has changed a lot," Evelyn speaks up again. "People can wear jeans and dress shorts to church."

Rick Warren comes to mind again. I suddenly regret wearing shorts to the interview and ask the ladies if this casual attire in worship bothers them.

"I always felt that when a pastor got up there, he should be in a suit, and that shows respect for the job." Cora laments. "I'm guilty of it too. Years ago I wouldn't have thought of going to church in slacks. I think we haven't shown respect for our church when people come in jeans or shorts or ragged clothes."

Then I ask the ten-million-dollar question and brace for the volcano to blow: "What do you think of the worship style?"

"We grew up when there was just one song leader," Evelyn responds. "Now we have worship teams, and sometimes they are not dressed very well either."

"Loud seems to be the criteria of being good. Loud is not good," Helen says emphatically. "Do you think it has anything to do with lack of training? People get put into a leadership role and they are not trained for it?"

Cora interjects: "I think of the hymns, that so many times after the preacher preached a sermon, those old hymns could emphasize the message that you just heard, and it would be very touching and draw you closer to the Lord."

Lavinia Worthen recalls that her own family left a Church of the Brethren congregation to attend the Church of God in Grandview, Washington, back in the days when people were expected to dress more conservatively for worship and yet women pastors filled the pulpits—something that has waned dramatically in recent decades.

"The Church of God was worshiping above the feed store, and Sister Gray was the pastor. Someone questioned, 'Can you wear earrings?' And she said, 'Not in the church!'"

"Incredible," I think to myself. "Nowadays I see male youth pastors wearing earrings." I refrain from saying this lest I cause undue stress.

I ask Lavinia if the people of the town thought it was weird that they had a woman pastor.

"No," she responds. "It was weird that we worshiped above the feed store!"

Lavinia's comments hearken back to a time in the early Church of God when it was common for women to be pastors and for Church of God meeting spaces to be very basic. It was only later, in the 1950s, as Church of God people entered into the middle class and became part of the Protestant mainstream that the movement became concerned with constructing significant church buildings. This was also a time of altar calls at the end of the sermon.

Lavinia continues: "I can remember the altar call. My brother Cal went forward, and I thought, 'If he needs to go forward, I really do!'"

It's hard for me to picture Lavinia sinning, but I suppose it's possible.

The women lament the fact that not only do the younger generations in the Church of God have no basic knowledge of the movement, but in many churches today, the various generations are split up and never interact with each other in any significant way.

"L. T. Flynt was our pastor for many years." Cora tells me. "Of all the pastors I had, he influenced my life the most. That was sixty years ago!"

"He cared for the young people," Violent adds. "My daughters really appreciated it. They still mention that."

Cora chimes in, "My kids still think of him as their second father. Every time we would gather, we would see two rows of young people sitting in the front, because he had that kind of influence."

"We were so thrilled to have Wilbur and Evelyn Skaggs. They were such a good influence on the young people," Lavinia interjects.

> Not only do the younger generations...have no basic knowledge of the movement, but in many churches today, the various generations are split up.

"That generation was interested in every generation," Helen says. "The pastors stood at the door and greeted everyone!"

"That's become a lost thing hasn't it?" Lee comments.

"Now so many of the churches have so many doors!" Evelyn says to great laughter in the room.

I make my own attempt at humor. "The pastor should say, 'I will be at door 7B today,'" The joke crashes like the *Hindenburg*.

Cora breaks the awkward silence and recalls the worship service of her childhood. "I remember that when I first went to the Church of God, we used to turn around and kneel to pray. You would hear the congregation agree with the pastors with their loud 'Amens.' The Church of God minister expected the children to sit and be quiet and listen to the message. And he always stood by the door and complimented you if you were a good child. And if you misbehaved, he would also let you know about that. It was the first church I had gone to where the pastor paid so much attention."

Lee Maddox recalls an interesting anecdote, "I would always get amused when people would mention the 'Church of God headquarters' and my father would say, "No," and point upward to the sky! My concept of the Church of God is the worldwide church of all Christians." This story reflects foundational ideas of the Church of God reformers: that there is no head of the church other than Jesus Christ and that the Church of God is not a denomination with a central institutional authority.

Helen Flynt hits upon another cornerstone of Church of God theology. "When you get into a conversation here (at Cristwood), as soon as you say, 'Anderson, Indiana,' they say, 'I know all about that church and your emphasis on unity.' One of my doctors recently said, 'I know all about you.' So the message has infiltrated other denominations, which is encouraging."

But today so few Church of God people are familiar with the distinctive ideas of the movement. What happened?

Evelyn responds; "I noticed something that started to happen when our young people went to our colleges. They changed. I remember when we were in seminary, some of the young people and a lot of the leaders would get together and make jokes about our heritage songs and change the words to make them funny. It seemed like they were making fun of our heritage. And it seemed like from then on, things began to change. They started questioning everything, especially about our heritage. When you went to meetings, there was always someone bringing up something new. It seemed like after that, we began to go downhill."

Helen recalls that her husband, Pastor L. T. Flynt, would often talk to students preparing for ministry about these issues. "I can remember L. T. would say, 'They have some very deep spiritual Church of God professors, and they have some others who are becoming more lenient. Be careful that you don't lose what you have, your passion and your convictions, because these changes are coming in the Church of God.'"

And L. T. was right. Much of the Church of God's identity was swallowed up by a larger mainstream evangelical culture (even though technically the Church of God is not part of the evangelical movement). The rise of Christian media and publishing, parachurch organizations, and the born-again movement have all played a part in the emergence of mainstream evangelical Christianity. The ladies in Seattle have witnessed over the course of their lives a dramatic change in the religious scene in America and the world. They pine for some of the old traditions yet understand that time marches on and that we cannot go backward in time. As we lose this older generation, we lose a powerful link to the past heritage of the Church of God. The younger generations have all been raised in an age when the heritage of a denomination or movement is not transmitted in a significant way. Many of the stories, the culture, traditions, and experience will disappear if we don't seek to preserve them (or renew them) in some form or another.

The Church of God was not started to create traditions or institutions that would need to be remembered and idealized. This goes against the spirit of the movement. However, what these ladies miss (and what I miss) is the fact that there was a time when our identity and our community were more concrete. While other generations today may have people who still care about the identity of the Church of God, these ladies are the ones who actually lived and breathed it every day. In some ways, their lives perfectly paralleled the golden age of the Church of God when the movement was at its pinnacle culturally, theologically, and organizationally. They saw the church at a time when it was more easily grasped and internalized. It is perfectly understandable why they find it strange that so many of us would want to dismiss this heritage without thought.

The Generational Divides

Throughout denominations and movements across the United States (and the world), generational divides have opened in the church. While every generation finds it hard to relate to the generation above or below it, today the differences have been exacerbated by globalization and the information age, which are ushering in rapid changes and creating entirely new ways to relate to one another.

In some countries, changes are reversing thousand-year-old traditions overnight. Take China, for instance, where for thousands of years in this mostly agrarian civilization, it has been accepted that the father is the head of the household and older people carry much more wisdom than the young. But what is a father to make of the fact that his seven-year-old daughter knows how to operate a computer better than he does and that she will most likely become the most educated person in the history of their family by the age of twelve? In India, what is the high-caste Brahman (who has been taught that lower castes are inferior) to think when he sees a low-caste Indian making five times his salary at a tech start-up in Bangalore and driving a BMW? In this latest round of globalization, the very linchpins of civilizations are being overturned and generational divides are occurring faster and on a larger scale than ever.

In the United States, I often visit small churches filled with mostly seniors who cannot relate to the new worship styles and feel as if all of the

Church of God traditions that they grew up with are being abandoned. Many of them are from the Greatest Generation, the generation that lived through World War II and helped to turn the United States into the world's most prosperous nation. Many members of the Greatest Generation and the Silent Generation (born between 1925 and 1945) experienced the largest expansion period in the Church of God. While things were always changing and being realigned, the movement grew substantially, moved toward the center of the Protestant mainstream, had its musical heritage valued across the Christian world, consisted of an emerging middle class, and grew internationally. Yet through it all, the movement managed to retain its Church of God identity. This generation was part of the expansion phase and the ascendancy phase of the Church of God, as Ramsey Coutta labels these periods of denominational growth in his book *Divine Institutions: The Nature of Denominational Growth and Decline in America*.[4] They have been to the mountaintop and are wondering why people want to get off the mountain, which offered quite a lovely view. In the latter half of their lives, they have seen many of the traditions they valued deemphasized or disregarded altogether. The changing nature of secular and Christian culture combined with the different style of leadership of the Baby Boomer generation has meant that the style of church they were accustomed to had now been labeled out-of-date or too traditional. Increasingly, they find themselves in churches that deemphasize Church of God particulars (perhaps even dropping the name "Church of God" altogether) or they keep those traditions only to see younger generations stay away in droves. Before long, they are either attending the one traditional church service offered by their changing church or they are surrounded by people mainly their age in a church struggling to survive.

The Baby Boomers are the generation that grew up after World War II in a time of affluence and social change (1946–64). They were part of the countercultural movement of the 1960s that challenged the old order on issues such as segregation, equal rights for women, and American involvement overseas. Vietnam and the Watergate scandal shook people's confidence in the U.S. government. Eventually, they became the wealthiest generation in history, helping to usher in the age of transnational corporations and high-tech industry. This generation seems to have perfected the art of marketing, not only in commerce but in politics and religion.

---

4. Longwood, FL: Xulon Press, 2006.

Concerned that the older traditional models of church were geared far too much toward people who are already believers, the Boomers sought to make changes that would make non-Christians feel more welcome. The music became more contemporary, the sermons less dogmatic, and the church architecture less traditional. Upholding tradition was far less important to this generation than doing evangelism on a massive scale in inventive ways. Under the leadership of Baby Boomers, the Protestant church in America saw the growth of nondenominational ministries, colleges, publishing houses, parachurch organizations, megachurches, interdenominational and interfaith dialogue and cooperation, the rise of the Religious Right and the evangelical political block, and the creation of a globally televised and marketed Christianity. For this generation, what works best for evangelism is often something unrelated to the priorities of the denomination, so they have acted around and beyond the denomination, sometimes disconnecting altogether.

In the Church of God, the Baby Boomers in leadership are mostly concerned with what works for winning souls to Christ, not necessarily what preserves Church of God identity and institutions. Of course, the Greatest Generation is not simply concerned with preserving the institution, but that generation came out of a paradigm where winning souls for Christ was done from within the Church of God movement (appealing to Church of God theology, using Church of God curricula, attending Church of God events, and supporting Church of God mission fields). Many Baby Boomers in the Church of God retain a love for the movement, remain connected through gatherings and support for Anderson, as well as mission support for Church of God people around the world, but they do not take their daily cues about what to do or how to form their church's identity from Church of God traditions, heritage, and theology. They draw from the ideas of a larger postdenominational Christian culture and are much more likely to be comfortable looking to the business community for advice on church management.

Then there's my generation, the Gen-Xers (born in 1965–81). Our parents and teachers belonged to the Silent Generation or were Baby Boomers. We're known as a cynical generation that is not likely to take things at face value. We grew up in the shadow of Watergate, with divorced parents and the church sex scandals of the 1980s, and were educated by Baby Boomers, whose distrust of institutions taught us to question tradition and be suspicious of truth claims. It should be no surprise that few of us entered into the ministry or went to the mission field. Those kinds of jobs struck us as dogmatic and intolerant. Many of us are now committed church members and pretty strict parents, and we work hard to keep our marriages healthy. But we will most likely not be in ministry in large numbers, nor are we prone to rally around a denomination's/movement's identity. Consequently, there is a stunning shortage of pastors in most denominations and movements, including the Church of God. Research funded by the Lilly Endowment clearly reveals that denominational decline among the mainstream has certainly been exacerbated by a failure to keep the youth connected.[5]

In the Church of God, there are some Gen-Xers in ministry. We tend to place a high value on relationships and far less on programs. Our ideal ministry setting is probably a small group, which may not even be meeting in a church. We may want to meet at a coffee house because we like to the see the church outside of the church building. We enjoy being the church everywhere; in that sense, we are even more removed from the Greatest Generation, which saw the Church of God grow and flourish within the movement's institutional organizations, and the Baby Boomers, who enjoyed seeing their own individual churches grow and flourish in their evangelistic capabilities through exposure to the greater evangelical culture. While Gen X's religious sensibilities may unnerve the older generations, our generation also puts a premium on bringing people together, whether it is by race, ethnicity, or class; we do not want anyone to be excluded. While the Baby Boomers wanted to make Christianity more inviting through their restructuring of the church, Gen-X wants to go out in the streets and do the inviting in face-to-face relationships.

There are no villains. In every case, each generation is trying to reconfigure itself to reach the world for Christ, but each generation tends to do that in a way that attracts its particular generation. So it should be no surprise that many in the Greatest Generation feel left out in the megachurch that strives to make its worship and its building overcome the prejudices against traditional denominational Christianity of their fellow non-Christian Boomers. Meanwhile, the Baby Boomers suspect that the Gen-Xers are dabbling in moral relativism when, in fact, the Gen-Xers are trying to tackle the cynicism of their generation by making church about relationships and au-

5. See James W. Lewis, "American Denominational Studies: A Critical Assessment" (Resources for American Christianity). http://www.resourcingchristianity.org

thenticity. We are more trapped in our generational culture than we realize in the Church of God. As a missionary in the Church of God, I am constantly navigating the various generations and the way they view the church. I am asked to inspire the Millennials, I am supported by churches led by Baby Boomer pastors, the actual donors are mostly from the Greatest Generation, and I myself am a Gen-Xer. Believe me, the differences are real.

One would think that generational differences would not be that great. After all, we have grown up in the same culture and society and even attend the same churches, yet there are barriers in our ability to completely relate to each other. How different can a generation be? I decided to take a closer look at the Millennials, a generation below me, to find out.

San Antonio: The Kids Are Alright

It is 95 degrees and muggy in San Antonio, Texas, a desert town two hours from the Mexican border. I am on the famous River Walk, which is filled with shops, swanky restaurants, and, of course, Starbucks. Numerous footbridges connect the river banks, and the trees overhang the walkways, giving this commercial area a tropical feel. Boats filled with tourists float by. I feel as if I am on a movie set or at a Disney theme park. Every few feet, there are stairs that lead people up from the River Walk to the streets of downtown.

Today the walk is particularly crowded as more than five thousand youth from the Church of God descend upon the city for the forty-sixth International Youth Convention of the Church of God (IYC). The River Walk snakes its way through the downtown area; on the northern end is my hotel, and on the southern end is the Convention Center. Walking toward the Convention Center, I see kids wearing matching T-shirts and on the street level vans and buses that say "Texas or Bust" and "Honk if you love Jesus." I see a van from a Church of God in Missouri and another one from the Tacoma Church of God. The Church of God in Pryor, Oklahoma, has a large bus. Many of these kids worked hard to get here to IYC, taking extra jobs or doing a paper route. Youth groups had car washes and bake sales. One group did cookbook sales and another did a 1940s-style dinner theater. One young person went around charging people to crack eggs over his head.

In today's denominational decline, there are many who say that large denominational events cannot be pulled off successfully. But every two years, Dr. Andy Stephenson, leader of youth ministries for Church of God Ministries, and the various teams assembled under his leadership prove those naysayers wrong. The event, which currently rotates between four U.S. cities, routinely mobilizes Church of God congregations from around the world to send their youth to an event that will challenge them spiritually and physically. Attendance can run as high as seven thousand, which calls for a breathtaking amount of preparation. At each convention, IYC invests heavily in planting a church in the host city or building onto a previous church plant. In addition, the host city itself is served by the legions of youth groups who do local ministry while in town.

I don't know what to expect. It has been twenty-three years since I have attended IYC. Back then it was held in Long Beach, California, next to the Spruce Goose plane and the Queen Mary ship. It was fun, but I don't remember it being spiritually challenging. Even when we had spiritual experiences, it was often hard to keep our commitment level high once we returned home.

Today's IYC, however, is a more holistic experience than the conventions I attended. Everything is strategically thought through so that there is more than an emotional encounter at IYC, that kids return home and experience change in their lives. Ministry, mentoring, follow-up—it's all part of the package of today's IYC. The kids will hear the gospel, they will have opportunities to make a commitment to ministry, they will be connected with a mentor and followed, and they will do service projects before and during the conference. The kids are deeply challenged on a number of levels.

Gina Shaner, a twenty-four-year-old currently in the process of ordination with the Church of God, is helping me to navigate the large convention center and the packed schedule of events. Gina suggested that I show up early. It's a good idea. But even though I arrive early, there is already a line of at least two thousand kids just waiting for the doors to open. These kids are seriously pumped.

Excitement hangs in the air. There is literally a countdown going on to the opening of the doors. Behind me, a couple of youth groups are chanting at each other, "We love Jesus, yes we do. We love Jesus. How about you?" as a staffer with a camera films them.

The doors finally open and we enter the arena. Christian rock videos play on three giant screens. There is a countdown on the screens and occasional snapshots of IYC attendees. The winner of the Facebook competition is announced on screen. I still don't get what Facebook is and can't imagine what the competition would have involved. The convention hasn't even started yet and already I can tell that this is nothing like the 1985 IYC.

The countdown hits zero, the lights dim, and the musicians walk out. The worship leader is bald, has two earrings, and sports a very long goatee; he's nothing like the preppy leaders that led the music when I was a kid. The music kicks in; the sound is deafening as the kids yell. The floor vibrates, and images of Jesus flash on the large screens behind the band. It is Charlie Hall singing, and his face is softer than in the picture found in the program book, his voice nice, and his countenance gentle and loving. You can tell that he's not just up there for himself. He's conscious of the kids and the importance of this event. The music is hard driving, complicated, with lyrics that seem meaningful and honest. The kids know the music and sing along. Many of them have their hands raised, the way we used to raise our hands for hymns and praise choruses. "My dead heart now is beating. My deepest stains now clean."[6]

By the second song I am hooked. The sincerity in the audience and in the worship leaders is clear. Large cameras are flying over the crowd as Hall sings and speaks to the crowd. "Jesus is your life, your whole life, your whole *strange* life." In this generation, Christian artists communicate more openly about the journey and the struggle of Christianity, which is a major difference from the era that we have just come out of, which emphasized music and messages with unambiguously happy messages. Authenticity and transparency are key for this younger generation, known as Millennials, Gen-Y, or Mosaics.

After the band finishes, the 2008 Student Leadership team is introduced—a team of ten Church of God youth from places like Elicott City, Maryland; Lebanon, Tennessee; and Dallas, Texas. These teens have spent the past two years of their lives helping plan the event, developing their leadership skills. We also learn about Spread the Word, a program that enables the youth to make a difference in the world. At every IYC, the youth are asked to bring about $20 for missions. With such a large attendance, it means that the young people usually raise $50,000 to $100,000 for missions during the three-and-a-half-day event. On screen are pictures of the various places where Spread the Word funds have been distributed. The program has supplied bicycles for pastors in Uganda, purchased a sound

---

6. "Marvelous Light." Lyrics by Charlie Hall. © 2005 worshiptogether.com Songs / sixsteps Music.

system for the Church of God in Honduras, and given money for the Hong Kong GodTeens program, among many other things.

Then we watch a skit by two improv actors, followed by a video drama starring high school kids from the Church of God. The video is about a girl who gives in to negative influences in her life and becomes overwhelmed with shame as Satan robs her of her belief in herself. It is well done. Andy Stephenson then takes the stage and explains that mirrors have been placed in the back of the arena; he invites the youth to write on the mirrors the destructive messages that they are carrying around about themselves, asking them to be very vulnerable and transparent. I think to myself that perhaps this might not work, that it would involve way too much vulnerability in front of peers. But I am instantly proven wrong. As soon as Andy says the word, the kids—many of them—go up to the mirrors and begin writing. These kids want to be set free.

> Youth is a time when so much of our core identity is formed.

I go to the back of the arena and watch as the kids bare their souls on the mirror.

"A Stupid Loser"
"Fat"
"A Failure"
"Weak"
"Lost"
"Shame"
"Worthless."

The number of kids who have written down the word *worthless* brings tears to my eyes. These kids are inundated with demoralizing and dehumanizing messages about themselves daily, and they are absorbing it. I did not know.

Efrem Smith, the day's speaker, gives an illustration about African impalas, wihch can jump fifteen feet straight up and thirty feet in distance. At the Minneapolis zoo, however, they are held in by a wall that's a mere three feet high. How does that work? "Because from an early age, they are taught that they cannot do what they naturally can do." As he says this, I wonder if that is what we do in the church?

It's a wonderful illustration and gets to the heart of why events like IYC are important. Youth is a time when so much of our core identity is formed, and in today's world young people are being bombarded with messages of superficiality. Anything that seeks to develop their identity in Christ is important, particularly in a culture that tells them that they are made for sex and superficial self-fulfillment.

But Andy and the IYC crew are not just interested in putting on a show. They are seeking to make sure that the kids have a "life change moment" (a phrase I would hear many times) and that these encounters are processed, so that these kids ultimately become agents-for-change out of this experience. By the end of the day, I am more fired up than I have been in a long time, and I am curious to see how IYC keeps the momentum going.

After the first evening's service, the kids divide into groups by geographic region and meet to discuss the evening's message. I decide to go to the Central Region room, randomly choosing to tag along with youth pastor Nate Hultz and his group from Sikeston, Missouri. Tonight's questions focus on people's images of you. I think back to when I was that age and the words "complete dork" flash through my head. One of the young men shares that he is teased because he is clumsy. Another shares that his old ways are changing because his life was recently transformed at youth camp.

Since Nate is twenty-something, I ask him if it is easy for him to relate to the teenagers.

"I feel I am already out of date. And most of our youth counselors are in their forties."

One thing that I hear over and over at IYC was that even people in their early twenties, like Nate and my assistant Gina, are having a hard time relating to today's teenagers. Things are changing *that fast*. Change is hard no matter what age you are at. I ask Nate what he would say to a more traditional, older Church of God person uncomfortable with the music and the presentation at IYC.

"I would first of all thank them for being faithful through the years and continuing to follow God through the years because we look up to them and they have a lot of knowledge and a lot of wisdom that we don't want to forget. But I would say, change is normal and we have to be willing to put aside the things that we love so dearly about worshiping God that we can do on our own time, to understanding that for so-and-so, who is seventeen years old, this is the only way he understands God. So we have to be willing to say, 'If he is getting it, then I need to love it because God is loving him through this and using this to reach him.'"

Nate reminds me that Jesus challenged the traditions of the church of his day.

"I'm only twenty-four years old and there's music and things that are happening now where I say, 'I can't worship that way,' but I am willing to take my students there. And I am willing to do the things that they enjoy even though I can't stand it because I know they can hear it; God is reaching them through it."

It's All About Transparency and Authenticity

By the second day, I am feeling old but loving IYC, and I'm anxious to attend one of the many breakout sessions offered for the kids at the convention center. There are classes on unleashing your gifts, world religions, spiritual warfare, family issues, mentoring, going deeper in your spiritual faith, discerning God's voice, and many others. There are also sessions for twelfth graders transitioning out of high school life and for college students. There are even classes for the adult leaders. I decide to start with a session by Chap Clark, a Fuller Seminary guru of all things teen.

Chap begins by saying that, "Most of the rhetoric about youth ministry has stayed the same for thirty years." Apparently, puberty now begins at twelve and adulthood starts in the mid-twenties. "What was cute and cuddly has taken a harder edge. If you have been working with students for the last six months, even if you are brand-new to this, you know that sometimes frivolity and craziness shifts into damage, violence, anger, and hurt that goes so deep. It is really easy for us to kind of think, 'Hey it's just youth ministry, play some games, prepare a talk,' but we are dealing with a completely different brand of kid now than we were even ten years ago."

Chap is on a roll. "Nothing is hidden from our kids, but we haven't been there to filter and help them process these things." Today's youth world, he tells us, "has stolen all innocence and hasn't given them any reason to mature."

I think back to what many of my former professors have said about this current generation of youth, the Millenials: "They are smarter and have a lot more information than Generation X did, but they are a lot less emotionally mature."

The formation of their identities can't be helped by today's more complicated family dynamics. "Their family tree includes my second dad, and my third father," Chap tells us. For a generation that has often grown up with not only one stepfather but various stepfathers, stepmothers, and stepsiblings, simple cliché definitions of God the Father understandably ring hollow. We shouldn't underestimate the degree to which broken families complicate how Christianity is perceived and understood.

"This generation of kids has been abandoned," Chap says. "They know adults like them when they perform, conform, and have an image that works. When they show up, sit down, smile, and shut up, they are welcome. Because almost no one is there for them—that is their perception, and we studied thousands and thousands of these kids in the largest study ever done of the inside world of these teenagers."

As the issues in teenagers lives have gotten more serious, so has IYC; this is one of the keys to its success. These kids are facing issues of cutting, anorexia, bulimia, obesity, sexual confusion, molestation, and other issues that the church has traditionally been slow to engage.

I decide to attend courses that would not have been offered at the IYC in 1985 when I was a teen. Marsha Reeder is teaching on "The Love Connection." She discusses alcoholism, drug addiction, cutting, sex addiction, addiction to pornography, and many other heavy issues. She then shares her personal testimony. Marsha's transparency is key. She doesn't stand high above them but engages them at a deep level out of her own fallenness. Today's youth carry a lot of pain, and simple clichés ring hollow.

I sneak into room 214, where Ricky Chelette is talking about what Scripture says about homosexuality. The room is packed. For the most part, you could have heard a pin drop in the room. There is the inevitable giggling as he talks about bodies changing during puberty, but that laughter is mostly coming from me. Ricky then says something shocking. "In today's schools bisexuality is cool."

In an afternoon session, we hear from Craig Gross, the founder of the XXX Church ministry, which reaches out to porn stars. Consider Craig's words about the teenagers of this generation: "They are downloading porn on their phones. The average age for exposure to porn is now eleven. One-third of porn addicts are now female." Craig shows us a video of a pastor's daughter that at age eight was exposed to porn and now works in the porn industry. It's a massive wake-up call. Pornography has the power to alter the brain. The fact that kids are being exposed to pornography in huge doses at the exact age that their sexuality is being activated is a very serious problem. When the youth are called to confess their sin of pornography addiction and to repent, many, both male and female, do so in front of thousands of their peers. I write in my notebook, "We can't afford to be squeamish about this anymore. The future health of these kids depends on our engaging this stuff in a serious and faith-filled manner. If we want to preach holiness to Church of God youth, these are the subjects we must deal with."

On Wednesday morning, the kids go to work to serve the city of San Antonio. When these youth groups left their hometowns, many headed first to other locations for service projects or mission trips before even getting to IYC. And now that they are here, they are spending one of the mornings doing something called IMPACT San Antonio. I decide to tag along with the large crew from East Side Church of God in Anderson, Indiana. Today, the kids are painting park benches.

Standing in the shadow of the 750-foot San Antonio Tower of the Americas, which provides a 360-degree view of the city, I listen as Jordan Sandefur tells me that the group just came from Corpus Christi, where in two and a half days, they painted six houses, scraped down and washed off houses, and mowed lawns.

One of the crew is Libby Parker, a seventeen-year-old who has been to two IYCs and is now on the planning committee for the 2010 IYC in Orlando. "It's a real honor for me. I just want to serve."

I ask, "Why do you want to do it? It's a lot of work and pressure."

"I love to serve. It's one of my passions. And here's my chance to help people have life change."

"Why is IYC important?"

"It was life changing for me last time. You feel a big sense of community when you are with a bunch of teenagers who have the same beliefs, the same passions, and praise the same God that you do. It provides a safe environment for you to really open up and work through some of those issues."

"What would you say to older people who say that you are just getting a temporary high at IYC?" I ask her.

"I would challenge them to take it seriously because we are the leaders of the Church of God for the next generation and we are passionate about God and we are passionate about this. And if they were to invest in our lives, they could help shape the future instead of being critical. You can tell the difference in our church of those who want to invest in us and those who don't. We have such better relationships with the ones who don't just want to criticize us because we are teenagers. Teenagers can be just as powerful and work just as well for God as anybody else."

I like these kids.

Brandon Mott is telling me that he has a car that runs on wasted vegetable oil.

"We get it from local restaurants, and it's really easy and really cheap."

Okay. Wow! I was wrecking my parents' new car at that age—not caring about the environment.

Brandon wonders if "we just need to be weird." He has my attention.

"Jesus was weird. He told Peter to pull money out of a fish. If we were just different, if we looked different. John 13:34 says that they will know that we are Christians by our love for one another. Love is radical. If people came to church and said, 'You guys are weird,' I feel that that would be very attractive because they are looking for something. They have the iPods, the cell phones, they've heard the church messages, they've gone to church, sung the songs, passed the plate, prayed the benediction, and gone home. They've done that their whole lives. But what if they saw church as this right here or as hanging out with their friends and having an intentional conversation about life?"

It's inspiring. But I'm even more impressed with Brandon's next comment.

"One of the problems with that is that it leaves out the older generation, and I don't want that because it won't do any good. So there's got to be a way to intermingle those two, and I'm not saying I know what it is, but I want to."

On the final night, I help with an anointing service. Anointing was a common practice in the Church of God, but is something that has slowly disappeared from most church services. Not at IYC however.[7] The youth have been told that they can make their way to anyone standing and wearing a red shirt. I am one of those people. Since there are so many of us in red shirts, I wonder if anyone will even show up for me to anoint. Will these twenty-first-century kids do something so nineteenth-century?

---

7. Anointing was also part the Youth Conference of the Church of God in Germany a year later, at which I was asked to speak.

At the word "Go," a huge line forms in front of me. I begin putting the oil on their foreheads in the form of a cross. The line is long, and all look eager and expectant. Each person tells me their name, and I say a few words to them and call them by name as I anoint them with oil. They are short, tall, big, small, smiling, have been crying, and have come from everywhere. About half way through my time anointing, a young boy of about twelve comes up to me, his body literally shaking, and through his loud sobbing he cries out to me: "I'm so lonely!"

I'm stunned by the depth of his pain. I hug him and feel led to whisper a number of things into his ear as he holds on to me, his body heaving. This is totally unexpected. As my line gets held up, someone else in a red shirt comes over to assist me and the anointing starts up again as I continue talking to this boy. Eventually, I have to let go of him since there are so many people behind him waiting to be anointed.

I spend the rest of that night a bit shaken, kicking myself for not having told that young man to meet me immediately after the service. I can't get his face out of my head. I spend the time after that service looking for the young boy with the very blonde hair. I never find him.

IYC ends the next morning, and I am still thinking about that young man. Did I pursue him enough? I begin to wonder that about the whole Church of God. We are concerned about preserving our identity, but have we done enough to pursue those who will carry it on into the future. We've had youth groups, we've tried to make it fun, but have we mobilized and pursued the youth where they are? I fear not. I find myself leaving San Antonio very grateful to Andy Stephenson and his crew for being willing to enter into the world of today's youth. They have created an event that mobilizes the whole movement. They have created a convention that is open, flexible, and under constant revision. In organizing it, they are training young twenty-somethings and teen leaders, and within the event itself they connect youth to mentors on the spot. As if that's not enough, they invest in the host city and leave it better than when they came. They also invest in a local church, they encourage missions, and they drench the entire thing in prayer. It's a model not just for youth ministry but for the Church of God as a whole.

But I leave feeling convicted that perhaps we have wanted certain behavior from our Church of God youth and have not been willing to change our behavior enough to invite them into holiness and unity.

As I walk out of the convention center, I pass the mirrors where the kids wrote about how they now feel about themselves. This time the words the kids wrote were different. On the mirrors I see the words:

"Chosen"

"Child of God"

"Disciple"

"A Temple"

"Complete."

Uganda: Transferring Leadership to the Next Generation

Sometimes, the negative messages that young people get in the Church of God come not only from society but from the church itself. In many countries where the Church of God movement exists, the unwillingness of the older generation to make way for the new generation is extinguishing the church. Here are three reasons why the Church of God in many nations is experiencing a shortage of young people in the church.

1. **Lack of Strategy:** In some countries, the lack of youth and emerging leaders in the church has to do with cultural shifts and a failure to understand and engage young people at a serious level in the church. In these countries, there is a desire for young people to go into ministry and emerge as leaders, but there has not been an effective strategy and young people have fallen through the cracks. In most cases, approaches to attracting youth were never re-evaluated over the decades, and now the church is very ill-equipped to engage or even understand the young generation.

2. **Cultural Ambivalence:** In other countries in the Church of God, however, there have been intentional efforts to prevent young people from emerging as leaders. This occurs in countries that place great value on elders and seniors and view anyone under the age of fifty as youth. It also occurs in countries and cultures where authoritarian tendencies run strong and top leaders occupy their positions until death. The irony, of course, is that this lack of investment in the younger generation means that the work of the older generation will most likely end with

their deaths. The legacy will not be carried on. While there may be cultural reasons for this skeptical attitude toward youth (especially in agrarian cultures where strict hierarchies were important to maintaining order in the family and village), the end result is that these fellowships often have calcified leadership, and when the top leaders vacate their offices, a leadership vacuum emerges and the whole church in that region suffers.[8]

3. **Monopoly of Power:** In some cases around the world, a particular tribe, family, husband and wife, or ethnic group has a stranglehold on leadership and prevents talented young leaders from emerging.

Uganda is a country where these problems could easily have occurred. But because of wise leadership that values young people and emerging leaders, the Church of God in Uganda is flourishing and has a bright future.

John Walters, the director of Christians Broadcasting Hope[9], and I drive to the capital city of Kampala to meet Tim and Colleen Stevenson as well as some of the top leadership in the Ugandan church. Their home is on the shores of Lake Victoria, a lake so large that after six hours of driving close to the shores, we have only driven about a quarter of the way around the lake. In this lush, tropical country are roughly five hundred Church of God congregations.[10] The Stevensons have helped to start more than 120 schools, including a gorgeous international school in Kampala named Heritage International.

The Church of God in Uganda is young because Uganda is young. Life expectancy is only in the fifties; 60 percent of the country is under the age of fifteen, and 80 percent is under the age of thirty. This means that Tim

---

8. Allow me to return to my example of the young low-caste Indian driving a BMW in Bangalore. For thousands of years, the caste system brought order to an agrarian society with too many people and not enough resources. Today, however, not only does India make enough food to feed itself (most shortages are due to corruption), but high tech industry is a valuable part of the national economy. The tech company doesn't care how old the low-caste Indian is; all that matters are his skills. He is no longer operating under the restrictions of an agrarian economy because India now has an industrial, service, and high-tech economy as well. However, when the young Indian goes to his church, he may very well be constrained by the traditional agrarian-culture views of leadership, which view age and experience as nonnegotiable requirements for attaining leadership.

9. Christians Broadcasting Hope is the umbrella organization for the worldwide broadcasts of the Church of God in nine languages.

10. Due to an insurgency in the north, some of the people from churches have had to move to camps temporarily.

and Colleen—both raised as missionary kids in Africa—have been living in Uganda longer than most Ugandans. They are busy. In addition to the schools they have started, there is the TAPP program (Tumaini AIDS Prevention Program), the identifying of sponsors for more than four thousand children, works in Rwanda and the Democratic Republic of Congo, the hosting of various work camps, leadership training, and the identification of new ministries in projects throughout Africa. They also serve as the field representatives of the Church of God in Germany's mission efforts through Kinderhilfswerk. I was primarily interested in talking to them because as far as leadership and the utilization of young emerging leaders in the Church of God is concerned, Uganda is a model of health.

As I speak with Tim at his lakeshore home, the equatorial sun sets rapidly and the sound of a Guineafowl provides background noise. Tim explains to me that in Africa, the lack of emerging leadership can be not only generational or tribal but even clan-based.

"There's a very narrow power structure," he tells me as we sit on the back porch. "It's not just a generational concern; it is a tribal concern and a clan concern." From the beginning, veteran missionaries Stan and Marion Hoffman, Colleen's parents, were concerned about the issue. When the Hoffmans arrived in 1983 to restart the Church of God in Uganda, there were only two churches. Within nine years, there were three hundred more. The Hoffmans knew they needed solid leadership training and that they would have to be proactive about avoiding tribal divisions. The Stevensons arrived shortly thereafter and continued the vigilance.

Today, the key leaders in Uganda are in their fifties—young by the region's standards. But more importantly, there is plenty of young leadership already at the executive level. In the Ugandan Church of God, the requirement for leadership has to do with how long you have been in your specific post. "You can't have someone run for office unless they have been in leadership for twelve years," Tim informs me. "Young people who begin working in the church can be eligible for leadership by their late twenties and early thirties. Some key leaders are already in that age range. It is experience and a proven track record as a wise Spirit-led leader that makes one eligible for leadership. "This prevents untested but charismatic leaders from working their way into leadership," he says.

This is very wise since there have been times in the Church of God when charismatic leaders have been able to work their way into key leadership positions without having much of a track record within the movement as healthy leaders. Many problems could have been avoided by clearer expectations of those eligible for leadership. But the Church of God in many places suffers from a lack of organizational safeguards (an issue explored in chapter 4).

Nor can one Ugandan clan dominate the Ugandan Church of God. There are six districts in the Church of God in Uganda, and there are at least fifty tribes in the country. People select the leader who best represents them (perhaps from their tribe) as district chairman. There may be forty different representatives chosen, but there is very little overlap in tribes.

> **Leaders who are not threatened by emerging leadership (and who actually encourage it) can be very rare in the church.**

"When we look at students going to KIST [Kima International School of Theology], we get concerned if we see that only one area is sending young people to KIST. It's not about creating quotas but about being alert and trying to have equal development."

The continual emphasis on leadership training also helps to prevent one block of leaders from obtaining a monopoly on power in the Ugandan church.

"We really promote leadership training, even if you are a gifted leader or are part of a family of strong leaders. Getting trained, getting skills, getting equipped is important. We want other people to look at new ministries, to develop their own gifting."

As obvious as it may sound, finding leaders who are not threatened by emerging leadership (and who actually encourage it) can be very rare in the church. New leadership means new ideas and new directions, which can compete with or replace the vision of the older leaders. Movements need to be revitalized constantly, but what happens more often than not is that a status quo is found and the leadership becomes too deeply entrenched to want change. Fortunately, in Uganda all the leaders I am meeting are enthusiastic about seeing new leaders emerge.

The new infusion of leadership also serves as a balancing force that prevents abuse of power or the misdirection of the church. As Stan Hoffman has said, "Believers who are not properly taught are a bigger threat to

Christianity than paganism. All kinds of cults and heresies have had their beginnings in this manner."[11]

Tim elaborates: "The more leaders being trained, the more people who are being equipped, and the more people getting information and knowledge, the less likely it is that individuals will misdirect the church, because you will have a core group of leaders who will understand decisions being made. They will be better equipped to articulate to the leader if they go down the wrong path. I don't see age, tribalism, or family control to be things that can't be broken down by training."

Another challenge for the Church of God has been that some non-Western (and Western for that matter) pastors receive education and then feel that they are "too educated" to return to the people in the local church. When young people and pastors are given assistance to train for ministry, it needs to be clear that they are being trained to be servants, not to enter some higher realm that makes them inaccessible to the people they were meant to serve. Just having a degree or a title behind your name doesn't necessarily win you points in the Ugandan Church of God.

Tim continues, "There are leaders who are educated but don't have knowledge. We should look at the fruit they produce. An understanding of church structure, interpersonal skills, social development—all of that is the part of the knowledge that we are looking at."

A day later we leave the lakeshore home behind to speak with Moses Abasola, the legal representative of the Church of God in Uganda. We are headed in the direction of his home in the eastern part of the country on a beautiful sunny day on the equator. We drive past bright green mountains, fields of tea, tiny villages, and a shocking number of mosques—evidence of Islam's push into sub-Saharan Africa, where Christianity has been the dominant religion. Some of the mosques are miniature and made out of mud.[12]

Moses is filled with a gracious spirit and a bright, warm smile. He refused to allow me to sit in the back seat as John drives us across the country. I shudder to think of what kind of cultural faux pas I am committing by sitting in front of this great man who speaks nine languages. He really does allow inexperienced youth to move up!

---

11. As quoted in Lester Crose, Cheryl Johnson Barton, and Donald D. Johnson, *Into All the World: A Century of Church of God Missions* (Anderson, IN: Warner Press, 2009), 248.

12. Jonathan J. Bonk points out that there were four times as many Muslims as Christians in Africa a century ago, but today there are two hundred million more Christians than Muslims and 46 percent of the continent is Christian ("Africa Unbound," *Christianity Today*, November 2007, 49).

"We have tried so much to train the younger leaders in places like KIST because we know that they are the leaders of tomorrow. Now we have a good number of pastors who have passed through KIST. If we want the church to grow and to stay strong, we must have these leaders trained," Pastor Abasola says, as John steers us toward the Ugandan border.

The result of this willingness to train the young is that dynamic ministry is occurring in a variety of settings, such as the work I saw being done by KIST graduate David Wafula, who heads the TAPP office in Kampala.

Abasola is encouraged. "I see the church growing and many good things happening, like social works, schools, reaching people with sickness, and we have a wonderful relationship with the USA, Canada, the Germans, and we have gone to Sudan, Congo, Burundi, Rwanda, and even Ethiopia. We go when there is a need to help leadership there." The Ugandan Church of God is an example of the way the African church is increasingly mobilized. An African renaissance is occurring as countries that once only hosted missionaries are now reaching other countries and sending more than 18,400 missionaries abroad to places such as Brazil and even Indiana.[13]

The Church of God in Uganda has challenges according to Abasola. "We still cannot stand on our own. There is a need for support in different areas." This is understandable, considering the huge size of the church in a country with a per capita income of only $1,000 per year. The Stevensons and Pastor Abasola are emphatic that there is still a great need for partnership and support between the Western world and the non-Western world. Uganda still needs help—not just financial, but in every area imaginable. But despite the lack of financial resources, the Ugandan church taps into its greatest resource for the future—the youth—and is creating a healthy structure to support this emergence.

It also leaves plenty of openings for foreigners to help out in unique ways. Tim had told me, "The church is so young here that you can just be a normal Joe in North America and have some great experiences that you can share with them. As a couple, as a parent, you can share with 60 percent of the Ugandan population because they haven't had those experiences."

The threat of dependency, the avoidance of which can sometimes be taken to an extreme as a response against the colonialism of the past, can be greatly lessened if the leadership is actively mentoring a new generation of leaders and shows a willingness to continually look beyond their borders

---

13. Ibid.

as part of their mission. The Ugandan church is not inward looking. Quite the opposite, they give back with what they receive. It is not only extending training programs to other African nations. Pastors and other visitors from Europe and North America are totally revitalized after spending time in the Ugandan church.

For instance, in 2006, a group of Anderson University students took a trip to work with the TAPP program. The TAPP members in Uganda were making crafts to sell but did not have a market in which to sell them. The group of Millennial youths from North America took the beads back home and began to sell them. The result was not just a few sales of beads but the birth of TAPP USA, a grassroots effort with a U.S. office at Park Place Church of God in Anderson. This, in turn, led to a regular internship program. When we see this kind of healthy synergy occurring, we have moved beyond the post-colonial issues of dominance and dependency toward one of mutual support based on bottom-up needs, not top-down demands.

Pastor Abasola gives perspective about the need for more creative interaction and relationship between the regions of the world: "We have a common goal: the Great Commission that the Lord gave us. If we stand together, I think we shall be able to fight the enemy—that is the devil. If we break up, we may become weak on both sides. There's so much that the Western church can learn from the African church and so much the African church can learn from the Western church. We need a common platform to discuss these things. Each country doing their own thing is a weakness." Amen.

Giving Birth in the Dominican Republic

The Church of God in the Dominican Republic is firing on all cylinders. One of the key reasons for their growth is that youth and gender are not barriers toward entering into church leadership. Unlike so many countries I visited, there is no shortage of young, emerging leaders in this country. But in order to have this kind of success in raising up young leaders, a number of other things have to be in place as well. Let's take a look.

The Dominican Republic is known for its great baseball players. As we make our way to the home of Pastora Yira and her husband Benito Rodriguez, we drive past the blue waters of the Caribbean Sea. We pass through Sammy Sosa's hometown and pass the 30/30 Plaza, a commercial center built by the famous baseball slugger. We are headed to an area called La

Romana, where, although located on the Caribbean coast, it hardly ever rains. The weather, which starts sunny, quickly turns, and before long, it is raining. We pass children huddling under the water falling from the roof drains—a common sight here.

This traditionally Roman Catholic country has crossed the tipping point, and evangelical Christianity is growing rapidly throughout the country. The D.R. has always been a religious culture. Juan points out a school building that has the national shield on it, its motto clearly visible: "*Dios, Patra, Libertad.*" "Notice that God is first," he tells me. The Spanish Conquistadors and their priests set up the first cathedral, the first hospital, and the first university in the Americas on this part of the island of Hispañola, and the Roman Catholic Church has been dominant ever since. But today, 20 percent of the population is evangelical, and only 4 percent of professing Catholics are practicing their faith. Moreover, as is happening in other parts of the world, there are now many charismatic Catholics with parishes structuring themselves more like evangelical churches, much to Rome's chagrin.

Juan Santos was the first Church of God convert in the Dominican Republic. Now in his early forties, he is a widely respected leader in the community. His church of five hundred has planted two other congregations; his own congregation was a church plant.

"It used to be that evangelicals were viewed as crazy people, but now it's becoming respectable and mainstream. People now commonly use the expression, 'God bless you,' and people know how to respond: 'Amen.' I think in ten years this country will be 40 percent evangelical." The well-known Latin musician Juan Luis Guerra is an evangelical Christian, and so is Freddie Veras Goico, the Oprah Winfrey of the Dominican Republic, who was very hostile toward religion until his recent conversion experience.

The land is mostly flat and green in this part of the Dominican as we hug the shoreline and enter La Romana. As we arrive at Pastora Yira's house, a torrential downpour begins that lasts the rest of the night. This is apparently very unusual. Pastor Yira and her husband came here to La Romana to start a church. The Church of God in the Dominican Republic has a dream to have a church in all thirty-two provinces of the country. Thus far, the mother church in Santo Domingo has birthed six daughter churches and two granddaughter churches. There are currently churches in three provinces as well as the capital city. Their vision is also to eventually plant churches in Spain and Puerto Rico and to work with the Hispanic Council in the United States to plant a church there as well. Juan tells me that Dominicans are particularly good at planting churches because they are friendly, sociable people. This is obvious. As soon as I step into Yira and Benito's home, I feel as if I am with long-lost relatives.

The couples being sent out are young. In some cases, they have been Christians for less than ten years, but the guidance and experience they receive upon becoming part of the church is so comprehensive that despite their youth, they have been well-trained for the difficult job of starting a church.

Yira and Benito Rodriguez were both in secular jobs a few years ago. But God began to put the area of La Romana on Yira's heart. A little while later, Pastor Gerardo Taron, the Argentinean pastor who started the work in this country, asked her if she had any feelings about helping to start a church in La Romana.

"I started to laugh," Yira tells me, "because God had called me there."

Yira's mother also felt that God was calling her to La Romana. The big surprise came when Yira told her mother that God was also calling her to go! In the end, Benito and Yira left their secular jobs and, along with Yira's mother, set off for La Romana without jobs or much money. Two other young ladies from the church came with them to live for those initial months. This kind of support surrounding the church planting pastors has been very effective in helping church planters battle the loneliness and discouragement that can come in those initial months. People never go alone.

As we sip coffee, Pastor Juan tells me about the mentality of pastors in the Dominican Republic. "In the USA," Pastor Juan says, "nobody thinks about being a pastor without knowing what will be involved regarding salary, insurance, and all of those things. Here, the words *pastor* and *salary* are two words that are not connected...We adapt to the resources we get."

"Our first offering was seven pesos," Yira says, laughing (that's about twenty cents U.S.). The mother church in Santo Domingo, however, provided finances to help, and so did Pastor Billy Franks in Louisiana. The Dominicans have developed strong relationships with partners in the U.S. church that give the right amount of support at the right time—enough to keep the ministry expanding, but not so much as to foster dependency. This goes for the mother church as well. "The mother church is decreasing its support to us. We are increasingly more indigenous financially, but not relationally," Yira says. This is key! Too often in the Church of God, churches have been planted in isolation with little support offered to church planters. If the church is successful, the ties to the original supporters are often broken and a new, overly autonomous Church of God congregation is born. In the Dominican Republic, that relationship is always maintained, which helps to not only preserve Church of God identity but to strengthen both the mother church and the newly established church. Members of the mother church continue to have a connection to a nearby mission field where they can use their gifts and make a difference on a regular basis.

When Pastora Yira came here with her family, a whole caravan of cars came to drop them off. And on weekends and on holidays, it's not uncommon for large groups from the mother church to come and stay to offer encouragement and help the ministry. "We plant with people," Yira says, "because this is a highly relational culture. It is a real trauma to leave the church family behind."

This culture of community and mutual support begins when they first become Christians and become part of the church. The Church of God in the Dominican Republic has had success attracting youth because they are willing to be flexible. It is not uncommon, for instance, for outreaches to utilize Christian rap and reggae instead of hymns or traditional praise choruses. Dressing casual is also acceptable. This is a big deal among other evangelical and Pentecostal churches, which are often very legalistic and even have a problem with girls wearing pants instead of skirts and people wearing tennis shoes. Pastor Juan can often be seen wearing jeans and a black T-shirt. This is highly unusual for evangelical pastors in this country, but it has enabled Juan to connect with more people. In the Dominican Church of God, adult pastors mix with the youth and meet them where they are at in life. This integration between the older generation and the young remains a constant in their church experience. Segregating young people from older people robs the young of having older mentor figures in their life. In this country, everyone seems to grow up with spiritual fathers and mothers in the church.

Once the youth accept Christ, they are quickly informed about the expectations that the church has for them. They are introduced into a new life, which includes replacing secular music with Christian music, not watching TV, and committing very seriously to fellowship in the church. There is a series of nine lessons that introduce them to the Christian life. Lesson 8 deals with the theology and beliefs of the Church of God. Lesson 9 introduces them to a new concept—the spiritual father. They will be mentored by a man or a woman in the church, and it will be an intimate relationship—not just a designated leader, but more like a parent. The concept of tithing is introduced at the very beginning, "before they get in the habit of not giving," Juan says. There is talk about managing your finances and how to live as a Christian in the workplace and among your non-Christian friends. There is also a weekend retreat. The integration and mentoring of youth is all very intentional in the Dominican Republic, and that intentionality is what is often missing in other Church of God countries.

Each church here is divided into cell groups. Each group has a leader with twelve disciples (the number does not always have to be exactly twelve, but it will not be much more than that). That leader is deeply involved in mentoring each person and preparing them to eventually mentor others. "These groups are not simply Bible study groups," Juan tells me. "It's living together. It's how Jesus and the disciples interacted. They see us leaders with our families, in our weak moments, even in our anger. It's a natural transfer of the Christian life. Our primary goal is to develop people who will influence others, not to build up the local church. Church members don't help you get a vision; disciples do. We are all leaders in this church."

Of course, not all people are natural-born leaders who can one day start a church. In fact, there are always people in any church who are pretty immature. That is why this church is sensitive to the individual capacities of people. Pastor Juan and the others are aware of this. "From the beginning, people are given jobs in the church. Their skills are used. If they are not mature or they are not good with people, they won't be given those kinds of jobs. But they will be given something else." People grow up in this church constantly using their talents for the Lord. The servant heart of the people is pretty obvious to me as I meet with the brothers and sisters here. But inevitably, jealousy and competition arises in situations like this. That is why the church is very strict about everyone being humble and non-competitive. "There are no battles to be the top leader here. Nobody wants to be the top leader, but everyone is a leader," Juan tells me. "In twenty-six years, we have had no division in the church of God in the Dominican Republic." There are few countries in the Church of God that can say that! Avoidance of schisms and competition between pastors and laypeople, as well as maintaining unity, is something that has to be infused in the DNA of a church at the very beginning, and it must be constantly reasserted and safeguarded. Pastor Gerardo has been careful to make sure that this Dominican Church of God DNA is reinforced. Unlike so many Church of God congregations, the churches here are not so easily moved to and fro by outside theological influences.

At the same time, neither is negative talk about other denominations or religious groups tolerated. People have taken notice of the Church of God in the Dominican Republic, and some churches, especially Pentecostals, are critical of the lack of speaking in tongues, the "liberalism," and the "absence of the Holy Spirit." The Church of God does not retaliate, however. Pastor Gerardo, the national leader, has taught his congregations that when someone accuses them, "you must channel all those negative thoughts you initially feel into prayer for these other churches." Pastor Gerardo has lived that out and modeled it by example. His disciples have internalized this message.

The Church of God here reaches out to many other denominations, including those that are critical of them. One year, a hurricane hit the country and damaged the roof of a nearby Pentecostal church that had been critical of the Church of God. The Church of God responded by donating their tithes for an entire month to help the other church build a new roof. The other pastor was taken aback and changed his tune about the Church of God. "You can't convince people by talking," Juan says. "It's done by actions." There is widespread respect here for the church, and the result is that the Church of God in the Dominican Republic is often asked by other churches and organizations to give conferences on every subject under the sun.

Avoidance of schisms and competition ... has to be infused in the DNA of a church at the very beginning.

I say goodbye to Yira and Benito, and the next day we drive into the mountains of La Vega. I am told that unlike La Romana, where it supposedly never rains, it always rains in La Vega. When I arrive, it is completely sunny. So my presence in La Romana causes the sun to go away in favor of rain, and in La Vega it causes the constant rain to turn into sun. I seem to be having a disconcerting effect wherever I go, and I begin to wonder if it's an omen about the reception of this book.

I find twenty-seven-year-old Pastor Carmen Mejia de Soreono and her motorcycle-riding husband Francis in the town of Jarabacoa. Carmen is a product of Juan's congregation and joined the church as a teenager. She was given many opportunities to develop her leadership skills over the years and developed a burden for this beautiful area in the mountains. This is not an easy area to start a church. "It's an idolatrous city," Carmen tells me as we sit in the back porch of a house they are renting. There is a beautiful creek behind us, and the sound of the water makes for a relaxing atmosphere. "Every community has an altar with the Virgin Mary. If you visit the houses, you will find the Virgin inside. Now it is starting to change, and there are changes happening now that evangelicalism is growing, but it's a slower growth here than in Santiago or Santo Domingo. It is more traditional here."

The people tend to not be as outgoing and personable in this part of the country. That takes some getting used to for the very sociable pastors who come out of the Santo Domingo churches. "Here the people are nice, but a bit cold," Carmen tells me, as her husband Francis sits down to join us. "They all have a dream to go to the United States. We call the people 'Dominicanyork' because 40 percent of the people from around here live in the United States for part of the year and here for the other half. It's an unstable environment. Even though it's a small community with an economy that's strong because of tourism, the people here live on foreign remittances. In Santo Domingo, a person who doesn't work, doesn't eat. But here, the people don't feel that they need to work or do anything because they get money from remittances."

This affects the church culture. "The hardest thing is that the people here say yes when you ask them about Christ or whether they want to accept Christ. But to disciple is tough. They don't like commitments. If you ask them, 'Can you help with a scripture?' then they don't show up to church anymore. They don't like to commit."

Although neither Carmen or Yira were educated in seminary, they found that the in-house leadership training schools in the Dominican Church of God congregations prepared them very well. "We were part of the school of leaders," Carmen remembers, "and it is a year and a half of training. Every church has a school of leaders. We learned a lot in that school, and it was stuff that is relevant."

The primary tool of evangelism is friendship. The churches are like families, and they invite their friends to join the family. In the Dominican Republic, people's lives revolve around the church. Church is the center of everything, as opposed to many countries where church is just one activity among many that take place during the week. Church in the Anglo world, in particular, is the spiritual activity of the week. In the Dominican Republic or Hong Kong, where we served, church is everything. As for the family atmosphere, in a country where almost everyone comes from a broken home, the healthy family dynamics in the church prove to be life changing for many people. While divorce rates are extremely high in the Dominican Republic, in all of the Church of God congregations, there has currently only been one marriage that didn't make it. That's a remarkable testament to how this church is transforming the culture around it.

There are a number of things that they do right here. First of all, they have a leader who is not afraid of seeing other pastors surpass him. "How could you not want your own children to do better than you?" Pastor Gerardo said to me one evening as we drove through a poorer part of Santo Domingo. It is a great attitude that too few leaders possess. Second, Pastor Gerardo is not only an intelligent leader, he is an intuitive leader. He has a high emotional intelligence quotient (E.Q.). In other words, he reads people well and knows how to deal with people and situations well. He understands that people are different, and he can adjust to those differences. I have found that a high E.Q. is pretty much make or break for a pastor. If a pastor has a low E.Q., the church will probably not do too well. Third, the core DNA of the church is well established. Theologically, organizationally, everyone is intentionally mentored on the way to do things. People learn how the church runs best by a leader who is an active teacher and chooses wise leaders to join him at the top. Fourth, after centralizing the system, the system is then flexible and open, allowing people to adjust their own churches to the culture in which they are working and to work in their own style. There is unity in the core values but openness in how the people and the other churches work. Fifth, the people that make up the church are willing to follow the leader, but that leader doesn't abuse his power and he empowers others. Sixth, there is a grand vision that everyone understands. They are here to evangelize every part of their country and their communities by planting churches. "We claim our communities for Christ," Pastor Gerardo says. "We don't just exist in the community; we aim to steer it."

"We want to raise a Church of God here," Carmen says, as I get ready to leave. "We want a church that can transform people and that can restore families." It has been done in Santo Domingo, and with the young leading the way, it is bound to happen again all over the Dominican Republic.

3
how should we
then teach?

The Theological Challenge
Portland, Anderson, Germany, Kenya, Thailand, Akron

The age we now live in has been described as a post-theological age. Few Christians decide which church they will attend based on a denomination's theology. Instead they choose churches that make them feel at home. The atmosphere, the style of worship, and the programs provided seem to be the deciding factor. As long as the church is Christian, few bother to find out the specifics about the church's theological heritage. This is very different from the atmosphere that existed when the Church of God began—one that was very theologically competitive and in which even minor theological differences could lead to schism.

The early Church of God reformers coalesced around some very specific theological issues facing them in the late nineteenth century. First of all, they affirmed that the foundation of the Christian faith is the Bible. Second, they held that religion is essentially experiential and that a second work of grace was vital to salvation from sin. Furthermore, they believed that God was specifically "calling them out" in the last days to be a united Christian community not associated with sects or denominations. These beliefs propelled the movement forward, and it grew quickly to the point that now, more than a century later, the Church of God exists in nearly ninety countries around the world. We are now at the beginning of the twenty-first century, however, and many of the theological concerns of the believers in these nations are far different than those of the nineteenth-century reformers. Even in the American Midwest, the religious atmosphere has changed dramatically since the beginning of the Church of God. The theological ground has shifted beneath us in a variety of ways that were not foreseeable to D. S. Warner. But how much has it changed?

The Road Map

In this chapter we go to Portland to visit the president emeritus of Warner Pacific College, Jay Barber. This Church of God college exists in one of the most post-Christian environments in the United States, the Pacific Northwest. Providing a Christian education and raising pastors has never been more difficult, and Dr. Barber explains why. We then visit the Anderson University School of Theology to hear how even within seminaries, which exist to train people for ministry, fewer and fewer people are interested in serving in a traditional setting. From Anderson, we go to Germany to learn about the things that the Church of God there does to prevent the total loss of theological identity. In Western Kenya, we will visit the Kima International School of Theology because even in a non-Western society where Christianity is growing rapidly and education is at a premium, it is increasingly challenging to run a Bible school. In Thailand, we will learn about the considerable expectations placed upon pastors to understand Church of God theology before ordination. Finally, we will go to Akron to see how African-American culture has been able to retain a sense of authority and tradition in their churches despite the weakness of the Church of God in these areas. But first, we briefly look at how the movement's theological understanding of itself is changing.

The Changing Theological Landscape

Were D. S. Warner to join us today in the twenty-first century, he might be confused by the changes in our theological emphases. So much has changed since Warner's time. He would hardly recognize the theological landscape around the world today.

The theological issues that Warner was concerned with were a direct response to the situation in the American Midwest in the late nineteenth century. As historian John W. V. Smith wrote: "The foundations of the religious reformation were laid in the soil of rural America and fashioned of basic Christian principles as they applied to the life of the people who lived there."[1]

In those days, they preached the need to end denominationalism, the need to be empowered by the Holy Spirit so as to live truly Spirit-led lives, the need to live as a community of saints, the need to stay true to their Wesleyan-Holiness roots, and the need to resist the secularization forces within America. Warner's voice needed to be heard on those issues in towns and cities across America in the nineteenth century. But those are not the most pressing issues that Christians in China, Nepal, Kenya, Guatemala, and Burma are facing at the dawn of the twenty-first century. What the Church of God reformers may have been preaching was true and important, but it was also addressing a situation in America—specifically the nineteenth century American Midwest. Warner and the reformers could not foresee that the movement would exist for so long and take in so many different countries and cultures with different theological landscapes.

Second, Warner might assume that the church has completely lost its way and is far removed from the first-century church that we read about in Acts. Ironically, however, if Warner were to travel the world today, he would see that the church in much of the non-Western world looks more like the church in Acts than the Church of God reformation did in the nineteenth century! This is because the Church of God reformation took place as an extension of various Christian reformations as they manifested themselves in countries with a strong Christian heritage. In other words, the Church of God reformation movement was very much a product of Western Christianity and Christendom.

Today, however, many Church of God Christians live outside of that Western society, and Christendom is no more. For the twenty-first century Church of God believers, Christianity is spreading in non-Western (non-Judeo-Christian) societies primarily through Scripture and the Holy Spirit. The non-Western experience of Christianity thus far has been devoid of the large-scale theological and military wars, reformations, and sometimes painful schisms that formed Christendom and that ultimately produced the Church of God reformation movement. Non-Western Christians are reforming their respective non-Christian societies, not critiquing Western Christian practices as the early Church of God did.

---

1. John W. V. Smith, *A Brief History of the Church of God Reformation Movement* (Anderson, IN: Warner Press, 2006), 19.

The believers in China have never experienced denominations because they were forbidden. New Christians in Nepal are not familiar with Calvin or Wesley because they do not come from churches, a country, or a civilization shaped by those debates. African believers come from an environment in which it is assumed that we are surrounded by spirits and that God most emphatically exists; there's no sense of the secular or atheism to fight against. The question is not, Is there a God? but rather, Which God do you follow? Guatemalan Christians cannot articulate a doctrine of sanctification because the only Christianity that they have ever known is a very Spirit-centered, borderline Pentecostal Christianity inspired by the Bible, not by the theological works of Europeans and North Americans. And Burmese believers are puzzled that the importance of community has to be articulated because amid the persecution in Burma one could not survive without community. Only in a country as powerful and wealthy as the United States (even in the nineteenth century) could such a radical individualism take hold.

The point is not that Church of God theology is irrelevant (we shall see in later chapters that indeed it may be more relevant than ever); rather it is that 130 years later, the terrain in which we operate is far more expansive and the theological challenges are, in many cases, quite different and more complex.

This is the natural result of becoming a global movement that is more than a century old. Today, many are coming to Christ not because it has been presented to them by Westerners or by some denomination but simply because the Word of God is spreading around the world with no strings attached. Many people—Muslims in Bangladesh, for instance—are learning about Jesus through visions. This is a shock to many in the West who still assume that Christianity must be spreading because Westerners are sending missionaries. The Westerner thinks, "Surely they will only get it right if they are building upon Augustine, Calvin, Wesley, or Warner." But for millions of Christians now, their only guide is the Bible—particularly the Book of Acts. This is something that would please the early Church of God reformers. Today there are more non-Western missionaries in the world than Western missionaries, and in many cases, they are not carrying the doctrinal suppositions of European and North American denominational Christianity.

As I see it, in the twenty-first century, there are basically three theological worlds that the Church of God exists in around the world.

1. **The Traditional World:** This is a world where churches are structured in a traditional style, people have an understanding that they are part of the larger church, and the culture around them knows and understands the role of churches. The average church in Indiana or Costa Rica exists in this world.

2. **The Post-Christendom World:** This is a world where Christianity was once widely understood and adhered to, but over the course of time the Christian church and its influence on the culture has declined so much that people rarely know much about the faith and may in fact be hostile or suspicious towards Christianity. Churches structured in a traditional way have a hard time growing in these places. Germany, New Zealand, Australia, much of Canada, and a growing portion of the United States fit into this model.

3. **The Book of Acts World:** In this world, society at large tends to be very religious, and evangelical Christianity may be a new phenomenon that is seeing explosive growth. There is a strong belief in the supernatural and the miraculous. Community life may also be considerably stronger than in other parts of the world. People in this world may know a lot about the Bible, but little about Christian history or Western denominations. There is a great respect for the authority of Scripture, and people tend to be more conservative about moral issues and issues of biblical interpretation than in the other two worlds. India, Bolivia, and Uganda are examples.

A country may inhabit one of these worlds or all of them. In the United States, most Church of God congregations inhabit the traditional world, but more and more Church of God churches (in places as unlikely as Indiana and Kansas) are structuring themselves for the post-Christendom world. One church in California that we will visit later has all three worlds present within it. Churches existing entirely in the Book of Acts World may have an advantage in terms of their growth. It is not necessarily the case that a developing nation will only inhabit the traditional world or the Book of Acts world, however. While in Lima, Peru, I shared this with Pastor Jose Flores and he pointed out to me that in Peru all three of these worlds exist. In the posh suburbs of Lima, there are middle-class and upper-class youth who have postmodern tendencies that place them in the post-Christendom world. They know little about Christianity despite having grown up in a "Christian" country, and they are not particularly interested. His own church on the northern side of the city inhabits the traditional world, while in the Andes, the indigenous communities inhabit the Book of Acts world. "We tried to read *The Purpose-Driven Life* as a country," he told me when we met at his church, "but existential issues about 'What is my purpose?' made no sense to the indigenous people in the mountains who spend their day wondering, 'Where am I going to get my next meal?'"

It is within this more complex theological environment that we must examine how Church of God theology can be transmitted. The good news is that Church of God theology is structured very well to reach all three worlds. The bad news is that theological transmission has never been more challenging.

In this post-theological age, very few people look toward systematic theology for answers, and they are often not very familiar with their denomination's or movement's creeds or beliefs. Theology for many people is primarily "experiential," meaning that it's not about adopting the right doctrines but about experiencing God day to day. People do not look to theologians or doctrines but rather examine the Bible and various voices to determine "what is right." This weakens a denomination or movement, which has core beliefs that have brought it into being and separated it from all the other denominations or movements in Christianity. The irony with the Church of God, however, is that as an anticreedal movement, the nineteenth century reformers were more in line with today's thinking. So is this new "experiential age" good news for the Church of God? Yes, in the sense that global theological trends are moving in our direction. But no, in that it also means that without a creed, there is currently little to appeal to theologically if we want to make the case that we should have a strong specific identity as the Church of God.

It gets even more complicated. Today in the Church of God, some regions of the world are accepting the traditional "church" as it has been understood for the past century. But in other regions where the Church of God is located, Christianity is brand-new and tends to be more charismatic. These churches are living in a pre-theological age in the sense that, like the early church, Christianity is spreading so quickly that issues of doctrine are low on the list. Meanwhile, other parts of the Church of God exist in a post-theological age, meaning that people are not interested in issues of denomination or right theology because they have become completely suspicious of the church. In other words, there are different theological landscapes in different regions of the Church of God world. When D. S. Warner and his friends started the Church of God, they were dealing with one reality in one culture: denominations had lost their holiness and division was destroying the church. Today it is far more complex.

Furthermore, as the world becomes more multicultural, people around the world simply identify themselves as Christian as opposed to Buddhist or Muslim or Hindu. This is particularly true outside of North America where Christians face hostility from other religious groups. Being associated with the Baptists, the Methodists, or the Church of God is not helpful. As a minority group in a non-Western, pluralistic setting, "I am a Christian" or "I'm an evangelical" creates a sense of camaraderie amid hostility and persecution.

Portland: A Theological Earthquake

I needed to find out what America's theological landscape looks like first before looking at other regions of the world. I decided to visit the president emeritus of Warner Pacific College, Jay Barber. Founded in 1937, Warner Pacific College is one of a number of Church of God theological institutions in the United States and Canada that also include Anderson University, Mid-America Christian University, Warner University, and Gardner College.

A denomination or movement can preserve its theological identity by having scholastic institutions that educate a new generation of pastors and laypeople in their theology. Despite the importance of training and imparting specific theological knowledge to young people and pastors, when the Anderson Bible Training School was founded in 1917, there was a considerable outcry. There were those who opposed the establishment of any kind of institution and so initially the school was unaccredited and did not hand out diplomas. This was in keeping with the Church of God beliefs about not giving people titles, not ordaining people, and not building institutions—the things of "man-rule." In time, however, the school became accredited and evolved into a fully accredited university. Over the years, the school has produced generations of pastors and missionaries.

Distrust of education runs strong throughout the evangelical Christian world, and the Church of God is no different.[2] Throughout the years, the schools have been attacked for being too morally lenient and theologically liberal. Sometimes there may have been truth to these charges, but more often than not, the schools (which primarily deal with youth) had to evolve with the culture and the times. A church can afford to see its youth dwindle away a lot longer than a college can. The local church can survive even if it is down to its last ten parishioners, all of whom might be over the age of sixty as long as they are paying the bills. The university, on the other hand, cannot.

Consequently, Church of God educational institutions have often been on the cutting edge as far as analyzing trends in the religious atmosphere. Their proximity to the young generation helps them to see the shifts more clearly than the rest of us. However, the schools are caught in a trap, because as soon as they point out these changes, they can easily be branded as liberal or caving in to the culture. It's a catch-22. We need the input of the colleges to help us read the next generations, but if they tell us something we don't want to hear, we brand them as useless. Regardless, for most of the life of the Church of God, these institutions have consistently trained many pastors and the movement grew.

We have now reached a turning point, however. There are a number of trends that are making it difficult for Church of God educational institutions to produce large numbers of pastors for the movement. Churches are getting older and smaller and thus have fewer youth to send to college. The few young people in the church may or may not choose a Christian college, and if they do, it may not necessarily be a Church of God school. Since the mid-1980s, tuition costs have soared, rising faster than the rate of inflation, limiting young people's choice of schools. They must go to the one that they and their parents can afford. Whether it's a Church of God school becomes less important if the price tag is $25,000 per year versus $15,000 for a local school. Those who can afford Church of God schools go, but they may not necessarily be from the Church of God.

The fewer students who enter into Church of God schools, the fewer the chances that future educators and pastors will be familiar with the Church of God. When a Church of God school needs to hire new profes-

2. This is ironic since evangelicals like Ockenga and Billy Graham had wanted evangelicalism to avoid the anti-intellectualism that was propagated by fundamentalists.

sors, it may not have the luxury of choosing a Church of God anthropology professor or New Testament scholar, because there aren't any. Thus, Church of God culture within the school erodes, and it is beyond the control of the institution. They may then seek to hire someone who is at least from the Wesleyan-Holiness background. But the question is unfairly asked: "Why don't you have more Church of God people on your faculty?"

Pastors and concerned Church of God people may also challenge the college administrators and ask, "Why aren't you producing more pastors?" But college administrators can easily say, "Why aren't you sending us more youth?" The absence of youth is taking its toll on the movement, and we have not made it easy for them to choose ministry as a way of life.[3]

I knew that the religious atmosphere in America has changed a lot since the beginning of the Church of

What is happening is nothing short of a theological earthquake.

God, but I wanted to find out what exactly is happening today in America. What is happening is nothing short of a theological earthquake. Ineffective outreach and mentoring to youth combined with the secularizing culture of America and the high cost of education is resulting in a significant crisis for the Church of God and other movements and denominations. The bottom line is that there is a lack of young people wanting to go into professional ministry. Most interestingly, this trend is becoming rapidly visible in Church of God regions outside of the Bible Belt where the traditional church model has lost much of its effectiveness. In other words, parts of America are rapidly becoming postmodern, post-Christendom societies. This has serious implications for the traditional church.

---

3. Young people in America are often criticized for not choosing to become pastors or missionaries. When these young people cite financial reasons as their primary reason for not going into ministry, they can easily be labeled as materialistic or lacking in faith. However, most people (especially outside of the United States) don't realize that students today usually leave college deeply in debt—mostly to the government. The average debt for a student graduating from a private-for-profit university in 2008 was $33,500 U.S. See http://projectonstudentdebt.org/files/File/Debt_Facts_and_Sources.pdf. The cost of education for Gen-Xers and Millennials has far surpassed the rate of inflation over the past twenty years and is in a league of its own compared to what their parents or grandparents would have paid. In the West, denominations and mission agencies have been slow to deal with this reality. In the case of many mission agencies, people with debt are often not allowed to become missionaries. This pretty much excludes the average person under thirty-five, who is most likely still paying back a ten-, twenty-, or thirty-year loan. My wife and I attended a Church of God college and have paid back enough money on our college loans to fund the government of a Central American nation—and we still have another twenty years to go.

I spoke with President Emeritus Barber at his home in the hills of east Portland. When he's not surfing at the Oregon Coast with his grandkids, he is advocating for the school he loves. It was a beautifully sunny August day, and from the hills, I could see the "Rose city" in the distance. Under his leadership, Warner Pacific has done extremely well. Enrollment is up, new facilities are being built, and a new satellite campus is operational. I have interacted with Warner Pacific College students numerous times, and they are unusually smart and engaged. Their questions are superb, and their commitment to Christ is significant. They are a very globally aware group of kids, and Dr. Barber believes that they will be change agents. Yet in the Pacific Northwest (as in many other regions), the kids are not attracted to institutional ministry.[4]

Jay explained to me why this is the case: "The young people are disillusioned with their experience in the local church. They find it irrelevant and obsolete. They also come from very troubled congregations."

Dr. Barber made a point I had not thought of at all: the effect of our divided and demoralized churches on young people. Do our churches look like the kind of places that someone would want to be in over the long term, particularly as a leader? Increasingly, pastoral tenures are short and the rate of burnout is high. Is this inspiring to the younger generation watching us from the pews?

Dr. Barber continued: "There was one kid who was fourth-generation Church of God, and I sat down with him and I said, 'What are your plans?' He was a religion major. I asked, 'Are you going to take an assignment? Seminary perhaps?' And he replied sarcastically, 'You are speaking of the Church of God reformation movement. The problem is there's no reformation and there's no movement.'"

Ouch.

"They want to do missionary work. They are passionate. They want to go into the third world or get involved in a parachurch organization," Dr. Barber told me. "But they are not interested in the traditional model."

Just like the first reformers of the Church of God, this generation is very suspicious of institutions and suspect they prevent one from doing ministry effectively. "What are we missing?" I wondered.

---

4. This has happened before. Val Clear points out that prior to the rise of the Holiness Movement, there had been a decline in the prestige of ministry and that from 1865 to the end of the century there were many vacancies in pulpits across the country (*Where the Saints Have Trod: A Social History of the Church of God Reformation Movement* [Chesterfield, IN: Midwest Publications, 1977], 26).

"As I look at our Department of Bible and Christian Ministries, what I have concluded is that these programs are doing a tremendous job of preparing kids to minister in yesterday's church. They are stuck in yesterday's models as well. There's Hebrew, Greek, and Pauline studies—the staples. But there's nothing there to teach them, to challenge them, to minister in the postmodern context. This is a major concern to me."

The fear that many have about what Dr. Barber is saying, of course, is that without the old model the church will be awash in trendiness and moral relativism. Does this mean the end of serious biblical scholarship and the end of sound theology? Dr. Barber assures me this is not the case.

"We need good solid biblical knowledge," he responds, "but that knowledge needs to be in a context of postmodernism. We need teachers and professors who work in that postmodern context instead of the traditional model."

Dr. Barber says there's something else we need that is sometimes hard to come by in the U.S. Church of God, which has often been so centered around small-town, homogenous, middle-America with its Bible Belt values: "We need people who have an affinity for the postmodern setting and are not intimidated by it. We need people who understand the multicultural and the multiethnic."

What does Dr. Barber mean by the term *postmodern*? Postmodernity is a reaction to the certainty of modernism ("we know how things work"). The postmodern mentality says that no one is personally objective, that the world is filled with uncertainty; it is skeptical of easy answers and believes that all points of view must be taken into account. In the postmodern view, Christianity can often seem unreasonable and unnecessarily harsh. Rigid dogmatism is uninspiring to postmoderns, who feel that truth must be presented within the context of love and relationship first. To older generations, this seems like wishy-washy moral relativism, but to postmoderns looking at Christianity in America, they see the hypocrisy of expensive churches, high divorce rates, church scandals, and a judgmental tone that repels their friends away from Jesus. When a society gets to the point that most people are not only skeptical about Christianity but are totally unfamiliar with the basics of Christianity, we call this a post-Christendom society. Consequently, much of Europe, Canada, and North America can now be labeled as part of the post-Christendom world I described earlier.

Warner Pacific has had to adapt to the postmodern, post-Christendom setting more quickly than institutions in the South and Midwest because of its unique setting. The philosophical landscape in the Pacific Northwest is very different. It is the most underchurched region of the United States. In many ways, it is closer in temperament to Germany (which I will visit later in this chapter) than Anderson—and that goes for the weather too! Portland is a unique city. It is consistently rated as one of the most livable cities in North America (as is Seattle and Vancouver), and it is highly progressive environmentally speaking. It boasts more bookstores than any other city in the country, and its streets give right of way to those on bicycles. It is a model of urban planning for the rest of the United States, and it is one place where the center of the city was never abandoned but remained relevant and alive. Like Germany, Portland is famous for its beers and appreciation of art. Politically, it is liberal and is known as one of the most gay-friendly cities in America. Young people flock to Portland, attracted by its multicul- turalism and tolerance, which is deeply ingrained in the DNA of the people. For people in the Bible Belt, Portland sounds like Sodom and Gomorrah. And for Portlanders, the Bible Belt sounds like hell—even though they don't believe in hell.

That is precisely why churches in Portland and any Christian organi- zation or institution trying to reach youth have to find new ways to pres- ent the gospel. It is not about watering down the gospel but rather about breaking down the prejudices that exist against the institutional church. The same challenge can be found in Boston, Chicago, Miami, Phoenix, and many other U.S. urban centers.

"Ignoring the centers won't work," Dr. Barber says, "because American youth are overwhelmingly choosing to live in those urban centers. And if they go into ministry, they want to do it in a multicultural city as opposed to a rural area.

As I listened to Jay, it occurred to me that a new generation cannot enter the Church of God if the Church of God is not geographically located close to the new generation.

The world that the young generation is growing up with is not being engaged by a majority of our churches, many of which are located either in rural areas or are run by pastors originating from rural areas. Many Church of God congregations located in cities are pastored by people originally from small towns in Michigan, Ohio, Indiana, or Illinois. There is a new disconnect between where the pastors come from in our churches and where the youth in their cities are coming from.

Warner Pacific is located right in the middle of this very new theological environment. Either Warner Pacific needed to be relevant to this unusual city or they would slowly die. Jay Barber saw, however, that Portland didn't have to be a curse to the school but could be a blessing instead.

"One of the top marketing experts came in and questioned five thousand of our church leaders and said that the most potent tool that we have as an institution that we haven't taken advantage of was our location, and that became a key to us to think about an urban studies program that is at the graduate level." The college moved to take advantage of that urban setting. With more and more of the country becoming like Portland and less and less like Wichita, Warner Pacific is actually positioning itself ahead of the curve.[5]

Another problem the school has faced is that the younger generation attending the school is not being mentored in their local church to the degree that they once were. Jay is in agreement with the sentiment expressed by the ladies at Cristwood in chapter 2 that today's pastors are not engaging the youth as much as they once did. The youth are usually given their own pastors, segregated from the rest of the church body, and often entertained instead of challenged and educated.

"The kids do not want to be segregated," Dr. Barber tells me. "They want to be part of the church."

Dr. Barber thought back to his years as a pastor in Red Bluff, California. "I believe the key responsibility of the church is to mentor. We used to call it discipleship; everyone saw it as their role. We put a lot of money into scholarships, and I would sit down with the kid and say, 'What are you thinking about in terms of college?' Not all of them wanted to go to a liberal arts school. Some of them went into engineering. But if you were willing to go to a Church of God school, we saw to it that you could afford to do that. We had as many as fourteen students at Warner Pacific."

Dr. Barber says that the kids who do go into ministry are the ones who were mentored and come from churches that offer a good model of the church in the local setting. It seems clear that if we want to see more young

---

5. Even Wichita is not looking like Wichita anymore. While the traditional church is more effective and respected in the Midwest and the Central Plains, Hope Community Church in Wichita is an example of a growing number of Church of God congregations in the Bible Belt that are configured in a way that is nontraditional and that can speak to people in the post-Christendom mindset.

people choose a Church of God education (and certainly ministry within the Church of God), a much larger effort will need to take place in the local church, not just in the schools.

"The schools have a key role, but I think our training programs in the local church are crucial. One of the pessimistic things I will say is that students coming in from our local congregations have no theological grounding and little biblical knowledge. They are just being entertained. There is no structure of preparing and teaching them basic and theological standards. We have to start with the basics: 'Genesis is in the Old Testament and there are two testaments.'"

For their part, Warner Pacific is doing all it can to lower tuition costs. Warner Pacific has chosen to reduce its tuition by 22 percent. Tuition, which was once as high as $30,000 per year, has dropped to $16,000, with 98 percent of the students eligible for federal and state aid. The general director of Church of God Ministries, Ron Duncan, also has a vision to see tuition underwritten through the Church of God Foundation for any Church of God young person attending one of our schools.

If the future of the United States looks more like Portland than Wichita, then we are not in Kansas anymore. The more predictable theological landscape that produced our traditional churches is dying. Perhaps that may be good for the Church of God. Those in the younger generation who are familiar with Church of God theology resonate with the historic skepticism within the Church of God toward institutions, its emphasis on experience over creeds, and its loose structure focused on "being the church," as well as the value the Church of God places on unity.

> "Students coming in from our local congregations have no theological grounding and little biblical knowledge."

The older generations tend to think that these kids just want to create a Christianity of moral relativism, but that is not the case. They are primarily concerned with being part of a Christianity that is not so dogmatic and dualistic that it can no longer interact with the culture around it. They want to be relevant and engaged. In their world, if you are a Christian, you don't get a fair hearing, and they suspect that it is because we Christians have not given the nonbelievers a fair hearing. We have not valued their culture; why should they value ours?

Anderson: New Paths to New Ministries

One would think that at seminary there should be an abundance of students who are committed to ministry behind the pulpit. But as I found out in talking to Dean David Sebastian of the Anderson University School of Theology, that is not the case. I met with Dean Sebastian at his office overlooking the scenic valley that separates the School of Theology from the main offices of the university. Like President Jay Barber, Dr. Sebastian is one of the most respected voices in the Church of God. As the dean of the only school of theology in the Church of God that can award master's degrees and doctorates, he holds an important office that gives him a unique vantage point into the challenges we face.

"There are an increasing number of students coming out of college who are going directly into seminary," he tells me one evening as we sit in his office. "But many are questioning whether they are willing to pastor my mother's and grandparents' churches. They are not."

The School of Theology has seen an increase in enrollment with this new Millennial generation of youth, but as at Warner, they are shying away from pastoral ministry. The master of divinity program, which prepares students for pastoral ministry and which has traditionally been the degree with the highest enrollment, has seen a decline in enrollment for the past five years. He pulls out some recent reports on enrollment at the SOT as I sit in his office. "We wonder if the MDiv will be a viable degree in the future."

He agrees with President Barber's assessment that something fundamental is changing. The AUSOT has seen enrollment rise for the past ten years, but the degree that is growing is the master's in intercultural service (a hands-on, mission-oriented degree), not the MDiv.

Dr. Sebastian is finding the need to help students think about their future options. "If I feel called to ministry, but not to pastoral service in a church, what is that ministry going to look like? If the students do not want to be in pastoral ministry and don't have an MDiv, placement in churches will be a challenge for them, or they may need to be bivocational. They want to do hands-on service, but we're not quite sure that we've identified populations of where they are going to go to serve.

"A lot of these students are attracted to new models of church, such as the Emerging Church movement (which we will look at in chapter 5), but there are just not a lot of those around, unless you start your own. And there is so little history of sustainability of those trying to do it in a new way. Will they be there in ten years? That remains to be seen."

The seminary environment that Dr. Sebastian described to me sounded very different to the environment I was exposed to when I studied at Anderson. And as I spoke to some recent seminary graduates while researching this book, the language they used about Christianity and ministry was completely different from what I heard in my day. When I was in school in the late 1980s and early 1990s, it was a challenge for professors to get students to think out of the box and question their theological assumptions.

Sebastian continues: "There has been a dramatic turnaround in the last five years. They are questioning Christianity as we have known it. There's a backlash to what some have seen. Looking down on other people if you are not like us Christians is very distasteful to this generation. They want to embrace all kinds of people."

In my day, religious departments in the Church of God and the seminary were often challenged not only by their more rigid students but by the church at large, which often referred to the seminary as "the cemetery where faith goes to die"! With this radical change in the theological landscape, I wonder if Dean Sebastian is getting a lot of pressure from Church of God congregations worried about the direction of this generation of students.

"I'm in my fourteenth year here, and the first two or three years the issue was, 'The seminary is not producing leaders. We need people who can actually lead, not just brainy theologians.' But now, I don't get anything from the church, good or bad. I don't get letters, or many phone calls, as far as people wanting to discuss disagreements."

This silence toward the seminary seems to be linked toward a growing indifference about the issues that once created tension and dialogue in the movement. It should also be noted, however, that the seminary has also done a good job of connecting with the local church under Dr. Sebastian's leadership.

"Do people still accuse the seminary of being liberal?" I wonder.

"No, but there is the question of whether seminary will be the way ministers are developed in the future."

In this challenging environment, the seminary, like other Church of God educational institutions, has had to be flexible over the years.

"We are growing online, and this year we have thirty-six pastors or key laypeople in local congregations from places like California, Canada, and the East Coast. They come to campus twice a year, and they do the program online. They say that if we are going to have seminary, it needs to be accessible and affordable. Thirty-two of the students are nonresidential doctor of ministry students doing accredited degrees without having to live in Anderson, Indiana."

The recent construction of the York Seminary Village has enabled seminary students to live in Anderson in affordable housing. And in any given year, on average 70 percent of Church of God MDiv candidates are enrolled in the seminary. In 2008, the number of Church of God students was 77 percent. An even more impressive statistic is the fact that two-thirds of Church of God MDiv students are enrolled in the Anderson University School of Theology.[6]

The seminary is also still an important voice in the Church of God movement. Dean Sebastian and seminary professors are regularly called on to attend campmeetings, state conferences, and other functions to share their expertise.

Another innovative move by Dr. Sebastian has been the creation of the Roundtable. The Roundtable has been meeting twice a year since 1985. They have lunch at the North American Convention each June and then hold a special gathering time in a new city each year. The Roundtable consists of pastors from the fifty-two largest Church of God congregations ranging in size from five hundred to five thousand. When they go to a city each year, they visit a non-Church of God ministry that is having an impact. This year they are planning to visit Mark Driscoll's church in Seattle. "It is one of the most postmodern cities in the country, and he has a straight approach toward young people," Sebastian tells me. "We learn from their philosophy of ministry and look at their ministry. Spouses are invited and there's a support group and a time to visit another church." The agenda for the Roundtable is open each time. Discussions may deal with staff relationships or what is working or not working in their ministries.

In his fourteen years as dean, Dr. Sebastian has seen some large changes in the theological landscape. Overall, the Anderson University School of Theology is still a key player and catalyst for the movement. It is unclear

---

6. Asbury Theological Seminary in Wilmore, Kentucky, and Fuller Theological Seminary in Pasadena, California, are the SOT's primary competitors.

what direction seminary education will take or in what forms ministry will take place with this new generation, but Dr. Sebastian is optimistic. "In the nineteenth century, the Church of God was very engaged. If we claim that, we will not be out of step with the young people. If we don't, we can become irrelevant. If our theology is practiced and taught, I am very hopeful about it. Every generation has to do it differently to be fresh and alive."

Germany: Engaging the Post-Christendom West

If we in the United States are headed toward a more postmodern and post-Christian society, then perhaps it would be good to talk to those churches that are already deeply engaged in ministry within those societies. Europe, which was once the birthplace of Christendom, is now a bastion of secularism. Even those regions of Europe that remained fairly religious are seeing steep declines. Ireland, once a devoutly Catholic nation, now has to import its priests from Africa, for instance. Yet it is in the heartland of this continent that one can find one of the most cohesive Church of God presences in the world: the Church of God in Germany.

I find myself speeding down the German autobahn with Klaus Kroeger, the federal chairman of the Church of God in Germany. Despite his distinguished white hair and his serious face, Klaus is a gentle man with a very sharp intellect. He is urbane and global-minded, having spent his life in Europe but also having traveled extensively throughout the world. With all of his experience and his great knowledge of theology and the Bible, Klaus is someone I could spend hours talking to and learning from.

As we speed along the autobahn (Germany's no-speed-limit highway), the federal chairman is trying to show me what it feels like to go 200 km per hour (124 mph). He wants me to get a picture of the needle on the speedometer hitting the 200 km/h line. Klaus keeps looking for a clearing among the fast-moving traffic, but each time he hits the 200 km/h mark, I mess up the shot. Klaus's elegant wife, Gunhild sits in the backseat guffawing at our juvenile antics. The Danish-born Gunhild must have been thinking to herself, "Boys will be boys!" This is not my first time on the famous German highways, but it is the first time anyone ever dared to show me how fast people are allowed to drive in Germany. As we go speeding past the beautiful green hills of central Germany, I feel relaxed, knowing that I am in good hands.

The Church of God in Germany is in good hands as well and has been for a long time. It began 114 years ago when German speakers from the American Midwest returned to their motherland as missionaries. As a break-away movement from the Winebrennarians, the early Church of God reformers were surrounded by Germans (like my great-grandfather Abraham), and many of them, including D. S. Warner, could speak German. *The Gospel Trumpet* first had a German edition distributed in America as early as 1895. Today the Church of God in Germany is in many ways a model of cohesiveness in comparison to other nations in the Church of God. They have done a good job of preserving their identity and maintaining communication. A key to that cohesiveness is Klaus, the federal chairman.

I ask Klaus about his role as the federal chairman.

"I am responsible before the law, and it is a spiritual role."

As with the early Church of God, there is a sense that official leaders are primarily there for legal and spiritual purposes as opposed to hierarchical, institutional purposes.

As Klaus and Gunhild drive me around, I find myself very impressed with the caliber of pastors I meet in the German church. They are strong in their Bible knowledge, articulate (often speaking multiple languages), and very committed to the Church of God. The buildings are always nicely kept up with impressive decor. And the German brothers and sisters are warm and inviting. It all looks good to me, but Klaus feels much more needs to be done.

"There are twenty-two hundred people in twenty-seven churches. The older churches are not the growing churches. We need revival."

The problem Klaus identifies in Germany is one that we are facing in many Western nations and even in some non-Western countries. The people in the pews are getting older, and not enough young people are entering into leadership. As we tour around, however, I do meet quite a few young Germans in the Church of God and they are extremely sharp.

Klaus is concerned about the state of the Church of God in Germany, but he is also a modest man. As mentioned in chapter 1, there are a number of things that a movement can do to help to retain its identity and unity. The German church does a number of things that have helped it to maintain a strong, cohesive identity. To begin with, they have regular meetings. The Bundeskonferenz (the year I visited it was held at a magnificent convention center in Essen) is very well-attended, meticulously organized, and truly inspirational. Most striking to me is the fact that the conference is attended by people of all ages, including plenty of young families.

In addition to the Bundeskonferenz, they have conferences for co-workers every two years, an annual teen camp, and a large youth conference every couple of years. A commitment to meeting together in a variety of settings is key to retaining the movement's unity.

Second, ordination standards are high. Germany is not only the birthplace of the Protestant Reformation, but it is well-known for having produced some of the greatest theologians in history. My impression after meeting and talking with various pastors in Germany, Klaus included, is that they have very high expectations of their pastors as far as familiarity with the Bible and theology is concerned. In other Church of God regions, expectations for pastors as far as theological knowledge, long-term commitment to the movement, and awareness of the message of the Church of God have often been too low.

Third, they produce an excellent magazine called *Perspektiven*. It is filled with relevant articles and given to every family in every church free of charge. A movement has to have good forums (a magazine, journal, or at least an excellent Web site) to keep communication flowing among the pastors and the churches. The pieces need to be relevant as well and not just promotional pieces.

In other Church of God regions, expectations for pastors... have often been too low.

Fourth, the magazine is able to continue its publication because the German brothers and sisters are strong givers financially. There has to be a commitment to invest in the movement.

Fifth, the German church is outward looking and mobilizes to support projects throughout the world in such countries as South Africa, Brazil, Uganda, Zambia, Tanzania, and India. A movement has to retain a strong sense of global mission in order to mobilize and fulfill its part in the Great Commission.

Sixth, the movement in Germany has Fritzlar Bible College, which has educated many of its leaders and given them a strong sense of what it means to be Church of God. The German Church of God would probably be considered very conservative by North American standards. Women in ministry has not been something that it has traditionally, yet today,

Fritzlar Bible College has a large group of Church of God women from South American countries, including Chile, Argentina, and Brazil.

Klaus and I drive north, east, west, and south across Germany. Everywhere we go I am very impressed with what I see. But Germany, like much of North America, Europe, and Oceana continues to see a decline in church attendance. While 40 percent of Americans attend church weekly, that figure is 20 percent in Europe and a mere 12 percent percent in Germany.[7]

Europe is often called post-Christian, meaning that the people have abandoned and forgotten their Christian heritage. Perhaps it offers a glimpse of America's future.[8] The separation of church and state has enabled the United States to retain a dynamic religious society up to this point. Europe, on the other hand, has many reasons why Christianity is struggling. It was in Europe that Christianity got organized, institutionalized, and then deeply divided. Those divisions resulted in wars—not small wars, but wars that resulted in centuries of violence and millions killed. In Europe, religion is often perceived as dangerous in a way that it is not in the United States, where the separation of church and state protected the reputation of the church in the eyes of the people. Europe was also the birthplace of the Enlightenment, the period in which reason challenged the authority of God and the church. The trauma of two World Wars and the nationalistic racial hatred propagated by the Nazi regime has also made Europe skittish about any religious group claiming absolutes. And unlike America, the church has been sponsored by the state and has thus not had to rely on volunteerism, nor has it had to compete in the religious marketplace.[9] Churches do not have to innovate and reinvent themselves in order to stay afloat. Consequently, they do not stay relevant.

For Church of God congregations in Europe, the most pressing theological issue is making it clear to a population used to state churches that we are not a strange cult, but rather a legitimate orthodox part of Protes-

---

7. Phillip Jenkins, *God's Continent: Christianity, Islam and Europe's Religious Crisis*. (Oxford: Oxford University Press, 2007) 28.

8. A recent survey by Trinity College found that if current trends continue, 25 percent of the United States population will claim "no religion." It is currently the fastest growing segment of the religious population. This does not necessarily mean that the rates of atheism will match Europe, however. Americans tend to be more agnostic or deistic (Dan Gilgoff, "Survey: One Quarter of Americans Could Claim No Religion in Twenty Years," God & Country, *U.S. News and World Report*, online ed., September 22, 2009, http://www.usnews.com/blogs/god-and-country/2009/09/22/survey-one-quarter-of-americans-could-claim-no-religion-in-20-years.html.)

9. Patrick Nachtigall,. *Faith in the Future: Christianity's Interface with Globalization* (Anderson, IN: Warner Press, 2008).

tantism. Then there is the need to explain and demonstrate to the people that Christianity need not be a dead religion.

The Church of God in Germany has been surrounded by a secular culture for a long time; it is a challenging environment. What is clear is that the only hope a movement has for retaining its theological identity is to value that theological heritage in concrete ways as the German church does. Throughout the Church of God worldwide, when publications struggle, we will be tempted to allow them to fail instead of making sure there are forums for communicating with each other. As our meeting times become less well-attended or more expensive, we will be tempted to not have these events or not attend at all. With a decrease in pastors, we will be tempted to lower ordination standards. And as our colleges re-calibrate, we will be tempted to give up on them. As we navigate these choppy waters, we may be tempted to fall behind in our financial support as well as in our Church of God missionary efforts. Disengagement as a community will be the temptation. But the Church of God in Germany gives our countries and states an example of the importance of communication, connection, and high theological standards in retaining our identity.

Kenya: The Cross and the Computer

The theological landscape in the West is changing dramatically. Nations like France, England, and the United States that were once considered "Christian," are today places where the church is barely growing. Despite the fact that the Bible serves as the foundation for Western civilization's Judeo-Christian societies, today one cannot assume that people in the West know who Adam and Eve are or can explain the meaning of Easter. While the United States, in particular, remains a very religious society, knowledge about Christianity is decreasing and the way Christians organize and present themselves is changing.

The story is exactly the opposite in the non-Western world. Evangelical and Pentecostal Christianity is exploding in such unlikely places as Mongolia, Vietnam, Brazil, Nigeria, and China. In the Middle East, Christianity is growing without the help of denominations and Western theological explanations created over two thousand years. Muslims are seeing visions of Jesus, and Christianity is being taken to the Gulf States and Central Asia by Christian migrant workers from the Philippines and China.[10] The rise of the Church of God reformation movement has coincided with a massive expansion of Christianity in the non-Western world. When the Missionary Board of the Church of God was started in 1909, there were only 10 million Christians in Africa. In 2000, there were 346 million.[11] There are more Christians in Africa than there are people in the United States. By 2004, within the Church of God, there were 125 percent more believers and 40 percent more congregations outside of North America than within North American borders.[12]

I travel to Kenya, a country that has been a missions focus of the Church of God movement since 1922. My own father and mother, Harry and Jene Nachtigall, served as missionaries to this beautiful country in the 1960s. It is a thrill to travel to Emusire High School about forty miles from the shores of Lake Victoria and find a picture of my father on the wall, the last Western principal of a school that is now flourishing and being run by Kenyan Christians from the Church of God.

The real purpose of my trip, however, is to visit Kima International School of Theology. The school sits on six acres of land in the hills above Kisumu, an hour's drive from the border with Uganda and just two miles north of the equator. There is not much of the famous wildlife in this corner of Kenya, but it is a lush, green area with some of the richest soil in the world. Despite the lack of giraffes and lions, the less celebrated wildlife remains present as I found out when a bat dropped a present on my head and a frog jumped out of the toilet bowl.

Christianity in Africa is also considered wild by many. Despite the fact that the North African church was established far earlier than the church in the West, Christianity is mostly new to sub-Saharan Africa. In this new Africa, Christianity and tribal religions mix in different ways. African Christians often struggle to stop believing in traditional religious practices or consulting witch-doctors, for instance. This is unnerving for Westerners. However, Africans find it strange that Bible-believing Western Christians place their faith entirely in modern medicine and don't even bother to have healing services in church. Sometimes African folk religion is mixed with Christianity, but the prosperity gospel—an American export characterized by the

---

10. Jennifer Riley, "Analysis: Why Muslims Follow Christ," *Christian Post*, November 16, 2007.

11. Lamin Sanneh, *Disciples of All Nations: Pillars of World Christianity* (Oxford: Oxford University Press, 2007), 275.

12. Donald D. Johnson. "Looking Back to Go Forward," *Missions*, January-February 2004, 8.

obssessive materialism of Western societies—is also making unfortunate and dramatic headway on the continent. Consequently, the teaching of contextualized but orthodox theology is very important in Africa—now more than ever.

The growth of the prosperity gospel, which teaches that God provides material wealth for those in his favor, is a theological challenge affecting many Church of God congregations and institutions outside of North America. Although it originated in the United States, it is experiencing tremendous success in Asia, Africa, and Latin America. Living Faith Church in Nigeria, for instance, has three hundred branches across Nigeria, and three hundred thousand people worshiping at a single service at its 565-acre headquarters north of Lagos.[13] In a previous book, I argued that the prosperity gospel "could only originate in a culture that is relatively free from suffering and persecution and that has an economic system supported by multiple safeguards, including the rule of law and strong governing branches that enable upward mobility." I continued by saying, "The prosperity gospel is the product of a culture that is so wealthy it can hardly relate to the agrarian societies portrayed in the Bible stories—filled with persecution, famine, war, locusts, refugees, and untrustrworthy government."[14] The question then is why does it grow in poorer, non-Western environments?

This is because outside of the West, in places such as Africa, religion is utilitarian. While questions of theology are more abstract in Western societies, (e.g., Who was Jesus? Is the resurrection possible? Does science support the Genesis creation account?), the question in poorer, non-Western societies is more about how religion can help a person in this life, with their present concerns (e.g., Can God cure my child of malaria? Can Jesus break the curse on my family? Will we be able to feed our children?). The prosperity gospel taps into those earthly needs, reducing the gospel to a way of prosperity instead of the way of the cross. This approach has been so successful that a significant number of Church of God congregations have lost pastors and people to this movement. Schools like KIST have the opportunity to balance genuine utilitarian theological concerns with the need for orthodoxy.

---

13. Eliza Griswold, "God's Country," *Atlantic Monthly*, March 2008, 49–50.
14. Patrick Nachtigall, *Faith in the Future: Christianity's Interface with Globalization* (Anderson, IN: Warner Press, 2008), 121.

KIST, which was started in 1995 under the able leadership of Dr. Steve Rennick, has one of the most impressive campuses in Western Kenya. Under Rennick's leadership, eleven buildings were renovated and fourteen new buildings were constructed. The school drew students from nineteen tribes and eleven different countries, began to offer an externally accredited bachelor of arts degree, established a $100,000 (KSH 5,000,000) endowment, and became debt free. KIST is a much-beloved Church of God institution, and over the past fifteen years, more than five hundred Church of God people have volunteered their time and energy to come to help build up the physical campus. On my particular visit, a group from CBH *Viewpoint* was dedicating a newly-refurbished recording studio, which will not only carry Christian broadcasts from the campus but also offer local musicians a place to record.

> "People are not sending their children to ministerial training, because pastors don't get paid."

For the past seven years, Dr. Donald Smith has been the principal of KIST, and the school has 122 students on campus and through extension. Under Smith's leadership, KIST has embarked on a journey to a higher level of accreditation. The school has been validated by the Kenyan Commission for Higher Education and has been moved to affiliate status with ACTEA (Accrediting Council for Theological Education in Africa). Over the next four years, KIST has to continue developing to receive candidacy status. In a continent where there is such great need for education and so few schools able to provide it, one would think that the head of a Christian school in Africa might have it easy compared to one in Portland or Anderson. Not so.

As KIST moves into this preferred future, there will be even more internal and external obstacles. "Africa is changing rapidly," Principal Smith tells me as we sat down in his office in the Ludwig House. "Computers and cell phones are revolutionizing Africa, and people want their children to tap into that world." Africa is now one of the world's largest markets for cell phones, and this technology is revolutionizing people's lives, enabling them to do business far better than ever before.

"People are not sending their children to ministerial training, because pastors don't get paid. And if you were a peasant farmer, that would make complete sense! So we have had to make an adjustment. Our scholarship program is so vital. We give scholarships and have a deferred scholarship where the students pay the first year but we pay for years two and three."

The good news is that Africans value education. Kenyan youth and the Kenyan government are desperate for better schools. KIST is viewed as a continuing boon to the area, but as was the case at Warner Pacific and the Anderson School of Theology, to survive and flourish as a ministry institution requires some changes.

For Don, these changes need not be threatening. It is not just the school that needs to change; the training of pastors in today's globalized world must change as well. "If the church is going to survive, grow, and make a difference in society, I believe we have to provide funding for ministerial students and, secondly, develop programs of education that will train them in communications, computers, science, counseling, and business. You have to develop that liberal arts training so that the church will have educated people, and that's how we become the leaven of the bread and the salt of the earth."

After the trauma of the Kenyan riots in 2007 (as well as many other traumatic events that have occurred on the African continent), counseling is now valued to a much greater degree here. It is an example of how the definition of ministry most likely needs to be expanded to better serve Africa in this ever-changing globalized world. The goal of this broader definition would not be to water down the school's Christian mission but rather to produce more well-rounded pastors who could serve bivocationally (which the vast majority do throughout the non-Western world).

To make that next leap, KIST needs many things: more diversified sources of funding, Westerners and non-Westerners alike (missionaries and professionals) to start key programs in areas such as computers and counseling (both of which are still relatively new in this part of Africa), more renovations to reconfigure for a bigger program, and a core of African professors and staff who are ready to selflessly commit to KIST. The latter can often be a challenge in African schools where African staff may not view their institution's self-interest above their own. NGOs and Christian institutions alike can easily be taken advantage of; that is one of the sad realities of working in the non-Western world. Yet Don Smith feels that the core has been formed and the platform built to make KIST a brighter beacon of Church of God education on the African continent.

Throughout the world, ministry is changing, the market is changing, and society is changing. Schools that aim to teach theology and produce ministers need to recalibrate and readjust constantly. In some cases, even in Africa, a school may not be able to become self-sustaining and pull in students without offering subjects that will equip the student for a twenty-first century career. Church of God outsiders looking in will have to be patient with our educational leaders as they try to create new opportunities for the next generation of church leaders. At the same time, educators will need to do their best to involve the people of the Church of God and her message in their endeavors.

Thailand: A Testimony of Unity

Two hundred kilometers east of Bangkok, amid the rice patties and modest green hills, lies a farm that belongs to Silawech Kanjanamukda, the national leader of the Church of God in Thailand. Brother Silawech, as he is widely known, splits his time between his farm, the Church of God office in Bangkok, and numerous villages scattered throughout the country. I met him in Thailand to hear about how Church of God theology pulled him into the movement and how he now transmits that theology to the new pastors in the Church of God in Thailand.

Brother Silawech was born into a Christian family. He is a third-generation Chinese Thai. "I grew up in a conservative Presbyterian church," he told me when I caught up with him on the coastal town of Pattaya. "Growing up, I met Christians from many other groups. But in the 1970s when Pentecostalism began to grow, tension developed between these new groups and the Presbyterians."

Brother Silawech did not like what he saw. The "division and fighting," was too much for this peaceful man. "I had good fellowship with the Presbyterians and the Pentecostals. I felt that they were brothers and sisters." Silawech was often invited by both groups to perform baptisms and weddings. He was introduced to the Church of God by a close friend who joined the movement. "I thought to myself, 'This is what the church should be,' because it is a movement under God."

Throughout the world, many people have been attracted to the Church of God because of its emphasis on unity. It's easy to see how in a country like Thailand where 95 percent of the country is Buddhist and 4.6 percent are Muslim, unity among the Christian minority might be important.

In 1979, Brother Silawech's friend introduced him to Church of God missionary Sidney Johnson, who gave Silawech books about the reformation movement. Today, not only is he the leader of the Church of God in Thailand, but he is also the president of the Asia-Pacific Church of God Conference.

There are twenty-five churches in Thailand, with seventeen full-time workers, two part-time workers, and five ordained pastors. In the north, one church among the Karen minority tribe is led by a woman pastor, whose husband died of a brain tumor. The Church of God is registered as a denomination in Thailand (as it is in many countries) due to the need to receive government recognition in a country that is staunchly Buddhist. Freedom of religion exists, but the country is very partial toward Buddhism and has even considered becoming a Buddhist theocracy. For this reason, there is also the need to be affiliated with the Evangelical Fellowship of Thailand in order to appease the government and be understood by the people in the villages as a Christian minister. While most Church of God pastors do not wear robes, there is an official EFT robe that is worn here during baptism or Communion. In a deeply Buddhist society where priestly robes are associated with official religious duties, the Protestants must do the same lest they be misunderstood. Unlike in the West, there are also times in Thailand when pastors are required to meet with Buddhists, Hindus, Sikhs, and Muslims, and the robe identifies you as part of a recognized minority religion. It's important to recognize that non-Western Christians often have to interact far more with people of different faiths than Western Christians. While Western Christians can have more of a protective, or stand-offish attitude toward other religions, most non-Westerners have to exist in societies that are either very pluralistic or biased against Christianity in favor of a dominant religion.

Within the context of Christianity in Thailand, the openness of the Church of God is helpful to Brother Silawech, who views all Christians as his brothers and sisters in Christ. But he does expect his pastors to understand Church of God theology.

"They need to understand Church of God history and theology."

"Why?" I ask.

"Because they will be asked by other Christians about who we are and what we believe." To that end, Silawech has been proactive in making sure that important topics are covered. "I have collected Church of God materials and put them into a Thai handbook that covers all the key issues."

I ask him what the requirements for ordination are in the Thai Church of God.

"You must be twenty-five years of age and have five years experience working in the church. You must also have a BA and have three years of Bible study. There is also a five-hour test."

Five hours! Wow! I'm really glad I was ordained in the United States.

"You have to get more than 70 percent on the test. If you fail, you can retake the test in three months. If a candidate continues to struggle, they may need to write a four- to ten-page paper in their weak area.

In Thailand, there is a great need for pastors, and many do not have access to the kind of education we do in the West. Nevertheless, the standards for ordination remain high and the theological heritage of the Church of God is taken seriously. In a country where there are so few Christians to begin with, a theology that encourages cooperation between Christians of various traditions may play a very important role. In the pluralistic non-Western world, the Church of God reformers' message of unity among Christians is an example of how our theology can have a new role in the twenty-first century that is every bit as important as the role it played in the nineteenth century. We will see more ways that Church of God theology is still relevant as our journey continues.

Akron: The Way of the Preacher

Perhaps the primary way that a movement's theology gets transmitted is through preaching. The Church of God has been blessed with many great preachers including D. S. Warner, Lillie McCutcheon, James Earl Massey, and many others over the course of the movement's life. While the early Church of God movement did not put stock in creeds and membership, expectations regarding living a sanctified life and being a part of God's church were expounded on in the sermons and music of the pioneers. Revivals, camp meetings, radio programs, publications, and hymns were just some of the ways that the message spread in the early decades. But the influence of these methods has decreased significantly today. One of the key ways of transmitting theology that everyone is still exposed to is the pastor's sermon. But over the last twenty years, the role of the preacher and the role of the sermon have changed significantly.

In Anglo-American culture, the pastor's authority, biblical interpretation, and theological beliefs carry far less weight than they used to years ago. Today, when trying to find out what to believe theologically, many congregants look to books at the Christian bookstore, listen to teachings of well-known evangelical personalities like James Dobson or Rick Warren, or decide their beliefs on what feels right to them. The idea that the pastor is the shepherd of the community and that his understanding of Scripture is authoritative has mostly been lost. So if, for instance, a Church of God pastor is preaching on issues like sanctification, divorce, or homosexuality, there is little chance that the congregation will base its opinions solely on what the pastor says is the proper belief.

In addition to the loss of pastoral authority, expository preaching, which includes carefully examining Scripture to look for the meaning of a particular text, has now taken a backseat to topical sermons wherein a particular subject or broad overview of a Bible book is presented instead.

There has also been a change in tone. While preachers a century ago were more confrontational, identifying sins and calling people to repentance, in recent years, preachers have made sermons less authoritarian and more conversational. Seeker-sensitive services in many churches make sure that the tone does not come off as judgmental. This effort to appeal to people skittish of the Christian church or uninformed about the faith has meant that sermons do not delve deeply into complicated theological discussions. Those may be saved for later times.

The idea that the pastor is the shepherd of the community and that his understanding of Scripture is authoritative has mostly been lost.

More recently, sermons have changed again, with many pastors preferring to have open conversations about theological and spiritual issues. In some cases, this may include pastors receiving questions in the form of text messages during the sermon, with the pastor responding on the spot or making it clear that he doesn't know all the answers.

Despite the growing influence throughout the world of the less doctrinally oriented preaching of people like Bill Hybels, Rick Warren, and Rob Bell, in the non-Western world, the pastor is still often a central figure of authority in the church community. American preachers are popular outside of the United States, but direct, confrontational preaching that takes strong theological stands is still the norm in Africa, Latin America, and Asia.

I visit Akron, Ohio, to talk with one of our most-beloved, well-known African-American preachers, Rev. Ronald Fowler. He has retired now, but he still sits on numerous boards and assists various organizations with leadership and community development. There's nothing about him that indicates a man who should be retiring. Still vigorous and healthy, it's not hard to believe that he was once an all-state high school football star in Ohio and a starter on the Kent State football team. As one of Akron's most influential people, his considerable impact on the football field has been surpassed by his influence in the city of Akron, in the Church of God, and beyond.

While the role of the pastor has diminished in the Anglo-American world, in the African-American community, the pastor still has significant influence. In their structure, African-American churches bear a close resemblance to churches in sub-Saharan Africa. The black church, which is centered around the pastor and the immediate community, respects the minister's authority. For a movement or a denomination seeking to transmit its values, it seems easier to do so in churches like this than in ones that look for authoritative voices from the broader Christian culture or secular world.

The Arlington Church of God is located on Arlington Street just south of Interstate 76. The homes on the street itself resemble other lower-income areas of Akron, an industrial city in America's Rust Belt. At one time in the mid-1920s, Akron was the fastest growing city in America, but today it is a city of two hundred thousand that is struggling economically. Arlington Street, many years ago, was the poorest place in the whole county. The streets were drug-ridden and lined with bars, and soliciting prostitutes was done in the open. Today the bars and prostitutes are gone, and higher-income homes have been constructed not far from Arlington Street. The Arlington Church of God brought stability and preserved property values by creating youth programs, being committed to social activism, building a family life gymnasium, and constructing a K–8 academy in an African-American community—the first of its kind in the area. The majority of people in the church today are from the middle and upper classes, a large part of the African-American community that is rarely represented in television and films.

The church started in 1917 when a few African-American families living together moved from Alabama to Ohio—part of the Great Migration when more than one million African Americans left the South and settled in the northern states and in California. These families initially met in a house and a few other places before eventually settling in a storefront on Arlington Street. In the early 1940s, the community purchased a Russian Orthodox social hall on Roberts Street. Rev. Fowler's father became the pastor in 1946. As often happens in the African-American church, Rev. Fowler and many others were mentored very well by Rev. Fowler's father, and the church grew and eventually resettled back on Arlington Street.

In 1969, Dr. Fowler became the senior pastor and held that position until December 2008. He is now the pastor laureate, a title of great respect, and the church is now led by another one of the finest preachers in the Church of God, Dr. Diana L. Swoope. Pastor Fowler is a great supporter of women in ministry and feels that the movement will not survive if we don't break out of the male dominance in the pulpit.

Unlike Anglo-Americans, African-Americans do not tend to become as skeptical about issues of faith and authority when their income and educational levels rise. "The black church has been able to maintain its cultural identity while modernizing its process. It still retains that sense that it is an African-American church," Dr. Fowler teaches me as we sit in his new office. In his previous office, he had two pictures from the pre-civil rights era of his father and Pastor Elmer Rich, a white Church of God minister. In one photo, Robert Fowler was washing Pastor Rich's feet, and in the other, Pastor Rich was washing Pastor Fowler's feet. It was a picture of the belief within the Church of God that we are all equal in God's eyes despite the color of our skin—a belief that once got D. S. Warner hit in the face with a brick.

While Anglo churches have seen pastors preach in styles that are less confrontational and that even intentionally subvert the authority of the speaker, in the African-American church that is far less common. "Expository preaching is still holding its own in the African-American church," Pastor Fowler tells me. "The pastor is still viewed as God's man, and that's why preaching in the African-American tradition is prophetic. That gives the leader more authority to say things that are not as acceptable and still be accepted. He says what is on his heart. And people will judge if it is of God or not. It's not carte blanche freedom, but he's free to be creative, he's free to explore the parameters of issues that are deemed politically incorrect.

"Worship in the African-American community is community-based, it is prophetic, and it is a celebration," Dr. Fowler says. As he points this out, I think back to the time in my life when I attended an African-American Church of God in Oakland, California, and I can see the difference. There does seem to be an air of celebration dominating the services in African-American churches, and in Sub-Saharan African churches as well. In contrast, the average Anglo church tends to view worship as a time to proclaim the truth. It's a primarily a dialectic approach as opposed to a celebratory approach.

"I think the intent behind black preaching is affirming the here and now. That means affirming people's worth, affirming their value, affirming God's favor upon the people present, and declaring liberation, thus setting people free from cultural constraints to become what they have the capacity to become." While Anglo audiences tend to be more passive, worship is highly participatory in the African-American church. "It is call and response," Rev. Fowler says. "It is people engaged!" This difference in the expectations, I think, helps to explain why unity services between blacks, whites, Hispanics, and Asians are often infrequent. The basic presuppositions of what worship is about are different for each group. We are often not comfortable outside of our own paradigm of church and worship, even if we like and respect the other style.

Because the vast majority of African-American history took place during periods of oppression and inequality, the black pastor and the church have often offered the validation, direction, and security withheld by American society and institutions. The pastor and the church became the people African Americans could turn to in times of difficulty. Within black preaching and the classic Negro spirituals, one finds a message of a God who acts in history and redeems his people. Worship is not simply about affirming God's truth; it is about celebrating the fact that God is in the process of delivering his people and bringing justice now. It's a little more Exodus and a little less Mars Hill.

The general trend in preaching in the wider American culture, however, has been toward making people feel welcome in the church and comfortable with Christianity.

"I find a lot of worship today is driven by performance," Pastor Fowler says as he assesses our contemporary situation. He shares a story that illustrates the point: "Once I was speaking in Anderson and when I got up to preach, they dimmed the lights. I asked them to please turn the lights back on. The reason they had done that is because they were concerned about the stage lighting for the videotaping. I was concerned about people not being able to see to take notes!" I laugh at this illustration that captures the different set of underlying expectations so well. Pastor Fowler hits on something else I had not thought of: there does seem to be a decrease of expectation that the people in church will be actively engaging their Bible. "I'm concerned that the Bible is becoming a relic. Something we carry around and seldom get into.

"When you look at the churches today, I think the average preacher will probably tell you that they are a teacher; they feel more comfortable in this role. We colored the preacher in one stripe—as being the dispenser of judgments. That may be part of it and it does have to be part of it—but the preacher should also be viewed as a mediator, one who passes along wisdom gleaned through study and preparation."

The African-American pastor is often a revered pillar in the community, a father-figure, and a social activist. That high level of respect is channeled into not only impacting the community, as Dr. Fowler has, but also toward serving as a role model and mentor. Like the Hispanic church in the United States, the African-American church has been very good at producing leadership from within. This means that when an African-American pastor takes Church of God theology seriously, he is able to easily transmit it to the younger generations. While Anglo pastors often pursue ministry in a more individualistic manner and go to an outside institution, such as a seminary, for training, African-Americans have been more likely to be raised and mentored from within the church.

"Mentoring is something that I have always taken seriously." Dr. Fowler says. "My father did it, and I started under my father. He raised a significant group of young ministers and trained them."

Because seminaries and Bible colleges were off-limits to African-Americans and many of these pastors had to work long hours in factories, getting sufficient training was not easy. In addition to the mentoring, many African-American pastors were trained through the In-Service Training Institute.

"What was that?" I ask.

"It was an educational ministry started by the National Association of the Church of God (the African-American Association within our movement) for the purpose of training people in local congregations because so many could not go to seminary. A lot of us cut our teeth in the In-Service Training Institute long before we got to seminary in these leadership development programs. The big benefit to all of that was the transmission of core values and traditions—a love for the movement's heritage. It got deeply engrained in us, so that the few who were able to go on to seminary were still able to hold on to that heritage even if they went to Moody or a non-Church of God seminary down South." Leadership, doctrine, preaching, and executive training all were developed in young African-American pastors through this combination of formal study, special training programs, and most significantly, hands-on mentoring. "The older ministers did not hesitate to require some degree of accountability," Pastor Fowler tells me. Perhaps more Anglo churches will need to think about this style of training and mentoring as it becomes more difficult for churches to support full-time pastors and for pastors to pay seminary tuition.

With the authority of the minister intact, the unapologetic use of prophetic preaching, and a strong sense of accountability to community, the African-American church has some key components that enable it to preserve many Church of God values more easily than most cultures in the Anglo-American church. However, the strong spirit of autonomy and the lack of organizational structures in the Church of God have meant that even within the African-American community, it is not easy to maintain complete theological cohesion.

"The biggest issue that I see on the horizon as the Church of God goes forward is that we have got to solve the issue of what it means to be a member in this church. What are the expectations? And we need to develop a structure that holds people accountable. Even in our bigger churches, there is an isolation and autonomy there that leads them to drift away. We haven't found the gumption to draw that line in the sand and develop the biblical structure that can administer it.

"You see this when there are pastoral-congregational conflicts. Who is going to step in and resolve it? Nobody can! The hope is that there is a pastor close by who has enough influence to settle things. That works in some situations, but in the majority of situations that doesn't work because our churches are too steeped in being autonomous. There's no way to help people be responsible."

I mention to Pastor Fowler that even in cultures that have no sense of this kind of radical individualism and autonomy, the Church of God manages to import those values into the local church. He sees this as well.

"Our fear is that somehow to have structure destroys freedom, takes away initiative to be creative, and leads to bureaucracies. I believe you can have all three of those things and still have structure. It doesn't have to be either/or; I think it can be both/and. Autonomy can do well, but it has to have accountability alongside of it, to make sure it stays healthy. I fear that until we solve the authority issue, our church will continue to drift because we have no way to call people back to a responsible position. Even in the New Testament in Acts 15, the council meets to decide what we should say to the Gentiles. They recognized the need to speak with some degree of unity. I wish we had not developed such a fear of organization."

"Autonomy can do well, but it has to have accountability alongside of it."

Pastor Fowler hits upon one of the most challenging aspects of our Church of God experience: our unease with organization. It is an issue that crops up too often in the Church of God, and as Pastor Fowler shared with me, it has become too easy to reap the benefits of being part of the Church of God without having to give much back. It is to the issues of accountability and organizational structures that we now turn.

to centralize or to decentralize?

The Organizational Challenge
Salem, Clayton, Bolivia

The Roman Catholic Church has Rome, Islam has Mecca, and the Church of God has Anderson, Indiana. More than a few ironic jokes have been made over the years about this city in the Midwest which since 1906 has served as the main organizational center of a movement that does not believe in having an organizational center. The Church of God seems to have a love/hate relationship with Anderson for what it symbolizes. On one hand, it is at this geographical location that a hub was created for Church of God ministries that touch the world. The Church of God institutions in the city are a concrete reminder that the movement grew and became global. At the same time, Anderson also has come to symbolize, for many, centralization and bureaucracy—everything the original saints tried to avoid. Our traditionally antagonistic stance toward Anderson is akin to the movement's unease with organization and structures. As the Church of God has grown, it has never reconciled itself with its need to create organizations, structures, and institutions. This has been the Achilles heel of the Church of God.

The early reformers hoped to see the end of denominationalism in the church. Like other Christian movements before ours, that antiorganizational stance was hard to sustain over time. Whether it's the early church in the first century, the Protestant Reformation in the sixteenth century, or the Church of God reformation in the nineteenth century, things never stay simple for very long. Time marches on, complexities arise for the various groups of believers, systems are created, schisms occur, and cultural, economic, political, and historical pressures press on that original movement and it morphs into something different.

The Apostolic Age can never be recreated, nor should it be idealized as a simple time. Looking into the book of Acts, the church of the Apostles was continually "pressed on all sides" and was forced to change, mutate, adapt, and transform in order to survive. The idyllic church of our imagination runs into a problem involving the widows of the Hellenic Jews (Acts 6). Moves are made to deal with this new issue, duties are delegated to believers, and the "perfect" church must increasingly deal with organizational and cultural issues. Things got even more complex after Antioch. The more people and cultures accepted the gospel, the more complicated it all became. Growth (especially cross-culturally) leads to more complexity.

Neither can a golden age of the Church of God reformation movement be recreated or preserved as it existed in the late nineteenth century. There are too many moving parts, too many variables that keep a movement, well, moving. The first believers within the Church of God were also quickly pressed on all sides by the environment around them and were forced to answer charges of sectarianism, they had their theology challenged, they needed to organize, and they had to begin dealing with issues of doctrine and practice more often than they originally intended. They did not exist in a vacuum, even in the rural Midwest of the nineteenth century. Nor were they able to usher in an age free of the need to redefine their identity as time marched onward.

This is how denominations are born and how movements end up looking very much like denominations.[1] Legal issues, theological issues, and financial issues force us to change in order to stay together. Unity requires some kind of practical organization, even if we don't want our spiritual identity and reason for existing to be about becoming an institution. Change

---

1. Thomas O'Dea suggested that there are five dilemmas in the institutionalization of religion: (1) the dilemma of mixed motivation, (2) objectification versus alienation, (3) the dilemma of administrative order, (4) the dilemma of delimitation, and (5) the dilemma of power. Of the third, he wrote, "It is characteristic of bureaucratic structure to elaborate new offices and new networks of communication and command in the face of new problems. Precedents are established which lead to the precipitation of new rules and procedures" (Thomas O'Dea, "Five Dilemmas in the Institutionalization of Religion," *The Journal for the Scientific Study of Religion* 1, no 1 [1961]: 35).

is constant and new complexities arise. The question then becomes: as change comes (and it always does), are we moving with a purpose or just being pushed to and fro by constantly changing external forces?

The Road Map

Organization is the Achilles heel of the Church of God. Our often unrealistic view about the nature of organization is obviously linked to our desire for our movement to be Spirit-led. In the Church of God at the dawn of the twenty-first century, however, it would be good to concretely acknowledge that the business of the church requires organization, adaptation, and wise human leadership as well as Spirit leadership. Fortunately, at the local, state, national, and international level, Church of God pastors, administrators, and congregations are dealing with the fact that things are changing and we must proactively organize ourselves to address these changes. This encouraging and dynamic trend is happening, but it is underreported. So many of us have the false impression that "no one is doing anything" to deal with new realities or that we are all just accepting inevitable decline as our future. Nothing could be further from the truth.

As I traveled around the world, I was surprised and excited to see that there are many dynamic leaders and ministries in the Church of God that are reconfiguring and reimagining themselves organizationally in order to stay relevant and effective. These people are not just treading water but adapting to the conditions. Whether a church movement is stagnant, in decline, or booming, things are always changing. That's undeniable. The next big question is how do we separate the things which must inevitably change from those that must be preserved at all costs?

In this chapter we will travel to Salem, Oregon, where we will get a glimpse at the challenges district (state) administrators face in these changing times. We will then discuss the challenges faced by the organizational centers of denominations/movements in a so-called age of postdenominationalism and visit a national administrator in Ohio. We will conclude in Bolivia, with a look at a healthy national structure existing in a non-Western paradigm.

The State Level: The Penguin and the Camp Meeting

I am sitting in an office in Salem, Oregon. Across from me sits David Shrout and a large stuffed penguin. David seems a bit too old to surround himself with stuffed animals. David is the executive coordinator for the Association of the Churches of God in Oregon and Southwest Washington, one of many area administrators who are listed in the *Yearbook of the Church of God*. There are a number of Church of God districts in the United States—some are highly organized with significant budgets, and others are more loosely organized and have very little financial support. Regional districts have grown rather organically. There is no common title for their leaders, either. The district leader may be known as executive coordinator, state director, executive state minister, or general overseer, for instance. Sometimes the leader is a full-time pastor who has to care for a congregation as well as try to manage a district. Others spend all of their time focusing on their district and may even visit every church within it in the course of a year. One coordinator may be more of a pastor to pastors, while another may serve as a resource person and coordinator for regional events. As is so often true within the Church of God, there is no single way to do ministry.

I have come to Oregon to speak with David because his district is one of the strongest in the Church of God. Seven thousand people, two hundred pastors, and fifty-one congregations (forty-seven in Oregon, four in Washington) make up the district. There's a strong sense of unity among the Oregon and Southwest Washington churches in comparison to many other regions. This district has preserved some of the key things that help to foster unity and preserve identity. For 113 consecutive years they have put on a camp meeting, the third largest state/district camp meeting in the movement. Each year at the Eugene Hilton, they gather for a district Spring Celebration to deal with business issues, but this is also a time of education and renewal for pastors and their spouses. They have managed to publish a periodical called *The Contact*, which regularly updates people on what is happening in the district. There is also a state campground and an annual retreat at the Oregon coast. Churches in this district are generous givers because they see the value of having a strong district office that not only coordinates their business affairs but offers a missional and ministry-centered focus as well.

While the early Church of God reformers were not too thrilled about organization and structure, they soon found themselves having to do just that because of complex situations that arose. Today, it is nearly impossible to do without it. David and the other employees at the district office have to answer tax questions, manage endowment funds, advise churches on health insurance plans, ordain people, provide training, oversee commissions, help churches find pastors and pastors find churches, deal with challenging relational issues, and keep the widely scattered people of the district connected. To this end, David logs over thirty thousand miles each year visiting a different church in his district each week.

But such challenges do not intimidate David Shrout, who recently rode his bicycle from Astoria, Oregon, to the Mexican border. That was a short trip. He has also biked from Miami to Maine. Over the last eleven years, he's biked twenty-six thousand miles. On his East Coast swing, he rode alone and asked God to teach him something new every day. As a result of that trip, he wrote a book called *Wisdom Along the Journey*. David knows how to prepare for the long-haul journey, and that is what he is helping his district do.

> People resist change because they fear that too many valuable things will be lost in the process.

David is only the fifth coordinator for this region. The first was Edgar L. Busch in 1954. The second was Dwite Brown, who also built many of the churches in Oregon in a similar style. "I can walk into a building and know it is a Dwite Brown," David tells me as he sits behind his desk. That makes me laugh.

Sitting in his office, I wonder if the stuffed penguin is some sort of security blanket that he takes on his many road trips. "What do you do when you spend so much time on the road?" I ask.

"I am a member of audible.com and I listen to books. At Christmas time I listen to Charles Dickens's *A Christmas Carol*, William Bridges's stuff, business books, and *Our Iceberg Is Melting,* by William Kotter. I've listend to it three times."

That explains the penguin. *Our Iceberg Is Melting* is a fable by a Harvard professor about a colony of penguins facing extinction. One penguin named Fred realizes what's happening and attempts to help the other penguins through the difficult process of change. The story shows how to navigate successful change as well as why change is so difficult. The underlying premise is that organizations must adapt or perish. So the large stuffed animal in David's office reminds him of that truth.

The rate of change in our world is accelerating and it affects the church in major ways. Yet churches are often places where people resist change because they fear that too many valuable things will be lost in the process.

While some districts of the Church of God have struggled to retain identity, David's district has done very well because it is well-organized and there is a strong commitment to that organization and the regional Church of God community. The annual highlight is the district's well-attended camp meeting. However, there is a constant need to reevaluate even the most successful ministries, so the district is currently reevaluating its annual camp meeting.

"We are engaging in a two-year conversation about camp meeting," David says. "I think if we continue to do camp meeting the way we have done it, in ten years the attendance will be down to two hundred. A lot of regions have stopped it altogether or have low attendance."

The district office decided to deal with the issue before it was too late. "While we are still large enough and strong enough to make some major changes and survive, we are entering into a discussion. I have invited a group of people to be a part of the program, and a prerequisite to being part of the discussion is to read *Our Iceberg Is Melting*."

David goes to the back of his office and pulls out two clear plastic canisters filled with ping-pong balls. One is long and the other is short. He holds up the longer canister. "This represents the 7,000 people who typically show up on any Sunday morning at Church of God congregations in our district."

Then he holds up the shorter canister. "We have an average of 824 people who show up to our combined services at camp meeting. That's only one-twelfth of those who show up on Sunday morning." The visual is striking.

He then asks, "What are we going to do to increase the congregation that shows up at the district event? What are we going to do to better reflect our potential? This is just our own folks I'm talking about here. This is not even including the people of this community who could benefit from what we do."

The decision of whether to continue Church of God camp meetings is a sensitive issue in North America. Camp meetings started on the American frontier in an era when believers spread out over large areas without enough churches or preachers to feed them spiritually. As the country was settled, churches were built, and new methods of transportation became widely available, the need for camp meetings lessened. Camp meetings continued, however, because they served as places of revival and reunion with like-minded folks. In recent decades, young people have not shown up to camp meetings in large numbers, yet they remain a highlight in the life of the church for many of us. "We have a generational responsibility," David says. "We can't lose the young, and we also have people in their seventies and eighties that we have to minister to. There's the rub."

Tough questions surround the district's camp meeting: "Do we need to move closer to Portland? Do we need to use new facilities? Do we need to buy our own facilities? Are we willing to pay the price?"[2]

Such are the difficult decisions that the Church of God will have to make in the coming decade. The group exploring these critical issues for Oregon and Southwest Washington will begin by taking a look at the decision-making process itself. In other words, they are going to prepare for the conversation before having the conversation. This strikes me as a very wise idea. On issues this sensitive, perhaps it would be better to first examine the ways that decisions are made and how different people arrive at those decisions.

The willingness to change is an important part of ministry in Oregon and Southwest Washington. It is not just programs and ministries that are reevaluated and refined, it is ministers themselves. To this end, the district is utilizing the SHAPE (Sustaining Health and Pastoral Excellence) program to create healthier pastors with longer, more effective ministries.

Oregon/SW Washington was one of the first three districts to take part in the SHAPE pilot program, which also included Indiana and Florida. Today it has spread to districts in Northern California and Tennessee. SHAPE is a three-year commitment that begins with a major retreat assessing the pastor's personality and skills. The pastors then come together for all-day meetings once a month over the course of three years. A "player/coach" serves as the facilitator for the meetings. Together they pray and study. A lot of time is spent dealing with daily issues facing pastors and creating a LAMP (Life and Ministry Plan). LAMP is a planning tool that helps a pastor finish strong. It includes a personal ministry and personal mission statement.

---

2. The very next year, the Assemblies of God campground where the Oregon-Southwest Washington Association was having their meetings was sold. They were forced to hold the camp meeting at New Hope Community Church, using a Seventh Day Adventist campsite and Warner Pacific College dorm rooms. The General Council is currently in discussions about where and how to hold camp meeting in the future.

There are five hallmarks of a successful pastor, according to the Lilly Endowment, which has given the Church of God sizeable grants in order to run the SHAPE program: knowledge, spirituality, connectedness, leadership, and vision. (Dave Shrout has added a sixth for his district: health). SHAPE pastors seek ways to improve themselves in each area. Not only does David coach people through this process, but he also does it himself, and it has led to major changes in his life. When state and regional offices can offer resources to help pastors and churches position themselves for the long haul, the health of the movement improves. However, not all regions have the funds to be able to do such a thing.

I ask David what keeps him optimistic about the future. He mentions that he is very impressed with the young pastors in his district. "I know church will look different, but I am okay with that."

He sees a shift in the way ministry is being done by successful churches. "Churches are doing more and more community involvement. I see that the ones who are actively healthy and growing are ones that are out in the community, touching the lives of the people, without the hook. For instance they say, 'We are out here passing out bottles of water just because we love you. If you want to know where we go to church just read the bottle, our name is on it, but we are here to love you.' When a church goes out with a hook, people sense that and they don't respond. I think there are true leaders in the community who are looking for a church that is changing the community they live in. The church without walls is the church that will really be successful in the twenty-first century. And I see our young pastors as people who want to do that and are shaping those churches. That's why I want to be a coach and help them."

The stuffed penguin is nodding in agreement. Or perhaps I am too tired from my travels.

"I'm at the point in my life where I'm thinking not what I am going to do, but who I am going to invest in. Ann Smith [former Church of God missionary and well-known speaker] said it right when she said, 'Nobody got here by themselves.'"

Perhaps riding across America has built up David's endurance for the journey that he is now on with the Oregon and Southwest Washington District. For journeys this long, one has to plan and prepare carefully. There will be mountains, valleys, and unpredictable weather conditions every day of the journey. It's difficult, but if a penguin can do it, so can we.

The Challenge Facing Denominations and Movements

Denominations and movements are not only losing their cultural and theological identity, but their organizational identity as well. By the end of the twentieth century, the Assemblies of God, the PCUSA, the Southern Baptists, the Reformed Church of America, the Church of God, and many other Christian groups were struggling to maintain the place of their organizational centers in the life of the local congregations. What happens when a denomination loses its organizational center? Let's take a look:

After a long period of expansion, church attendance is dropping, and congregations that were once large and thriving find themselves considerably smaller. Soon churches do not have enough pastors, and the people in the pews are mostly older people. Denominational events that were once well-attended see a steep decline in the number of participants. People begin turning to more effective organizations to help them solve their ministry problems, since they see their own denomination as ineffective.

Frustration and anger at the denomination's central offices begins to set in as people sense a lack of relevance. The organization is slow to respond to the fact that things are changing, so it loses time and valuable people. There are still enough people committed to the organization that it misreads the speed at which things are changing, so it fails to notice its many competitors (many within the denomination itself).

Faced with a decline in financial giving and belatedly sensing that it is losing vital support, the organization tries to buy time and reinvigorate the enthusiasm of its people by restructuring the organization. In fact, restructuring may occur several times. The restructuring, however, only exacerbates the problem because it attempts to further centralize the organization when true momentum is moving outward. Mergers between various agencies begin to occur. National leaders claim that this will make the agencies more efficient and responsive to the needs of the churches. While some agencies may see genuine benefits, the overall effect is that they lose the flexibility they need to respond to their congregations' increasingly diverse needs. The resulting centralization further suggests to the local church people that their leaders do not know what they are doing. Meanwhile, the pressure builds from the local, state, and district organizations to have more control of their own ministries. The momentum toward local ministries grows stronger.

The central office staff may claim that they need greater support because they are doing important ministry. But the reality is that the bureaucratic organizational model is inflexible and uninspiring. People begin to view the organization as too concerned with self-preservation, resistant to out-of-the-box thinking, and unwilling to take creative risks. Leaders of the institution argue that they know what they are doing, by virtue of their years of experience, and they have a bottom line that they must meet. In droves, the organization's talented leaders migrate to other more flexible organizations to create new, innovative ministries. It does not matter to them whether they are part of the denomination or not.

The central organization is soon run mostly by managers who seek to preserve the status quo. With the leadership talent pool drying up, people are put into key positions by default. These leaders lack the proper skill sets to revitalize the movement or denomination. For example, people who are not managers get put into management positions; people who are not visionaries get put into visionary positions. This organizational mismanagement further turns people off, which further dilutes the talent pool. It is a vicious cycle.

Within the organization, morale begins to suffer greatly. Lay-offs and resignations occur at greater speed. Tensions between the newly merged agencies begin to threaten unity. Many of the leaders feel that they are in over their heads but cannot admit as much.

Eventually, aware that it can no longer count on the people to be loyal to the organization, the denomination tries to position itself as a service provider. But by this time, their churches have spent years (perhaps decades) going to other organizations that provide such services as church consulting, church planting, publishing, and missionary sending. The declining organization's poor cash flow cannot compete with other Christian organizations, each of which specializes in one thing and does it very well.

Eventually...the denomination tries to position itself as a service provider.

The lack of financial stability causes stress and causes its leaders to continue playing it safe. Attempts to generate enthusiasm through new programs or slogans fall flat because they fail to articulate why the denomination is particularly unique in its mission, compared to other Christian organizations.

Risk aversion is justified by the financial managers. They argue that they are acting responsibly. However, they fail to see that the church's money follows a bold vision. So vision and risk-taking cannot wait until the money comes in. The financial managers' attempts to protect the institution from going broke has precisely that effect. The organization's safe position is viewed as an unholy concern for self-preservation and fails to inspire big giving from churches or individuals. More than ever, talented, innovative, visionary people decline leadership roles, viewing the organization as a place where ministry dies and good ideas have no chance of surviving.

The denomination goes into survival mode. It no longer has the re-sources, time, or energy to do courageous ministry. Eventually, there will be so little money that the organization (long considered irrelevant) can no longer survive.

This is the pattern that church organizations have followed in the de-nominational world.[3] The Church of God is not unique in this respect. Con-sidering all the factors that led to centralization of denominations during the twentieth century, it is understandable that they found themselves in this trap at the end of the century, as decentralization swept over the world. Resuscitating the old paradigm does not work, so denominations are forced to create an entirely new paradigm to survive.[4] Ironically, the Church of God started with a nondenominational, decentralized paradigm and then entered into a more centralized one out of necessity, only to find

---

3. See the book by Ramsey Coutta, *Divine Institutions: The Nature of Denominational Growth and Decline in America* (Longwood, FL: Xulon Press, 2006.), for a look at the phases passed through by the Methodists, Baptists, Presbyterians, Assemblies of God, and Congregationalists. *Church Identity and Change: Theology and Denominational Structures in Unsettled Times*, ed. David A Roozen and James R. Nieman (Grand Rapids, MI: W. B. Eerdmans, 2005), was the most helpful book I found while doing re-search on denominations and the challenges they face.

4. Russell E. Richey proposed the five stages through which mainline denominations move: (1) ethnic voluntarism, (2) purposive missionary association, (3) churchly denominationalism, (4) corpo-rate organization, and (5) postdenominational confessionalism (Russell E. Richey, "Denominations and Denominationalism: An American Morphology," in *Reimagining Denominationalism: Interpretive Essays*, ed. Robert Bruce Mullin and Russell E. Richey [New York: Oxford University Press, 1994]). Despite the fact that the Church of God is not a mainline denomination, an examination of these stages is helpful. Richey writes "that denominations have lost or are losing long familiar adhesive and dynamic principles and are groping, often desperately, for tactics that work and unite." The irony with the Church of God is that the foundation for number five has been there all along, but we have not been able to fully emerge into that paradigm for a variety of reasons, many of which are articulated in this book.

that the most effective organizations in the new millennium are radically decentralized. The Church of God is a case study in irony.

The National Level:
Challenging "the Ecclesiastical Octopus"

While the Church of God does not believe in having a headquarters per se, the recognized center of organization has been Anderson, Indiana, where the general offices of the Church of God in North America are located. The early reformers were against any kind of human ecclesiastical organization because they felt it obstructed the Holy Spirit, and that suspicion of human organization has stayed with us for more than a century.

As mentioned in chapter 1, we are not the only movement to struggle with issues of organization because of an antidenominational theological heritage. The Assemblies of God, much like the Church of God, was an experientially-oriented holiness movement concerned with "baptism in the Holy Spirit," which viewed itself as the apostolic church restored. Like the Church of God, the Assemblies did not focus heavily on theology and initially resisted forming doctrinal statements. However, they eventually felt the need to clarify a number of theological points.[5] As with the Church of God, the autonomy of the local church was prized. There was great resistance to becoming a denomination and to interacting much with other groups.[6] There has consistently been a love-hate relationship with institutionalism in the AG.[7] Ultimately, the movement did become a denomination as it felt the need to credential ministers, establish schools for ministry training, clarify acceptable teaching, and organize for global missions.[8] The bureaucracy remained as spare as they could keep it, but from 1941 to 1953 the AG entered a period of bureaucratic growth. There followed a few attempts to restructure, in order to ensure that the services the bureaucracy provided

---

5. Gary B. McGee, "More than Evangelical," in *Church, Identity, and Change: Theology and Denominational Structures in Unsettled Times*, ed. David A. Roozen and James R. Nieman, 35–44 (Grand Rapids, MI: Eerdmans Publishing Co., 2005): 35. The Disciples of Christ and the Churches of Christ also had no intention of becoming denominations.

6. William W. Menzies, "The Challenges of Organization and Spirit in the Implementation of Theology in the Assemblies of God," in *Church, Identity, and Change: Theology and Denominational Structures in Unsettled Times*, ed. David A. Roozen and James R. Nieman, 97–131 (Grand Rapids, MI: Eerdmans Publishing Co., 2005): 104–5.

7. Margaret M. Poloma, "Charisma and Structure in the Assemblies of God," in *Church, Identity, and Change: Theology and Denominational Structures in Unsettled Times*, ed. David A. Roozen and James R. Nieman, 45–96 (Grand Rapids, MI: Eerdmans Publishing Co., 2005): 88.

8. Menzies, "Challenges of Organization and Spirit," 104–5.

were truly needed and to increase the efficiency of the organization[9]. Local pastors, who feel a closer connection to district offices, have felt alienated and ambivalent toward the national office. Attendance at the Assemblies' Biannual General Conference meetings has decreased.[10] Relations between the organizational center and the local church have often been tense, but "amorphous revival movements inevitably require some structure for survival," historian William W. Menzies writes.[11]

The Church of God held out a lot longer than the Assemblies of God.[12] For the first thirty years, the only organization that existed was the Gospel Trumpet Publishing Company, led by the "Spirit government of charismatic leaders" such as Warner and the second editor, E. E. Byrum. However, even in this early phase, the need to establish clear lines of authority and to deal with the realities of the publishing company forced a significant level of organization.[13] From 1900 to 1917 came what might be called "the era of expedient procedures." This saw the establishment of the General Ministerial Assembly and a corporate structure brought to the Gospel Trumpet Company. From 1917 to 1930 was the era of national agencies. From 1930 to 1950 came state structures, planned coordination, and developing democracy.[14]

Through it all, we felt ambivalent about organization. But if we want to continue to have fellowship with people who share a common history, heritage, and tradition, we will have to work together. To affiliate with each other on any kind of significant level requires some human organization. This is something Earl Slacum found out the hard way.

Slacum was a pastor from Indiana who preached an incendiary sermon in 1944 titled "Watchmen on the Wall." He expressed the concern of many that leaders in Anderson were centralizing the movement. Before long, many were joining Slacum in what came to be known as "The Watchman Movement." Slacum's challenge was probably a healthy reminder of the

---

9. Ibid., 106.

10. Poloma, "Charisma and Structure," 86.

11. Menzies, "Challengies of Organization and Spirit," 105.

12. See Valorous Clear, *Where the Saints Have Trod: A Social History of the Church of God Reformation Movement* (Chesterfield, IN: Midwest Publications, 1977).

13. As Historian Merle Strege chronicles in his book *I Saw the Church*, the early editors shaped and defended orthodoxy and were not above labeling challengers as heretics and having them shunned. E. E. Byrum seemed to have the gift of organization, even though his methods were authoritarian at times (Merle D. Strege, *I Saw the Church* [Anderson, IN: Warner Press, 2002], 48).

14. Final report of the Consultation On Doctrine, convened by the Executive Council of the Church of God, 1974.

need to avoid excessive bureaucracy and centralization, but soon Slacum's own movement became organizationally top-heavy, leading him to humbly admit that this new movement had "developed more structure in five years than Anderson had in twenty-five."[15]

The Church of God has tried to gingerly differentiate between being Spirit-led and being man-led by suggesting that human beings cannot "organize God's church," but rather under the guidance of the Spirit can "organize the work of the church." Nevertheless, the offices and agencies in Anderson continue to be viewed by many in the movement as—to borrow a term from Earl Slacum—a threatening "ecclesiastical octopus." Today, the concern is less often expressed as a theological one and more of an organizational one.

The current trend in media, politics, and military affairs is to decentralize to better deal with realities on the ground.[16] The form of national church government we recognize today evolved out of what Russell E. Richey has called the fourth stage of American denominationalism, which led to very centralized bureaucracies.[17] This mostly happened in the early twentieth century as denominations and movements felt the need to organize to do ministry more effectively. While the Church of God experienced tension, such as the Slacum controversy in mid-century, due to its early theology, the current suspicion regarding centralization comes from more recent events.

In 1987 the General Assembly established a Task Force on Governance and Polity in an effort to strengthen the ministry efforts of the Church of God. The effort lasted five years, and by 1995, Leith Anderson was hired as a consultant by the General Assembly's Leadership Council. The end result was that a new national structure for the Church of God was created. The Missionary Board, the Board of Christian Education, the Mass Communications Board, the Home Missions and Church Growth units of the Board of Church Extension, Vision 2 Grow, and the circulation and publishing departments of Warner Press were centralized under the newly created Church of God Ministries, Inc. This new organization was given a general director who

---

15. The Slacum Letter, Church of God Archives, Anderson University.

16. Everything from denominations to media, manufacturing companies to the local church, terrorist organizations to NGOs, to the government of the People's Republic of China is decentralizing. Even the U.S. military is decentralizing in response to the new decentralized assymetrical threats. More and more decisions in and out of combat are made by lower rank soldiers in the field.

17. Russell E. Richey, "Denominations and Denominationalism: An American Morphology," in *Reimagining Denominationalism: Interpretive Essays*, ed. Robert Bruce Mullin and Russell E Richey (New York: Oxford University Press, 1994), 76.

answered to the Ministries Council. The General Assembly overwhelmingly voted for this restructuring effort, and the agencies of the Church of God have been following a more centralized model since then.

As mentioned before, the Church of God seemed to centralize at precisely the moment that other organizations and denominations chose to decentralize. This centralization effort may have strengthened some agencies and enabled the Church of God to continue doing some types of ministry, but it also had the effect of looking like an outdated denominational model. The laity's skepticism toward Anderson now has more to do with decentralizing cultural trends than theological ambivalence (i.e., the influence of the Internet for curricula, megachurch pastors and their various competing programs, the Emergent Church movement placing emphasis on the local church, distrust of hierarchical government in general, and new corporate models that place more emphasis on decentralized innovation and decision-making). Why did we centralize so much at a moment in time when the forces in the world were pushing toward decentralization, and when our movement still retained such an autonomous spirit?

I am traveling to Ohio to speak with Robert Moss and ask him this question. Rev. Moss is currently the chair of the General Assembly and of the Ministries Council of the Church of God. He is a highly respected Church of God leader. I meet with Bob just as he is settling into his new office at the Salem Church of God in Clayton, Ohio. Bob has been a pastor and church administrator and has engaged the Church of God overseas. He has about as much experience as anyone having seen the Church of God organization from a number of different vantage points.

"In the Church of God," he tells me, "if you are in any administrative office, you are marginalized." As he took positions of administrative authority in the Church of God, his wife Renee expressed concern about this. Though he has remained one of the most respected voices in the Church of God, Bob has felt marginalized at times. "When I became a state minister, people began saying, 'What do you know? You are just a state minister paper pusher.'"

As with the early pioneers, nobody in ministry today really wants to be part of an inflexible bureaucracy. That is not what was intended with the agency merger, and it is not what Church of God Ministries strives to be today.

"The [Leith] Anderson model was viewed as a remedy to a lack of collaborative effort," Bob tells me. "The model was also a remedy for a lack of a leader. Baby Boomers were saying, 'Who is the leader? Where is our vision?' So the structure was supposed to be a way to bring people together, not to bring a centralized structure." At the time, national agencies were in deep financial trouble, and many Church of God people had a sense that there was too much competition and not enough cooperation among the national organizations.

"We thought we needed to create one entity," Bob tells me. "I still believe that we need one entity. But we took all the existing players [the various agency employees], put them in a building, and told them to all get along. It's taken more than a decade to get where we are today. But during that decade, we suffered a huge consequence: disengagement. People walked away from even caring. I believe that is such a huge danger."[18]

Bob Moss and the other members of the Ministries Council now function under a governance model that holds the general director, currently Dr. Ronald V. Duncan, accountable as well as to make sure that the general director has the freedom to do what he needs to do. Under Ron Duncan's

---

18. The centralization that took place just as we entered into an era of decentralization is worth examining closely. Leith Anderson warned in his report that aging denominations have entrenched bureaucracies and devote resources to institutional perpetuation, so he was not naïve to the way centralization can be damaging to denominations. The findings of Leith Anderson's report support what Bob Moss was telling me, which was that the goal was not to create a centralized bureaucracy but to enhance coordination. In the report, Anderson wrote, "Because each agency is independent and executives report to different boards, they are not organized to work as a team seeking to fulfill the same goals. The executives of the Leadership Council and general agencies hold few meetings. There does not appear to be adequate discussions of strategies. The system does not adequately identify or enable clear leadership." His report further suggested that despite their aversion to authority there was a strong "intellectual desire for the benefits of centralization." Clearly, this "centralization" that Anderson helped to usher in was meant to increase cooperation and accountability, and make it possible to follow a vision under strong leadership. This streamlining to end overlap, fiscal deficits, and excessive disorganization certainly needed to happen. The problem, however, is that this kind of "centralization out of necessity for coordination purposes" easily leads to another kind of centralization: bureaucratic centralization, in which the various departments, agencies, and ministries with different DNAs lose their ability to be flexible and respond to changing needs in their own particular way. In today's world, there is a need for what I call "decentralization on the other side of centralization." There is a core vision, a core ethos, and a core way of running the organization that is clearly articulated and understood by all employees, but each department or agency has the freedom to configure itself in its own particular way within that organizational core. The alternative can easily be a one-size-fits-all model that has radically different agencies with different realities trying to operate through the same uniform structure. This kind of excessive bureaucratization leads to a different kind of waste as energy and innovation are choked by a slow, risk-averse, red-tape-filled bureaucracy. Many have said to me that Leith Anderson did not understand Church of God culture. I don't think this is true. I think he understood but was saying that this culture needed to be challenged somewhat and reformed. The danger as he pointed out, however, was of the organization reforming too much in the other direction.

leadership, the Church of God regained a fiscal discipline that it had been lacking for decades. This was crucial. But as this difficult, necessary, and time-consuming transition was occurring, Moss saw too many people disconnect.

"At the General Assembly level is where I see disengagement at its worst. There's a desire from some to have a town-hall meeting type of GA, where people can make a motion from the floor and say, 'I think we ought to do this or do that.' That's exciting, but it's also dangerous to the organization because the organization can't stay on course when a new course is set during each GA. So the GA has become more of a reporting session. As a result, disengagement is rampant. We obviously need to address the disengagement issue."

As the movement grew, so did the spirit of autonomy.

The years of not having a direction have left their mark: "If you ask a hundred people to describe God's call for the Church of God, you will get a hundred different answers," Bob says. "In the earliest days of this movement, you could write our cause on the back of a card: Salvation, Holiness, and Unity. We felt we were initiating a great movement. We were one of the only voices preaching the combination of holiness and unity. We felt our cause was to show that salvation was a spiritual experience, not just joining the church." However, he admitted, we no longer have that kind of unity.

I understand what Bob Moss is talking about. It was very evident as I traveled around the world speaking to Church of God pastors. The lack of a unifying voice and message has taken its toll on the Church of God. When we were smaller, even with our disdain for centralization, a common voice and a message was possible. But as the movement grew, so did the spirit of autonomy. The most recognized voices for the movement (particularly the *Gospel Trumpet*) fell by the wayside or faced competition from other Christian voices. As a result, the message of the movement became whatever individual pastors thought it should be.

The tension between national offices and local congregations is not at all unique to the Church of God. Roozen and Niemen, who have both done a significant amount of research on the challenges denominations face, point out that "given the relative power of national staff in comparison to the national assembly, the ability of the grass roots to hold national staff accountable is episodic and arduous at best." They go on to say that "when questions about the accountability and representativeness of the national level are combined with concerns about the fundamental identity, direction, beliefs, and practices of a denomination, it is little wonder that denominational politics occasionally make the front pages of the secular press."[19]

The Church of God is at a disadvantage compared to other denominations in that it has even less of a cohesive center that can provide direction. But the Church of God is also blessed to have avoided the kind of schisms and bloody battles that other denominations have faced in the past few decades. We are too divided to divide.

"In our heads we still believe in this movement, but in our hearts we don't feel it," Moss says. "So the effect of the GA is that of being in a reporting session. 'Here's how our business is doing,' instead of 'Here's the hill we charge for this great global cause.'"

While all denominations have had a difficult time fostering loyalty for the past few decades, the Church of God is at an even greater disadvantage because of its antiauthoritarian spirit. "It's in our DNA," says Moss. "The principle that we have now is, 'If I don't like what the group is doing, I won't do it.' As pastors we are offended if we are treated that way in the local congregation, yet that's our attitude in the church at large. I don't think we should do like Nazarenes or Wesleyans and say, 'You give 10 percent or else.' There's a joyfulness in giving when you are on a team. But there is a frightening sense of abandonment when participation is not there." Another challenge for the organization has been competition from within the Church of God. Heart to Honduras, Project Partner, and the Church Multiplication Association are just three of more than seventy free-standing organizations affiliated with the Church of God that provide services similar to those of the central offices in Anderson and compete for the same money. There has been an explosion of these organizations in the past decade, and this can result in a duplication of services. The lack of common theology, identity, and loyalty to tradition has left a lot of denominational central offices configuring themselves as service providers for other groups, providing things such as health insurance, pension plans, mission opportunities, or church planting services. With such a flurry of Christian nonprofits growing

---

19. David A. Roozen and James R. Nieman, "Introduction," in *Church, Identity, and Change: Theology and Denominational Structures in Unsettled Times*, ed. David A. Roozen and James R. Nieman, 1–35 (Grand Rapids, MI: Eerdmans Publishing Co., 2005): 11.

even within denominations, the central organization's purpose for existence becomes less clear.

Bob Moss believes there is still a purpose for the Church of God and thus a place for a central administrative body that can mobilize people, but a central administrative body does not necessarily mean centralization. "There's an old Turkish proverb that says, 'No matter how far you walk down the wrong road, turn around.' I think the structure should change so that it serves the mission, not the other way around."

For Bob, this means turning over leadership to young people. "When older people go into a new paradigm, they tend to go back to the familiar. The move to the one Anderson office [Church of God Ministries, Inc.] caused a lot of staff to move into a new model with a sense of powerlessness, perhaps feeling herded like cattle. But they drifted back to the more familiar corporate model." I consulted many books, experts, and experienced administrators that echoed the sentiment. Adopting a new paradigm doesn't mean people will be able to implement it. The obstacles to that implementation have to be examined closely.[20] Bob's belief that a younger generation may have to play a part in that implementation is key.

However, the younger generation has mostly been disengaged from the Church of God. "I talk to a lot of young leaders who love the church, but they don't like the stuff we are selling," Bob observes. "To reengage the disengaged, we have to be willing to dismantle what is. Jesus said, 'Unless a seed falls and dies, it cannot grow.' I do not find any voices that are enamored with the offices in Indiana."

As Bob speaks, it seems to me that our primary problem in the Church of God is not so much that we have the wrong organizational model (although we do), but that this pales in comparison to our spiritual and theological problem: a lack of willingness to be accountable and a lack of the scriptural and theological understanding upon which to build such a relationship. Obviously, the central offices must cast a vision that can be followed and its organization must fit our inherently decentralized style, but even if Church of God Ministries changes into the right kind of administrative body, would we have unity as well as a willingness to communicate and—dare I say it—follow?

---

20. The book *Harvard Business Review on Change* (Cambridge, MA: Harvard Business School Press) has some excellent essays which deal with the obstacles to real transformation that companies and organizations face.

Bolivia: A Model of National Unity

Unity and a strong identity backed by an equally strong organizational center is hard to come by throughout the Church of God. So when I hear about a country where there is a great deal of national unity among the churches, I have to see it.

I travel twelve thousand miles from my home in Hong Kong to the country of Bolivia. As the plane descends into the airport at El Alto, I am surprised to see how flat the terrain is at twelve thousand feet. This is the Alto Plano of the Andes, a dry plateau where La Paz, the highest city in the world, is located. From the airfield at El Alto, my taxi begins descending into a mountain cauldron and the city of La Paz unfolds before my eyes. From within the canyon created by the Choqueyapu River, the brown mountains completely surround the city, and taller snow capped mountains are visible in the distance. It is a stunning sight. I am also stunned by what feels like an invisible belt being tightened around my head. It's *soroche*: altitude sickness.

I am here to attend the annual three-day Easter celebration of the Church of God in Bolivia, which is located at an even higher altitude than La Paz: fourteen thousand feet. That is the same altitude as the summit of Mt. Rainier in Washington State, one of the tallest mountains in the continental United States. Being a clever traveler, I arrive four days early to try to adjust to the altitude before the meeting. Bolivia mocks my pretensions, and I begin to suffer altitude sickness, which causes headaches, fatigue, dizziness, insomnia, shortness of breath, a persistent rapid pulse, loss of appetite, and nausea. Located as I am far from a decent hospital and three miles above sea level, my body decides that this would be a good time to not only get altitude sickness but to suffer from my reoccurring kidney problems. I am suddenly in a tremendous amount of pain.

I check into a good hotel, just in case I need medical assistance in the middle of the night. The hotel is more expensive than I would like, but it offers the guests emergency oxygen. I decide to get a room. I spend the next four days virtually immobile and in constant pain, with my usual medicine providing no relief. Suddenly, La Paz doesn't look so beautiful.

From La Paz, I was given instructions to take a bus to the small town of Lequepalca, which is located at an even higher altitude. At this altitude the clouds look low enough to grab, and the wide-open spaces make distances seem smaller than they actually are. I spot what I think are some flowers on a hill, but they are actually sheep. As we continue to climb, my head feels more pressure, and it is clear to me that by the time I arrive, I will be practically catatonic.

The bus drops me off in a miniscule town in the middle of nowhere next to a five-hundred-year-old adobe church. It looks like the remotest corner of Nevada. I proceed to walk along a river bed for two kilometers in the mountains before turning a corner and stumbling upon thousands of people. It is a surreal experience, made even more surreal by the fact that I'm slowly dying. Indigenous Bolivians have come from all over the country in shared vans, trucks, buses, cars, and even on foot. Full of smiles and friendly waves, not one of them struggles from altitude sickness. Tents, blue tarps, and many people dot the hillside. The scene contrasts dramatically with the sparsely populated land I have been riding through for hours. This is the annual junta of the Bolivian Church of God in Chacarillas.

Every year at Easter, up to eight thousand people from the more than 235 congregations and forty house churches in Bolivia make the journey. For a few days, the believers gather to worship together, pray, listen to various speakers, and reconnect with each other. It all cumulates on Easter Sunday with a massive baptism ceremony, which has included as many as five hundred people.

The mountains create a natural amphitheatre. People sit on bricks and rocks or on the ground overlooking the great camp-out. The church in Bolivia (much like the country itself) is predominantly Native American. It is not a Latin church culture. The people are Quechua or Aymara, and some speak languages I've never heard of, such as Puquina and Chipaya. The women are adorned in black hats with colorful sweaters and skirts that have streaks of purple, red, violet, blue, and lime green. To me, all the outfits that the women wear look beautiful and are of one style. But I am told by missionary Kattia Jones that the different styles, designs, and even the skirt lengths indicate which region of the country they come from.

Many of the people do not speak Spanish, so the service is interpreted into Quechua and Aymara. The stage is a flatbed truck with a white cab and the musicians play beautiful traditional Andean music—music that was once frowned upon by the evangelical churches in Bolivia. The music seems to continue whether there is a service or not. The first services begin at 5:00 AM, but even at 2:00 AM large groups of people are awake, singing heartily. Some climb the mountains to repent and pray. (Not me, however.

I spend most of my time in pain, lying down, and mostly delusional.) Nevertheless, in one of my few lucid moments, I learn about this unique part of the Church of God body in Bolivia.

The Bolivian church is the largest church in Latin America and the least subsidized by foreign missions funding. Organizationally, they base their model on the New Testament. The Bolivian Church of God is lay governed. Everybody in the Bolivian church is eligible for ministry. Anyone can be a deacon, missionary, elder, or evangelist, depending on the gifts that they display. There is no separation between the laity and a professional clergy. There are national business meetings and a national board of directors, which is elected by the general assembly. On the local level, however, the lay ministry operates through a diaconate. Five men and two women are elected every year to do the ministry of the local church. They divide the pastoral responsibilities so that it is not too taxing on any one of the seven. Their responsibilities match their particular gifts and skill sets. At the end of the year, the congregation can reelect them or someone else. Everyone in the local church can expect to be a part of the diaconate ministry at some time. Those who have special ministry gifts may become regionally recognized as evangelists, but they do not make up any sort of hierarchy within the church. Nobody receives a salary.

The New Testament organizational structure of the Bolivian church would have greatly pleased the early pioneers of the Church of God. So consider this irony: the success of the Bolivian church at achieving such unity may have something to do with the fact that it did *not* start within the Church of God movement. The work was started in 1963 as an independent church known as Congregaciones Evangélicas. These Bolivian churches were attracted to the Church of God message of holiness and our New Testament understanding of the church. They practiced footwashing and found that very few other groups did. In 1976, they voluntarily joined the movement and finalized their affiliation with the Church of God. Only in time did they realize that their model of church government was actually out of sync with much of the rest of the Church of God. Their Book of Acts structure is considerably different from what we find in the Church of God in most regions of the world. Nevertheless, they have happily remained a part of the Church of God. They attend the Inter-American Conference and treasure their relationships with other Church of God nations.[21]

Although Christianity arrived in this country through the Roman Catholic Church in the 1500s, Catholicism has struggled in Bolivia because of its history of colonialism, the Spanish ancestry of the dominant *mestizo* minority, and the Catholic priests' toleration of indigenous syncretism and animism.[22] Bolivians have inherently strong communal social institutions due to their reliance on small-scale agriculture in a difficult land.[23] The highly communal and spiritual nature of the indigenous people in Bolivia more closely resembles the communities in ancient Palestine than societies in most of the West. Consequently, they inhabit an environment that I referred to as the Book of Acts world in chapter 3. Since the 1950s, the Catholic church, with its rigid hierarchical structure, has declined in influence while groups such as the Assemblies of God, the Seventh Day Adventists, the Quakers, and the Baptists have grown among indigenous Bolivians.[24]

David Miller, Church of God regional coordinator for Latin America, thinks that the Bolivian church's key to success is that they have organized their church in a way that is true to the New Testament and culturally relevant to the local culture. "The New Testament model is culturally appropriate and it is fluid," he says. "If we follow an ecclesiastical tradition that grows out of a particular point in history or a particular culture and then try to apply it to the two-thirds world context, it just doesn't work. But if

---

21. Another source of health for the region is the Pastoral Forums started by regional coordinators for Latin America David and Barbara Miller. One of the great things about these forums is that they are held in places that are accessible to people—for instance, Central Americans do not have to travel all the way to South America by plane to attend one. David Miller shares that the goal is to enhance the skills of active ministers (especially since a recent survey showed that nine out of ten Latin American pastors are bivocational). They also help to equip and raise up a new generation of pastors. Many of them have had a better education than the older generation, but they still need to enhance their pastor skills. There is also a need to have an in-depth knowledge of the Scriptures. Cults, false prophets, and sub-Christian teachings flourish in this region. When asked about this, David said to me: "Our goal in every place where the Church of God ministers in Latin America is not necessarily to be the biggest or most affluent church in town (although we are, in some places) but always be the healthiest church in town. We believe that our tradition of holiness, living a consistent, godly Christian life before the community while bearing the fruit of the Spirit, and unity, showing respect to and doing good for all those of the household of faith as opportunities arise for us to work together, is the Biblical prescription for health. We strive to be a New Testament church in the twenty-first century, led by the Holy Spirit and operated by the priesthood of all believers."

22. Andrew Canessa, "Evangelical Protestantism in the Northern Highlands of Bolivia," *Studies in World Christianity* 4, pt 1 (1998): 24–27, 30.

23. Ibid., 36–37.

24. Ibid., 29–30.

we follow the New Testament principles that we profess to in the Church of God, we come out with a sound structure. You have to find the connections between the culture and the New Testament."

The unity of the Church of God in Bolivia is a remarkable thing to observe. It is hard to find other parts of the Church of God that have such a strong identity and such a widely accepted organizational structure, and that are showing considerable growth. All of this is made more impressive by the fact that they actually seem to be following in the footsteps of the nineteenth-century Church of God reformation movement, which itself aimed to follow the apostolic church.[25]

There have been challenges. In 2000, nineteen of the churches decided to join the neo-Pentecostals, a movement that has also seen tremendous growth while operating with a nonhierarchical structure. However, these breakaway churches didn't manage to convince the rest of the more than two hundred churches in the Bolivian Church of God to join them. Their theological and organizational identity is too strong, and the role of lay leaders helps to prevent abuses by charismatic leaders in influential positions. Of the nineteen that left, only two congregations have survived.

The Church of God in Bolivia and their Easter service is amazing. For the baptism portion, hundreds of people dressed in white enter a cold river as people crowd the mountainsides and look down on them. At this altitude, I found it breathtaking both metaphorically and literally. As soon as the baptism service is over, I head back down to twelve thousand feet in a desperate attempt to catch my breath.

The Bolivian church's loose lay-led structure parallels the New Testament and the early Church of God movement. It even looks like the Emerging Church's missional paradigm, which is growing in influence in the West. U.S. Church of God congregations in places like Oklahoma are trying out these very ideas. But a word of caution is in order. It is hard to replicate the Book of Acts world in the Western world. Our Western societies are more atomized than communities in most parts of the non-Western world. Even something as basic as automobile ownership creates a level of autonomy and individualism that makes the non-Western communal experience hard to replicate. Education and urban living also create obstacles to faith-based

---

25. For an inspirational and in-depth look at the Church of God believers in Bolivia, see David Miller, *Song of the Andes: The Impact of the Gospel on the Andean People of Bolivia* (Nappanee, IN: Evangel Publishing House, 2002).

ways of communal living that are relatively easy in agricultural communities. It can be done, but the unity and mutual dependence of a persecuted Christian community (in China, for instance) are hard to replicate. As China's middle and upper classes grow, this kind of community will most likely wane.

Organization has always been a significant weakness of the Church of God. As a result of our anti-institutional heritage, we have prized autonomy to a degree that far surpasses most other movements and denominations. In some ways, this lack of a center with strong authority has been very beneficial; it emphasizes the fact that the church is primarily a spiritual community. We do not exist to build an organization or promote ourselves. However, throughout the world, Church of God congregations and organizations have paid a steep price for our lack of clearly-defined structural expectations. At the local, national, and international levels, one hears many sad stories about how a lack of accountability and an excessive spirit of autonomy have led to divisions and losses. Have we spent far too much time lauding our autonomy and not enough time considering the toll that this autonomy has taken on our movement?

5
the cross or the video screen

The Liturgical Challenge
Vincennes, Olathe, Phoenix, Fishers, the Philippines, Egypt

I begin with a confession and a story. It's the kind of thing that you are not supposed to say aloud to fellow Christians because you might get funny looks or possibly be viewed as hell-bound. But as I meet with Joe Gregory the music pastor at the Vincennes Church of God in southwestern Indiana, I confess, "'Shout to the Lord' is my least favorite song ever."

So why do I not like that song? "Because," I continue, "no matter what key the song starts out in, it's too high or too low for me. It's not an easy song to sing. I also don't like that it's mid-tempo but calls for this loud, shouting kind of singing. And songs like that make people hold notes for a long time, and most people don't sing well enough to be holding notes like that. It's a song for singers, not regular people." I am just getting started. "I feel uncomfortable singing that song. Hymns on the other hand, are more reasonable and make for better unison singing in my opinion. They don't have that performance quality to them, as if the songs are designed to be on someone's solo album." And lastly, "I much prefer the lyrics of hymns, which seem to me to have a deeper meaning, better theology, and resonate with my temperament a lot more."

I continue my whining session to Pastor Joe with a surprise ending: "I really had a strong aversion to that song, but then something happened.

My five-year-old son started school, and he began to sing praise choruses. Of all the songs out there, three guesses which one he liked the most? That's right, 'Shout to the Lord.' So every day I hear this little boy in the bathtub singing 'Shout to the Lord' with all of his heart, and I felt chastened. Now the song has taken on a different meaning for me. I actually still do not enjoy the song, but I am overjoyed when I watch my son enjoy the song. and that makes it a time of praise for me as well."

Joe listens patiently to my complaint masquerading as a story. It is only later that I realize that the story is a great illustration of what is happening in the church. An older generation is lamenting the music that is being lost, but it's undeniable that the young are responding to the less familiar new songs. The Church of God produced a very rich musical heritage. Today, much of that heritage is being forgotten as worship is increasingly made up of contemporary Christian praise choruses. In some cases, the music used might even be secular and the Sunday morning worship may be a less emphasized part of the Christian community than in the past. The traditional church, with services on Sunday morning, Sunday evening, and Wednesday night, is being challenged by new models that are growing quickly in the Church of God. The sound of the Church of God is no longer so recognizable.

The Road Map

In this chapter, we will begin with Pastor Joe by learning a little about the musical heritage of the Church of God and see how he is keeping that music alive in new, innovative ways. We will then look at the seeker-sensitive megachurch phenomenon by visiting one of the largest congregations in the Church of God, in Olathe, Kansas. In Phoenix, Arizona, we will meet a Gen-X pastor who is trying to bridge the gap between generations during worship in a way that encourages spiritual depth. Then we will travel to Fishers, Indiana, to learn about a church that is reaching out to postmodern, post-Christendom Americans. We will then go to the Philippines as we learn about how throughout the world, many Church of God congregations are being challenged by fast-growing Pentecostal and prosperity gospel churches. Finally, our journey will take us to Egypt to see how the Church of God's message of holiness and unity is finding new relevance amid Pentecostal growth and ancient churches. But first, we return to Joe.

Vincennes: The Music Man

Driving past the cornfields on the way to this town of eighteen thousand, I see a sign that reads, "Vincennes: Your Window to the Past." This is the oldest city in Indiana. It is older than the United States, having been established in 1732. And that is why I am here. To talk history and to hear from Joe Gregory about where we have come from musically and where we are going. After listening to my complaint about new church music, Joe offers some comfort as we sit in a quaint restaurant on Vincennes' main street not far from the church where he works.

"When I graduated from Gulf-Coast Bible College in 1983, it was a time when a music minister had thirty-five in the choir, you had a pianist and organist, and you led the singing out of one songbook and you had it made. It's all different now. It's complicated. It's difficult to get people involved in music because their lives are complicated. They are busy with their children and their lives. And the worship style has changed with a band, with vocals, technology, videos, dramas, and the way things are done. Thirty years ago we never thought of the term *seeker-sensitive*."

That sounds just like the churches I grew up in.

"Overall, worship in America has tended to get farther away from choirs to praise teams. I think music ministers are increasingly uneducated and lazy. It's easier to work with four or five people who can really sing than with fifty people who can't." His comment makes me laugh, until I remember that I was in the choir in one of those churches and I can't sing.

The fact that the focus is less on the congregation and choir is not necessarily good, Joe explains. "Music ministers often have not been trained. They only know how to play the guitar. As far as choral training or how to handle a bell choir, that's becoming a lost art. I recently watched Paul and Rita Jo Yerden [well-known Church of God worship leaders and musicians] play a concert and it was their own arrangements, their own creativity, and all that is being lost because that's not the way it's done anymore."

I think back to the Heritage Sing-a-longs that I occasionally watch or listen to on DVD that bring back the old music I grew up with and how it gives me a different feeling than the current music.

"What about the praise choruses that I don't like?" I ask. "Am I crazy or are they problematic? Most people are not Whitney Houston."

"But they would like to be!" Pastor Joe interjects. "I think that is why this music has done well. It's been done well by Sandi Patty and Michael

W. Smith, and they have brought this style into the church. It doesn't mean congregations can do it well. But how well they themselves can sing doesn't matter to the average person listening to the radio going to work."

Many people like this music Pastor Joe explains, but it has changed the nature of worship somewhat. "It is true that sometimes the first verse has sixteen syllables and the second verse has seventeen syllables and it doesn't always fall at the same spot and it's not congregational friendly. In the exchange that takes place with this new style, you have less participation from the people overall and more participation on stage. A worship team doesn't have to inspire anyone; they inspire themselves, as opposed to a song leader needing to inspire everyone when that's all there was."

Images of my old-school music ministers flash through my head—the lone figure behind the pulpit waving his or her arms to help us keep the beat.

"When this shift was made that led us away from the old hymns, which are a way of transmitting our Church of God theology," I ask, "was that okay or is it important?"

"I think it should have been done through the preaching more than the singing. If you are preaching it and writing about it, it shouldn't be that big of a loss. Why aren't there new writers? Why aren't there people taking Barney Warren's place? We have a publishing house that doesn't publish things like that anymore, and if I am a songwriter in the Church of God, where could I go? Sermons nowadays do not tend to focus on teaching the doctrine of the Church of God, and both the music and publishing industry are finding it hard to produce as they once did.

Pastor Joe thinks there is a spiritual dynamic missing in all of this. "I think we neglect prayer, fasting, dependency on God, and inquiring of God, 'How do you want us to do this?' We have relied on prayer choruses to bring people in. I think that's why we see little results, and the culture is going in the other direction. I think we fall in love with old strategies, like Sunday night worship. We love the strategy more than the God-given mandate to reach people. A lot of times in the church, if you give up the strategy, you are called out for compromising. When actually it's the ones not changing who are compromising because they are willing to remain ineffective and not winning the lost through those methods."

"Were the old hymns better?" I ask. I feel that they were, but who am I to say.

"I think the heritage songs had a deeper way of helping people through the issues of life, trials, and discouragement. It helped them in their daily experience with God. Praise choruses give you a buzz and let you express yourself in the moment. But they are not as reflective. They don't deal as much with temptation, failure, loss."

"It also seems to me that the older songs painted a more realistic image of where we are on this fallen earth and where we are going," I think to myself.

Pastor Joe continues: "We had a music that demanded good singing and parts singing, which is lost today—the running bass, the echoing parts, the harmony, etc. We are almost becoming musically illiterate, and we have even taken it out of people's hands, including musicians and music ministers. You listen to a CD, and this is how it sounds. You are getting a generation that is illiterate as far as how to make music on your own. And like you are saying, Patrick, a lot of the songs are keyed, not for the vocalist, but for the guitarist. That means they're not pitched in the right key for the vocalist. They're too high or too low for the vocalist. You didn't have that as much with hymns, because they wrote from the piano and not from the guitar."

"Praise choruses give you a buzz and let you express yourself in the moment."

So does this mean that we are going to lose all of these heritage songs? Not if Joe has anything to do with it. In Vincennes, they rework the songs and give them new life.

"We will take a heritage song and contemporize it. One of the young people's favorite songs here is 'Back to the Blessed Old Bible.' All we did to it was we put a little bridge in it, and instead of 6/8 time we made it in 4/4 time, which changed it and gave it a syncopated rhythm. We used the same words, the same notes, but we made it into a more modern song for today and they love it!"

"Wow! Do they know they are singing an old song?" I ask, with tears in my eyes.

"Yes!" Joe affirms.

The image of Joe leading young people into a rousing modern song that is really a heritage hymn is amusing and inspiring. "In this culture," Joe says, "the youth have a tendency to lead. My grandmother pointed out that when she was young, it wasn't the young people that drove the styles, the music, and the movies; it was their parents. And when you look back at the 1930s and 1940s, the people who were the stars were adults. *They* led. Now it's the other way around."

The invention and marketing of the teenager has had a profound impact on the church. It's an excellent point. I wonder if this is something that the older generation senses, even if it is subconsciously. The reality in our age, however, is that not only do younger people drive the trends, but older people seem obsessed with being younger. Fortunately, there are young people who still respect the music of that age as well as older leadership.

I am curious as to what Joe's favorite hymn might be.

"'There Is Joy in the Lord,' Joe responds. He tells me a story about a non-Church of God person who played the old music. "There was a Nazarene music professor who came to Mid-America and heard these Church of God songs, and he arranged them and played them to the people he knew at Southern Nazarene University. And they loved them. One of them was 'Child of God.' They thought that was the best song they had ever heard! We have a lot of secrets, if you will."

I mention to Joe that I have heard more than a few pastors resentfully complain about the traditional services that they have to put on early on Sunday for the older folk. The bitter attitude towards the older crowd upsets me, especially since I prefer their music.

"These pastors complain, yet it's those people who are paying their salaries. It's those people who show up on Wednesday night. I understand both sides, but the reality of it is that we are called to honor that generation. We are who we are because of that generation. It doesn't mean we cater to them though. On the other side, the ones who are most resistant to change are the very ones who have lost children and grandchildren that the change would help reach! Can you sacrifice some of your desires for the sake of winning the lost?"

While Joe Gregory is open to changes and finds creative ways to keep our heritage alive, there are some Church of God theological pillars he is not willing to part with. "The doctrine of living a holy life is one thing that I just could not abandon for the sake of my children. Now a Church of God heritage hymn, perhaps."

Vincennes looks like a pretty traditional town as we drive around, and the Vincennes Church of God has a beautiful building that looks very traditional. However, this is a church with visionary leadership. It is one of the largest Protestant churches in Vincennes, with four hundred people, and they recently birthed a new church with a coffee house atmosphere that meets on Thursday nights. It is only a year and a half old and already averages two hundred fifty people. Last Valentine's Day, this church plant advertised that any couples living together could get a free wedding in the church as long as they paid the $25 marriage license fee. The church provided the photographer, the cake, and the minister. There were eight or nine couples that took them up on the offer. That's not exactly traditional.

I ask Joe if he has any final thoughts.

"I think we need to have a holy pride about who we are. I sometimes think we are somewhat shy and reserved and closed-mouthed about who we are as the Church of God. Maybe it's because we don't know who we are. And I do think we need to be more encouraging to young people. I am having my nine piano students play in the service. That's what my home church did with me. They let me play when I was twelve years old. We need to foster that in worship."

We end our time together by going to the sanctuary of the church and Joe plays two versions of "Back to the Blessed Old Bible." The modern version has an extra bridge, a faster tempo, and a key change. The new version gets you dancing and shaking your hips, if you're Latin, that is. I can't help but wonder what D. Otis Teasley would think.

Olathe: "Only Do the Things That Multiply"

For struggling denominations and churches, it's hard to miss the mega-church. To them, megachurches have become like Christianity's Walmart—large organizations threatening to put the small mom-and-pop churches out of businesses and usurping the role of denominations as the central nexus of activity and dialogue regarding the future of the church. More than a few small churches have watched in frustration as church members leave them behind in favor of the large, sleek-looking megachurch with the first-class day-care center and hip coffee lounge. Megachurches patterned after Willow Creek Community Church in suburban Chicago, and to some extent Saddleback in Orange County, California, have shaken the Christian world. Although it can be said that churches of this style and size go back a few decades, it was really in the 1990s that the megachurch emerged as an influential part of the Christian world, producing many books and conferences on church growth.

Megachurches are churches with more than two thousand people attending worship services. With their theatre seats, large video screens, CEO pastors, massive complexes, coffee shops, and nondenominational names that sound more like the names of wealthy suburban housing developments than churches, the megachurch came off as a shocking rebuke to the traditional church and to denominations.

Baby Boomer pastors like Bill Hybels revolutionized the church-going experience. As a generation that was always rebellious and innovative, it comes as no surprise that when the Boomers decided to settle down spiritually and institutionalize, they created institutions that offered the best of both worlds. The megachurch was relevant, cool, sleek, and rebellious, yet it was done in a way that was very placid, family-friendly, and Orlando-like. The megachurch seemed to be an effort to rebrand Christianity to the Boomers' generational peers. Whereas the traditional church seemed tied to denominationalism, stuck to traditional hymns, and was full of religious symbols and language that made secular people uncomfortable and seemed to be geared toward people very familiar and comfortable with Christian traditions, megachurches wanted to provide a place where religion was not viewed as overly-dogmatic and traditional. The goal was to make church approachable to "Unchurched Harry," to use Willow Creek terminology. The interest was no longer in toeing the denominational line (or preserving its culture, music, and theology at all costs) but rather finding what works and doing it well.

Rebranding seems like an important word. I use this corporate marketing term because there is something about the megachurch that initially feels very corporate. Yet the interesting thing is that, as Helen Flynt pointed out when we were in the retirement center in Seattle, these churches are often more mobilized for missions than other churches. For skeptics, the shying away from religious symbols, the discarding of hymns in favor of up tempo songs led by worship teams, the large buildings with the large monthly overhead, as well as the numerous programs leave them feeling as though the church is trying to sell Jesus so much that the church is selling out altogether. There is the concern that being seeker-friendly equals low expectations for Christians and that it fosters a consumer mentality instead of a disciple mentality.[1]

For supporters, however, the megachurch model produces a culture within the church that takes organization seriously, exposes thousands to the gospel, and can mobilize millions of dollars toward the missionary enterprise. Megachurches often draw many professionals with management-level experience. The result is that the organizational skills that are often lacking in small churches and in district and national offices can often be found in abundance at a megachurch. On my journey, this resulted in a fascinating discovery: the age-old tension of organizational management needs versus openness to the Spirit is often best managed in these megachurches. Considering what I was seeing on this journey across the Church of God, that is no small matter.

Willow Creek has developed into a large network of churches that strive to reach the unchurched.[2] Rick Warren's church, Saddleback, launched the PEACE plan, which aims to accomplish things that secular organizations and international governments have failed to do adequately enough.[3] They are also assisting Rwanda to become a "Purpose Driven Nation" after having been invited to do so by the president of that nation. Consequently, churches like this have grown in influence and seem far more relevant than denominations. What about in the Church of God? Is the megachurch a threat to Church of God unity? The answer may surprise you.

As I drive up to the Church of God in Olathe, Kansas, Indian Creek Hills Community Church seems to fit the megachurch stereotype at first glance. There is the large parking lot surrounding a building that looks like a cinemaplex. There is nothing to suggest it is a church or a "Church of God." Inside is a large lobby with many windows, including some on the ceiling allowing the sun to shine inside. There's wood, stone, red brick, and even water used in the building's décor. The Café and Resource Centre offer

---

1. Recently, Willow Creek released the results of a REVEAL survey, which suggested that the effect of this new model of church has not been as effective in creating disciples as they had hoped. A quarter felt that they were "stalled" in their spiritual life, and many are dissatisfied with the church and considering leaving. "It is causing me to ask new questions," Hybels has said. "It is causing me to see clearly that the church and its myriad of programs have taken on too much responsibility for people's spiritual growth. The study included Willow Creek and twenty-nine other churches in the Willow Creek Association ("Willow Creek Finds Limits to Its Model," *Christian Century*, January 28, 2008: 16).

2. The Willow Creek Association is an international network that has more than twelve thousand member churches from ninety denominations in forty-five countries.

3. Saddleback has identified five global problems that they are seeking to address: spiritual emptiness, self-serving leadership, extreme poverty, pandemic disease, and rampant illiteracy.

places to sit with an open laptop and converse while drinking a cup of java or perhaps perusing the latest Christian books and DVDs on the market. Comfortable chairs and sofas abound throughout the building, offering a place for people to sit and visit. There is a large auditorium, a gymnasium, a lot of office space, and many multipurpose rooms. When constructing this building, the church intentionally chose an architect who had never designed a church before. The idea was to build a building that could be used by the whole community, and Indian Creek is, in fact, used seven days a week for martial arts classes, violin lessons, dancing groups, singing groups, drama groups, multimedia productions, the Boy Scouts ,the Girl Scouts, basketball leagues, and even a wiffle ball league.

Was the goal at Indian Creek to one day have a church so large that people would have to take a high-speed train from the parking lot to the narthex? Is it all about size and programs? After walking around Indian Creek's campus, I meet up with Pastor Gary Kendall, wife Belinda, and daughter Kristin at a local Panera Bread. Pastor Kendall doesn't exude the Gordon Gecko CEO vibe that I am expecting from a successful Baby Boomer pastor. Instead he comes off as the thoughtful quarterback of a winning football team, someone who sees all the possible plays in his mind and is confident that the team will get the touchdown.

> **The age-old tension of organizational management needs versus openness to the Spirit is often best managed in these megachurches.**

Pastor Kendall was as surprised as anyone at how large Indian Creek has become. He and his wife were pastors at a Church of God in Kansas City when they were tapped to help out a small group of people in Olathe (a suburb of Kansas City) who had a vision to reach their neighbors. Pastor Kendall, whose church had grown to about 350 people, gave advice to the Olathe people and six months into the advice-giving felt called to lead the church. Surprisingly, the elders at his church agreed and fully supported the Kendalls in their move to the suburbs.

The vision was to be relevant and contemporary. They also believed that it would be a church larger than one thousand. The church went from twenty-seven to seventy-five the first year. They hit 250 the second year, and by year three they were preparing their first church plant, which was done by year five and included sending out sixty of their people. They grew back the numbers given to the church plant the very next year. They spent the next five years growing to about six hundred and then planted another church. They believed that their job was to keep birthing churches, not simply to grow large for the sake of being large. They even planted a church as far away as Oregon!

In 1996, they built their own building and then added on to it in 2002 and 2006. Today, it is a church of twenty-five hundred with another campus in Gardner, Kansas, about fifteen minutes away. They are on the brink of their twenty-fifth anniversary, and for the next twenty-five years, they want to continue their plan of creating neighborhood-reproducing churches. Each church will have to reach their own neighborhood in their own particular way. These churches might start in neighborhoods, coffee shops, or movie theatres. So it is not all about being big and providing many products to religious consumers; it's about expanding the kingdom of God in creative ways.

"Actually, what we've tried to do is narrow the focus," Pastor Kendall tells me as I order an unusually healthy sandwich. "We don't try to do everything, because we can't do everything well. We have an outcome-based ministry. There are three outcomes: love God, love your neighbor, and live out the love of Jesus in a servant kind of way. We need to mentor, train, and release people to serve. We do children's ministry and student ministry. Then we have small groups for adults, mission efforts, and a class called Alpha." Overreaching is a common problem for churches, mission agencies, and denominations that try to do more than they are really equipped to handle. Indian Creek intentionally narrows its focus and births new congregations of different shapes and sizes that can take on other forms and do more than they could ever do on their own.

"When we started the church, we talked about a ripple effect," he says. "I reach my friends, with my friends we start small groups, small groups reach neighborhoods, eventually we start a church in one of those neighborhoods, and then we reach a whole city. The organizing principal in our church is this: only do the things that multiply. If something doesn't multiply or reproduce, we don't have time for it."

I ask Pastor Kendall about the criticism of the megachurch: that they are filled with fancy bells and whistles that attract lukewarm people.

"A missional church is attractional. The only way to reach our world in this culture is that they see something real, that is passionate, and something bigger than themselves. It's not going to be programs, buildings, or shows, because we can't compete with the world in that arena, and we don't need to. We do want to be passionate, authentic, and we want to serve as Christ served. There is something about that which is real attractive to the non-Christian."

The growth in influence of megachurches has not only made smaller churches nervous, but it has made denominations nervous. The Boomers have not been overly concerned with promoting denominations at any cost, which is why I classified them as a missing generation in chapter 2. Will megachurches ultimately supplant denominations? Pastor Kendall doesn't think so.

"There's not much brand loyalty. Not to Willow Creek, not to Saddleback, not to Indian Creek. I don't think it really exists, because there's so much opportunity on the Internet and everywhere. My belief is the very best thing we can do is partner; don't re-invent the wheel. If I can find something that has a good ROI—return on investment—and it's bearing fruit, then I want to partner with them. But if I don't see fruit, then I will find something that will, because life is too short to put money, time, and effort into something that doesn't bear fruit. We do see the value of long-term, but we want to have some first-hand involvement, we want to meet the people, and we want them to see where we live. If the Church of God can make that happen, then we want to be a part of that. There's a saying 'Christianity is only one generation from extinction.' We do very little if we don't see some pretty positive results from it."

The success of megachurch pastors at creating growing churches sparked a whole market for church growth seminars, books, and CDs. Pastors around the world have flocked to this literature in order to figure out how to make their smaller churches become large churches like Willow Creek or Indian Creek. It has not always worked out well, and I met more than one disillusioned pastor in the Church of God that is asking the question, "I've read all the growth books. Why don't I have my Willow Creek?" I ask Kendall about all those frustrated pastors who followed the church growth models and are now saying, "Why didn't I get my Willow Creek?" Is there a role for the small church if they can't become big?

"I think people saw the outside of Saddleback and Willow Creek and missed what was on the inside. Both of those churches have a huge desire to win people to Christ and disciple them. They might use different vocabulary, such as 'reaching seekers' or 'developing fully devoted followers,' as they do at Willow, and Saddleback may say their desire is to 'fulfill the five purposes of the purpose-driven life,' but at the heart of that is winning those who are lost and developing fully devoted disciples. If we didn't believe small churches could make a difference, we wouldn't be planting churches. Small churches are great for making disciples. But if you just do programs and activities, then you will not necessarily create disciples. If small churches take to heart mentoring and discipleship, they will find vitality. If they set a goal to plant by the time that they get to two hundred fifty to five hundred, then they could have multiple life cycles."

> "The hardest thing for small churches is that they are not willing to reinvent themselves."

Pastor Kendall is alluding to the fact that the average life cycle of an average American church is eighty years. The first ten to fifteen years are the steepest curve for growth. The churches plateau at fifteen or twenty and might have a five- or ten-year plateau, and then they begin a slow decline until they die at eighty.

"The way to jump that life cycle is to run your ride up and all along the way create new churches, which gives your church a new run. The hardest thing for small churches is that they are not willing to reinvent themselves. So if a pastor asks, 'Why didn't I get my Willow Creek,' it's because the culture changed and so did Willow. But the First Church on Tenth Street is still doing ministry the way they did ten or fifteen years ago, and culture blows by them and they can't catch up. Discipleship never gets old, though. If we could be more person-centered instead of program-centered, we could have multiple life cycles. And changing pastors a lot also doesn't help. It hurts continuity."

But what about churches that are older and have stalled in their growth for a long period of time? Can a church like that regenerate with such an ingrained DNA? Kendall believes they can.

"If they can't raise up a new generation and raise up new leadership, then they will want to partner with someone who will help give them life. They are loved by God, they are valued, and they have a rich community, but we are called to give our lives to something that outlasts us. I am at the place now where I want to invest in younger pastors. They have a whole lifetime in front of them, and the best thing I can do is help start the new ones. It's giving your life away. I don't know if we have enough of that kind of mentality. We think, 'It's about me.' But it's not about me at all. It's about Jesus. We really have to have that mentality in our pastors and our churches. If we ever lose that then we plateau and decline and we probably should."[4]

The inventiveness and creativity of the Baby Boomers has led them to form a lot of organizations that compete with denominations. Many times, they have started or invented ministries that the denominations have overlooked. The Church of God, for instance, has more than seventy freestanding organizations—many of these started by Boomers who saw a vacuum in the movement and filled it with their own newly created organization. Pastor Kendall was one of the initial founders of the CMA (Church Multiplication Association), a group of Church of God people who have planted churches and offered support to church-planters.[5]

"It started with Oral Withrow, who was a hero to me and a mentor. He believed in us and helped us with our church plants. When we launched Indian Creek, my friend Robin Wood launched Mountain Park Community Church in Phoenix around the same time. We knew we needed a network because it was hard to find ideas and emotional support. The Church of God did Vision 2 Grow, which was a real positive thing. A lot of churches were planted in that time. Then Robin went to Salem Avenue, and there was a vacuum. Spontaneously, other pastors started calling us, and I would get a call for pastors who wanted advice or wanted to be listened to or prayed for. It happened to Robin too. We pitched the idea to Anderson to develop a network, but it never came about. We raised the money and met in Phoenix and invited people who would be interested in supporting this kind of thing. We are now about to have our fifth conference."

In five short years, they have helped more than sixty churches get started in the United States. In the same way that Boomer-led businesses have moved away from heavy, centralized bureaucracies toward decentralized networks, CMA tapped into a need using a new paradigm and it took off.

---

4. Supposedly, about 80 percent of churches in the Church of God in North America have reached a plateau or are in decline. This seems to be what other denominations are reporting and what state and district directors said to me when I asked. It's also the figure that I would say as someone who regularly visits churches as part of my job.

5. Church of God Ministries in Anderson now has a department that does this as well and has cooperated with CMA, the Hispanic Council, and others to plant churches.

"The concept is easy. You find people who are doing it and partner up with people who want to do it. It's simple, it's not complicated, and it is not particularly expensive. It is a relational platform. We have conference calls, and then the next week we have breakout calls [in which pastors of churches under two hundred have one conference call and pastors of churches over two hundred meet with a different group]. It doesn't have a lot of hierarchy, and it's lean and mobile. We mainly focus on churches multiplying. If we are only thinking one generation, then we are thinking way too small. We're not anti-Church of God at all. We are planting Church of God churches.[6]

Will all these churches that are being planted be a part of the mega-church movement? Or will there be a reaction against the megachurch with its high financial overhead? Pastor Kendall thinks that these kinds of churches may have had their moment.

"I think we are in a whole new day and age, not just in the United States but around the world. Large buildings and large programs are never going to be the wave of the future. Personally, I don't think that's bad. One of the reasons why at Indian Creek we are interested in planting churches is that we can take advantage of this new movement that meets in coffee houses or whatever; then let's put energy into that and help light that fire. As long as we realize it's about being missional. It's not about being big, but almost about being small. It's about helping each person become a follower of Christ."

The bottom line for Kendall and the folks who make up Indian Creek is that it was never about being a large church and simply producing consumers. It was about expanding the kingdom of God, and it just so happened that in Olathe, that expansion started through a large church.

---

6. While making this book, I did not get the opportunity to attend one of CMA's annual gatherings, unfortunately. But I've heard that they are very electrifying. "What are church planters like?" I asked Pastor Kendall. "They can make decisions quickly, they are action people, they are highly relational, high energy, catalytic, and entrepreneurial." Belinda Kendall added that they often spend a lot of time talking out in the lobby. "The church plant is one of the most effective ways to reach people for Christ because people are more likely to get involved in something new than something that is older and more established," Belinda told me. Their daughter Kristin added that "church planters are continually thinking, but they are very in the know with the culture and wanting to meet the current needs and thinking how they may need to change to stay relevant. It's very different than a traditional church mentality." "They are movements like the original Church of God," Gary added. "Some people call them cultural architects. They find things that are moving and they add extra octane. You can do it anywhere in any culture. The ratio for winning converts for a new church is about one to fifteen, where in the older church it is one to thirty. That's why we want to continually plant churches. We can reach more people that way."

"The way we look at the kingdom of God is as a spiritual kingdom. It is that, but we talk a lot about the Lord's Prayer when Jesus says, 'Your kingdom come, your will be done on earth as it is in heaven.' If you take out the words 'Your will be done,' what you would have is a prayer from Jesus that says your kingdom come on earth as it is in heaven. So we want earth to be more like heaven. We want heaven to come to earth by how we love each other and through the person of Jesus Christ. We live with this concept that by the grace of God we can transform our community to become the kingdom of heaven on earth. We believe in heaven, but we want to make such an impact that our city becomes more like heaven because of the church. We want to change our community for Jesus. We want to be his hands and feet."

Indian Creek takes this seriously. They have an event called "The Church Has Left the Building" in which everyone comes to church to sing, listens to fifteen minutes of instruction, and participates in an offering; and then they all split up and go out and do thirty projects in one day.[7] They do this twice a year and do a service project once a month. The news has spread.

In Johnson County, there are now about thirty churches serving together, gathering one time a year and doing eleven projects in the inner city. In one day, three thousand to four thousand Christians go to the inner city. A week later they have a joint celebration with about four thousand people gathering together to worship the Lord.[8]

"We are trying to change the culture's perception of the church by the way we serve. The kingdom of God is advancing. If the church is who we are called to be, we should not be the victims. We should be the cultural architects, and the culture should be more like the church. Church has taken on a victim mentality. It's the opposite of what Jesus had in mind.

---

7. There were an impressive array of options in 2009. There were a variety of lawn care and minor home repair projects. Another option was landscaping, painting, and grounds cleanup projects in nine different schools. There was also a grounds cleanup and prayer walk in various Olathe parks. An option for people like me that are useless with their hands but can talk a lot was to visit the Ridgeview Village Senior Community and either visit or clean the grounds. They also gave people care kits to assemble for disaster relief; others wrote notes to policemen, firefighters, and soldiers in the military. There was also a local food kitchen taking the Indian Creek volunteers as well as teams to make snacks and cookies.

8. I also visited the predominantly African-American Jubilee Church in South Boston. This megachurch has had a very positive influence in South Boston under the leadership of Bishop G. A. Thompson. The Sunday I was there, his son Michael preached an outstanding sermon that left me both laughing and crying. Some of the largest churches in the Church of God are African American. In these African-American churches, the pastor or bishop is still a respected member of the community and the church aims to transform its environment. A lot of these churches raise up their own pastors from within to great success.

We're like football players in the huddle who never get out of the huddle to play. We should huddle less and play more. Jesus talked about the kingdom of heaven or the kingdom of God over 120 times. Only two times did he talk about the church. We really limit ourselves because we talk about the church all the time and rarely talk about the kingdom of heaven. The kingdom of heaven was a lifestyle, a kingdom of love, of joy, of peace, of sacrifice. Jesus preached the kingdom. We've made it about the church. The church is only part of what God wants to do in the world."

The next Sunday I attend one of the Sunday morning services. During the service, a new thirty-six-year-old Christian named Lenny talks about his recent conversion. He was a violent man and a drug addict until he went to church. He entered into a rehab program and during that time made his way to one of the Alpha classes offered at Indian Creek. It's been ten months since he last did drugs and five months since he became a Christian. "Drugs never felt like this," he said. His life is completely new. Lenny's story leaves me with my own high as I make my way out to Indian Creek's parking lot. Suddenly the long walk from the narthex to my car doesn't seem so bad.

Phoenix Rising

From the air, Phoenix is an amazing sight. As the plane descends on its approach to Sky Harbor International Airport, I am struck by the fact that Phoenix is much larger than most of us think. It looks like a slightly smaller version of LA, complete with brown flatlands, housing developments as far as the eye can see, and stunning mountains frequently obscured by smog. For the past decade, Phoenix has been a boomtown, and with more than four million people, it is now one of the largest cities in the United States when the Phoenix–Mesa–Scottsdale area is counted as one. Greater Phoenix culturally feels like Southern California as well. The weather is great, there is a laid-back attitude toward life, and people are not afraid to wear their success on their sleeves. Sixteen-year-olds driving Hummers and BMWs would not be a strange sight in this city.

Phoenix has its fair share of megachurches as well. Like Southern California, the casual church seems to fit well into this environment. The criticism that has most often been leveled at the megachurch is that it fosters a consumer mentality. The fancy buildings, the numerous programs, the large nurseries, the lively entertaining worship, and the gentle sermons lead to a body of believers who go to church primarily to have their needs met. Volunteerism is low and attrition can be high. Getting people involved in ministry and getting them to commit long-term is a challenge. On first glance, Mountain Park Community Church looks like the kind of church that might attract people seeking entertainment, anonymity, and low-commitment. There is the pre-requisite Southwestern-style building in earth tones, a brown hill with a cross, and a large sanctuary that seats nine hundred fifty. The building is beautiful, and more than fifteen hundred people attend the church each week.

MPCC is located on Pecos Road, a long flat road that takes you away from I-10 and wedges you between the brown flatland of an Indian Reservation to your left, the South Mountain Range in front of you, and to the right, the suburb of Ahuatukee—creating an area of ninety-five thousand people that is sometimes referred to as "the largest cul-de-sac in the world." The broad roads, palm trees, and Spanish-style homes that make up a façade of prosperity mask the fact that community is hard to come by in Phoenix. The homes have walls around them, people are not inclined to interact with their neighbors, and the families in these beautiful homes are often broken. Phoenix, in fact, has an astonishing 72 percent divorce rate. It is also a city that is being hit hard by the economic downturn as much of the new wealth that has permeated the city was built on debt. On the day that I arrive, the city of Phoenix is asking the government for a bailout.

While some large churches have made the mistake of being too accommodating to seekers at the expense of ignoring the more challenging parts of the gospel message, Pastor Allan Fuller makes sure that Mountain Park doesn't go down that road. Fuller—a tall Canadian who looks so much like Indianapolis Colts quarterback Peyton Manning that he would probably get asked for autographs if he put on a blue football jersey—grew up in the church and was not entirely sure that the church was relevant anymore. It seemed to have become an ineffective insiders club. Even the fast-growing megachurches were mainly pulling in people who were already Christians.

"That's one of the reasons I didn't want to go to church ministry," says the Gen-X pastor. "I saw that the church was important to people I trusted, but it very much lacked relevance. It wasn't until I was part of a church that came across as relevant that I decided I could do this—ministry."

That church was a Vineyard Church in Cincinnati. The services were dynamic and engaged the challenges of the day. There was also a strong emphasis on spiritual warfare and the reality that there are forces keeping people in bondage. John Wimber, the founder of the Vineyard Movement, had emphasized transformational prayer and intimacy in worship. It was a different atmosphere than Allan had found in the Church of God, so he prayed to the Lord, "If this is real, I want it." He emerged from his time at the Vineyard with a stronger awareness of the need to focus on prayer as well as worship where people would truly experience God instead of going through the motions or simply being entertained. Pastor Fuller also learned of the downsides that come with having a large church, which prevented him from having "a glossy view" of big churches. Little did he know that he himself would soon be the pastor of a large church.

Mountain Park is a church that was started as a church plant by Church of God Pastor Robin Wood in 1987. On the first Sunday, three hundred people showed up. Eventually Wood left, and the church, after an interim period of a couple of years—"having reached a certain level of desperation," according to the self-deprecating Allan—made the unusual decision of entrusting itself to a thirty-three-year-old who had never been a senior pastor. Upon accepting the job, Pastor Fuller called one of his old mentors, Church of God theologian Gil Stafford, and said to him, "I'm back in the Church of God!"

Stafford responded, "Allan, you never leave the Church of God."

"We have these expectations that we are unfolding with our church," he told me as we sat in his air-conditioned office. "One of the dangers of a church like this is of having a large front door and an equally large back door. They may love the relevance and authenticity, but they don't feel connected and they move on to something different."

As for the consumer mentality in many churches, Allan suggests that "it is the virus of the church."

It is not uncommon in churches like these for pastors to be bombarded by constant complaints with people threatening to leave the church if something is not to their liking. The pastor can end up being viewed, not as the shepherd, but as the master of ceremonies. The church community—the church family—seems to be optional for many people, a kind of "take it or leave it approach" to what should be a long-term commitment to journeying with fellow believers.

"When people are treated so well and everything is so glossy and beautiful for them, they just start to keep their eyes open on what they can complain about," Allan remarked.

In order to combat this spirit of detachment and consumerism, Allan focuses on a number of areas that he calls "A through G" that aim to keep people engaged and maturing in Christ.[9]

As I talk with Pastor Fuller, I am struck by how much he is a bridge between two different eras in American evangelical Christianity. On one side are the seniors and Baby Boomers who are looking for concrete absolutes. They want things spelled out very clearly and don't like anything that smacks of relativism. Yet on the other side are two generations (Gen X and the Millennials) that, much like the early reformers of the Church of God, are skeptical of easy answers devoid of concrete experience and a faith that doesn't demand very much. Gen-X pastors are uniquely qualified to bridge this gap because they grew up in the traditional church yet they understand the mentality of the new emerging postmodern culture.

> **Gen X and the Millennials… are skeptical of easy answers devoid of concrete experience and a faith that doesn't demand very much.**

This gap between the more traditional older generations and the younger postmodern generations was evident throughout my journey. Both sides tend to view each other as superficial. The younger generation views the older as naively dogmatic and attracted to superficial bells and whistles. The older generation views the younger as uncommitted and flirting dangerously with moral relativism. The truth is far more nuanced, but

---

9. "A" is Ask Questions. The church is given the opportunity to ask questions, and the pastor does not worry about having all the answers. "It breaks the bubble of 'I know everything' he tells me. Increasingly, younger generations in the church are very skeptical of easy formulaic answers that don't show that the issue has been processed in-depth. "B" is Be There. "There's a tendency to just show up once a month or something. If God is moving, you don't want to miss it. You want to be part of our story. It's a push against the kind of mentality that says church is something you go to when it's convenient." Fuller challenges people to make church the cornerstone of their week as opposed to one of many leisure events that make up the week. "C" is Connect with God. Fuller is pushing for a consistent daily intimacy in people's relationship with Christ. The spiritual disciplines are emphasized, but not dictated. "D" is Doing Life Together. "There's a group of five to twelve people who know your name, and you are doing life together." In other words, you are not alone, living in isolation on your spiritual journey. It's a challenge to the congregation to become dependent on community. "E" is Extending Yourself. "This isn't about you," Pastor Fuller cautions. "It's not just about *your* salvation. You are supposed to have an impact on other people." Here, Fuller seeks to correct the over-emphasis on personal salvation at the expense of cultivating a burden for others and a sense of mission. "F" is Freely Give. "We have a responsibility to give. The Bible tells us that where our heart is, there will our treasure be." "G" is Get in the Game. "Things will not get done if you don't get involved. It's not about simply filling a slot, but about finding what you have been uniquely wired to do. When we all start to breathe that deeply, it gets pretty exciting," Fuller says.

nuance is not something the other generations do well—but Gen X does. Pastor Fuller is one of a few Gen-Xers I ran across on my journey who are trying to strike the right balance in the church so that it can speak to all the generations in a deep way. It is a tough, underappreciated job for these Gen-Xers, and many would not put up with it. They are trying to serve as a bridge in a Western Christianity that has really been split into two types: the traditional and the postmodern.[10]

"I am accused of compromise. My desire for balance comes across as compromise," Pastor Allan says. He is referring to a time during the main worship service when he has a Q & A and people are free to ask all sorts of questions. "I'm no oratory master. But it's not about me having the answers. It's about modeling a journey of faith."

But Pastor Allan was criticized for not having the right answers ready. For the younger generation, the lack of rote answers is affirming and reassuring. They are comfortable with the mystery of Christianity that suggests that God is so great, we can only humble ourselves before him and experience him and yet never really understand him fully. For the older generation, the lack of certainty is not reassuring, but rather it is frightening. Are we not certain about what we believe? For the younger generation, the acceptance of Christianity is a slower process that requires accompanying them on a journey. For the older generation, salvation is something that should happen immediately, and there is a desire to create moments that close the deal. A pastor today has to navigate those two very different mentalities about what it means to discover Christ.

Pastor Allan also received blowback after a Sunday morning that was modeled after *The David Letterman Show*, complete with a set, a band, a top-ten list, and even a monologue of jokes. It was part of a series on stories that highlighted the seven different kinds of stories human beings tell (e.g., comedy, drama, tragedy, rags to riches). The idea on that particular Sunday was to celebrate laughter and to experience that as part of the world that God created.

---

10. I met many of these people I call Bridges on my two-year journey. They are Gen-X pastors who grew up long enough in the traditional church to understand it and value it, but they are close enough to the younger generations to understand the postmodern mentality and culture that the church in many places is now trying to reach. Although there are not enough, the ones who are out there are playing pivotal roles in the Church of God. It's vital that they be used in a more intentional way in the future as this divide between the older generations and the younger generations is more extreme than usual due to the rapid changes taking place in the world.

"People just walk out of church when it is didactic saying, 'I liked that.' You're lucky if they talk about the service at lunch."

Pastor Allan wants people to experience worship as a significant step in their journey of faith. If this sounds a little too much like feeding the consumer mentality of the people in the theatre seats, do not be so quick to judge. This church takes spiritual warfare seriously, and that undercuts those who might suggest superficiality is being created here.

"On one of my first Sundays here, I said, 'We'll be a safe place to visit and a dangerous place to stay.'" What does Pastor Fuller mean by that? He means that people will feel very welcome, but if they stay, they will feel challenged.

The feel of the worship service is more of a living room feel than a show. The language and the vocal tone are very casual. "I introduce myself every Sunday. I don't assume that people know who I am. Some people could be offended by the 'sloppy' language. But this isn't a slam on formality. The more intimate you are with somebody, the more casual you are. If you are going to do a job interview, that's when you put on a suit and tie. If you are with your family, you are going to wear a T-shirt and shorts; and if you are going to have a late night intimate discussion, you will be in your pajamas. We want to be intimate and casual in our Sunday morning experience."

But the casual vibe of worship should not be confused with a casual approach toward the Christian faith. "God's journey is a dangerous journey," Fuller warns. "To go from selfish to selfless, to go from 'all I have is mine' to 'nothing is mine' is a dangerous journey."

This seems particularly true amid the wealthy suburbs of Phoenix where intimate community is not greatly valued by the local culture.

"People say to me, 'Don't use the word *dangerous*.' But I don't want to tone it down. When you fully commit and have a growing intimacy with him, we will hear his voice. Our natural tendency is toward self-preservation, and it's dangerous to go where God wants us to go. A to G is a dangerous journey."

Pastor Allan talks about spiritual warfare all the time. And in this community of broken families, high divorce rates, and excessive materialism, there is a lot to oppress the people. "The presence of an enemy doesn't mean that we don't take responsibility," he explains. "There is an internal struggle, but there is an external struggle as well."

He gives me an example of the unique pressures on people in the Phoenix area. "In Phoenix, people are so beautiful here. But so many people are hurting so badly and are so insecure on the inside. People are constantly changing their bodies and their clothes. They make destructive decisions because they believe the lie that they are not good enough or they are not as beautiful as that person. The reality of the Holy Spirit blows those things away and says, 'I'm not interested in what the world is interested in.'"

Broken families and the 72 percent divorce rate also create a spiritual oppression, not just on the secular community, but on the church as well. A full 70 percent of the church staff have gone through a divorce. This may seem shocking to some, but it is very much a part of the Christian landscape in this part of the country and the wounded need healing.

"We are here to fight for the health, growth, and vitality of families" Pastor Allan says with conviction. It is amid this brokenness that Mountain Park Community Church exists. "Families are being slaughtered by the enemy, and people are listening to the lies of Satan that 'you deserve better.' People are not getting divorced for legitimate reasons. It is simply because they say, 'I am not happy anymore.' But we are going to bring in the power of the Holy Spirit to fight this thing that is defeating the people." Pastor Allan makes the point that struggles within the family are some of the most energy-engulfing experiences that we can have as human beings. The effects of divorce are devastating and hinder personal growth, he tells me. "Instead of talking about how they can impact the world, they are talking about their spouses. Divorce consumes their lives. We want to be on the offense instead of the defense."

Mountain Park Community Church prizes innovation, and there's an attempt to foster creativity. Pastor Fuller believes that being a part of the Church of God has given him and others the freedom to experiment with worship.

"I think the Church of God is the best of both worlds. If you look at independent churches, they have no affiliation and no accountability, but in the Church of God, I am connected to something larger than me. I'm connected to a state minister, I have mentors, and I have a group of pastors that I get together with. We have a history, a common educational experience, and an ordination process, and all these things you don't get out of the independent church concept."

"At the same time, we are very autonomous in how we get to do church, and I feel freedom in the development of my theology and in the development of my practice of ministry. Nobody is visiting us and saying, 'Here's a list of things you can't do or that you must do.'"

But encouraging those Church of God ties is increasingly more difficult. As churches grow and need to add staff, it is becoming harder to find qualified people from within the Church of God. "I just brought in two leadership pastors, and they are great, but they are not Church of God. They are more Calvinist theologically. We can do ministry together because we all agree that there are things that are more important, but it dilutes our 'Chogness' when I hire from the outside. When we talk about budgets, it becomes more difficult to make the case that money needs to go to state or national. It gets harder to support that."

Despite the challenge of trying to foster loyalty to the Church of God in a church with very few born into the movement, Pastor Allan remains committed to the Church of God. And he remains committed to trying to bridge the gap between the generations in the worship experience. It is not easy. If a young person with multiple piercings wants a position in leadership, the blowback against them might be considerable, even if they've proven themselves to be mature, responsible, and Spirit-filled. The definitions of piety are changing, and pastors like Pastor Allan who are trying to bring the generations together are standing in the line of fire.

After a time of prayer in his office, where he prayed for me, I bid Pastor Allan farewell. Feeling hungry I stop off at the Arizona Mills Mall in the suburb of Guadalupe. A few months earlier, it was here at a 1950s-style restaurant called Johnny Rocket's that I had eaten a cheeseburger and fries with my five-year-old son Marco, and I am missing him quite a bit as my journey across the Church of God hit the halfway mark. Somehow it makes me feel closer to him and his mother to sit in the chair where we sat and put coins in the jukebox. As I place my order, a man my age covered in tattoos and piercings sits down with his heavyset son, who looks to be about ten years old. I watch the two interact while I eat, and I notice that they don't seem to know each other very well. The man is shy and awkward with his son, trying to get him something that he likes for dinner. The boy doesn't know what to say either, but he is clearly thrilled to be with his father. I wonder if there had been a divorce in the family and this is a rare father-son outing.

As I watch the tough-looking guy with tattoos and piercings crumble in the presence of his son, I wonder, "Who is going to reach out to this father and son if we in the church do not?" That's the big question that is facing the church in America right now. Are we going to be a country club with safe membership rules, or are we willing to actually go into the community even if it changes our church? I smile because I know there is at least one Church of God down the road where they might one day find a home.

Fishers: Getting Out of the Christian Ghetto

Two thousand miles away from Phoenix, I visited a church plant in Indiana. I arrived a bit late to the worship service at Crosspoint which takes place at Fall Creek Elementary School in Fishers, a newly-developed area of strip malls and impressive homes on the outskirts of Indianapolis. My journey across the Church of God increasingly kept taking me toward suburbs and cities: a reflection that the Church of God is shifting away from rural to urban as is the world. The pastors and volunteers of this church have to arrive at 6:00 AM each Sunday to spend three hours setting up for the morning service.

As I settled into my seat, a clip from the secular movie *Meet the Parents* is playing on the two video screens at the front of the "sanctuary." In the scene, Ben Stiller is visiting his girlfriend's home for the first time and is asked by her father (played by Robert De Niro) to say grace before supper. Stiller, the non-Christian prospective son-in-law agrees and then stumbles through a prayer trying to get all the religious language just right. It's a scene that brings a lot of laughter as the viewers sympathize with Stiller being a fish out of water among the more pious family of Christians.

That scene from *Meet the Parents* captures the predicament that a lot of people in the West (including such traditionally "Christian" places as Indiana and Kansas) now feel when they are in church or exposed to Christians. More and more people do not feel comfortable in church and do not even know how to behave in church. For many of us who grew up in the Christian church, we think of it as a family and as the least threatening place in the world. But for those on the outside, church can seem like an insider's club where the language has to be exactly right or you may reveal yourself to be a condemned sinner. Curt Walters, Crosspoint's thirty-six-year-old pastor sympathizes with the awkwardness and fear that the Ben Stiller character portrays in the film, and finds that many in his church feel the exact same way. Today in the West, people's images of the church have been distorted. Some of this has been because of society's increasing secularization and some of it has been because the church has become more known for the things that it is against, than the things that it is for.[11] Many others have had bad experiences in the church or were raised by parents who have had negative experiences in the church and have not educated their children about religious issues.

"We're seeing a gap," Pastor Curt told me as we sit in a Border's café sipping mochas a few days later along with his twenty-seven-year-old director of creative arts, P. J. Towle. These interviews are making me gain weight!

"People are interested in God, but not in church," he says. "We would invite them to our homes and they would say that they would come if it wasn't overtly spiritual."

Fishers, located only about twenty-five minutes from Anderson, is the town with the third lowest church attendance in Greater Indianapolis, yet it is also the fastest growing area. Walters and Towle discovered that even though Indiana has a lot of churches, there were many people who did not feel comfortable in traditional churches or megachurches. In the case of Crosspoint, the church is reaching out to many Catholics and former Catholics who are looking for a deeper, experience with God but are wary of the traditional Protestant church.

The assumption that "Christian parts of the country" like Indiana, Oklahoma, and Kansas are well served by the traditional models of church is turning out not be true. There are many people even within the "Bible Belt" who are either so skeptical of the traditional church, or so wounded from previous church experiences, that the only church they are willing to take a chance on is a church that is presenting the gospel in entirely new ways. This often means worship services that focus on community, activism, and which don't shun everything secular—for instance a secular comedy starring Ben Stiller.

> The assumption that "Christian parts of the country"...are well served by the traditional church models is turning out not to be true.

Unlike the older traditional churches, or even the megachurches, that have put a lot of emphasis on their times of worship, Crosspoint focuses

---

11. The book *Unchristian* by David Kinnamen and Gabe Lyons (Grand Rapids, MI: Baker Books, 2007) is helpful in showing how American society's perception of Christians has changed in recent years. Being a Christian has become synonymous with many negative things for many people in our society.

more on reclaiming community. It's not that worship is not important, but rather that they want to worship in community and *within* their community.

"One of the big things for both of us was the increasing realization that we wanted to be effective in our communities," P. J. says between sips of his favorite Starbucks drink. "My wife Angie and I were driving thirty minutes away to a church...but we wanted to impact our neighbors. Two of our neighbors are now a leading part of our children's ministry."

This is a common refrain among younger churches like Crosspoint. There is a strong desire to re-engage the local neighborhood, the secular world, and the real challenges of the local community *as a Christian community*. In other words, it is not enough to come into a building and just worship together. The questions that linger in these churches are: What difference are we really making in the world around us? Are we just coming together each Sunday for worship and then returning to our various individual communities? Or can we grow together as a community and then mobilize for ministry in our community?

Curt chimes in following up on P. J.'s comments: "An older pastor told me that church is still at ten o'clock. We say, church is more than a one hour event in an auditorium on a Sunday. The core of Crosspoint is the small groups that meet during the week. We are not a church with small groups. We are a number of communities under the umbrella of Crosspoint. That's a pretty big paradigm shift for those of us that grew up thinking of Sunday morning in our church building as 'church.'"

"It's easy to remain anonymous in the megachurch model. You take your coffee into service and then go out," P. J. interjects echoing not only the thoughts of many Gen-Xers but even many who have championed the various church-growth models.

"What does it mean to reclaim community?" Curt asks rhetorically. "What does it mean to do that? How do we live together the way God designed. Because of our loose structure in the Church of God, we have the freedom to do this. We are trying to create a sense of what it means to be a movement. As Gil Stafford said, 'people on the outside should view us as a movement,'—a community that people are attracted to. Part of their conversion experience here is that they see that something here is making a difference." And people in Fishers have been attracted to Crosspoint. In its first year, the church plant that started with forty people grew to two hundred.

I couldn't help but notice that P. J. and Curt sounded a lot like Pastor Allan in Phoenix. All of them have a high regard for the original goals of the Church of God. They listened to their Church of God mentors, and are trying to commit to that original radical vision more than they are trying to commit to the generic model of the average American church. Despite their affinity for the early Church of God reformation movement , they can easily be perceived as radical and unorthodox. Of course this is how the Church of God reformers were viewed in their time also as they focused more on spreading the life-changing message of holiness and unity, rather than aligning themselves with the traditional church structures of the day (denominations). Many of those who pine for "the old Church of God" would not really be comfortable in the church of D. S. Warner. What they really pine for is the Church of God of the 1950s—the cohesive, established, re-spectable church. As much as we are loathe to admit it, "the Golden Years" we miss are often those years when the Church of God looked more like a denomination in its prime.

"We've taken flack for our methodology," P. J. tells me, "but when I read John W. V. Smith or the writings of the early Church of God reformers, I say to the others, 'Dude, if you haven't read this, it's spitting Crosspoint propaganda all over the place!'"

There might be those tempted to believe that worship is not taken as seriously as it should be at Crosspoint Church. They not only show clips from secular movies, but their time of preaching is called a time of "teaching." As in Phoenix, the pastor here is not presented as the know-it-all, but someone who reveals himself (transparency again) to clearly be on a journey of faith as well—every day seeking to be more and more like Jesus. Some aspects of the church look casual. I happened to show up on a Sunday when they were serving Communion. I've seen the elements come in many different forms over the course of my travels, but I've never seen it packaged in a cloth bag with a vial of grape juice inside and pre-packaged crackers from the Steak 'n Shake fast-food chain. But it's not the crackers that might raise the red flag of more traditional Christians, rather it's the music. At Crosspoint, they even sing secular songs at times during the worship service. The praise band is just as likely to break out into a rolling rendition of a U2 or a Coldplay song as they are an updated classic hymn.

Is this sanctified? Before we pick up the stone of blasphemy and hurl it at Pastor Curt and P. J., it's best to hear them out.

"Sunday morning is the starting point for presenting God's design for each one of us. Sunday is transformational, but the transformation actually occurs in our small 'life-change' groups. On Sunday, we are making a connection of life and culture and then trying to figure out how that goes together with God's way for us."

Curt and P. J. are dealing with a group of people who are not entirely trusting of the Christian world, so they are finding the need to build a bridge first. In other words, every Sunday at Crosspoint is like Paul standing on Mars Hill speaking to the people who are spiritually hungry but are worshiping an unknown God. Sunday worship is the "Mars Hill moment," and the discipleship primarily occurs in the small-group setting.

"Everyone believes in something," Curt says. "Music, TV, and culture connect us. We have had to learn to speak a new dialect. The dialect is key."

The old ways and the old approaches in presenting the gospel do not work for many in the secularizing United States. No one is denying that the "Christian culture" is dying in America. But where Curt, P. J. and others like them believe the church has really erred is in making non-Christians feel that they are not spiritual. During my travels, one Gen-X pastor in Vancouver, British Columbia, said to me, "These people are being exposed to the gospel for the first time. They have no problem understanding that the world is broken and that they are broken. They get that. What they don't believe about themselves is that they are evil and everything about them is evil." It might be true that these non-Christians are not in church, it might be true that they are not saved, but that does not mean that they are not spiritual. It's just that what moves them spiritually are other things often found in secular culture and art.

"Every single week we play secular music," says the Coldplay-loving P. J. "Even if we don't play something live, all of our pre and post music is all secular. But for us it comes to everything being spiritual. Unless it is specifically drawing us away from God, then we view it as something that is a product of God that allows all of us to create."

By this, P. J. is not saying that all secular rock music glorifies God, which is how this could easily be interpreted. Rather that secular art does have meaning—but it is meaning that falls short of what God wants for our lives. Yet this kind of art is what moves people and is spiritual to them. The key for Kurt and P. J. is to use secular music (and other things from the secular world) to identify the areas of longing in people. A secular song by U2 such as "I Still Haven't Found What I Am Looking For" is clearly a spiritual song that conveys a spiritual longing. Crosspoint is unafraid to engage the secular as it tries to tap into those longings and explore them further in the same way that Paul was not afraid to go to Athens and stand next to the unknown god statue. Paul didn't see the statue as a thing full of demons that he had to stay away from, condemn, or cut-down. He saw it as an opportunity to get an audience and expound on the unknown God so as to lead the people to the one true God. This is what Crosspoint is trying to do by using a new dialect—one that is the language of the street instead of the language of the institutional church. As with Paul, it's not appeasement to secular culture. It is engagement and refinement of culture. It is finding Christ amid what people already know.

Curt continues to elaborate. "The church is notorious for trying to create barriers between the culture we are trying to connect with. We, on the other hand, look at these songs and we say, 'they are very spiritual songs.' Most songs are about relationships, love, frustration, anger, hurt, and they are asking the right questions. We are taking those questions, bridging the gap, and then God meets us there."

Is there too much acquiescing to the secular mind and not enough time spent on dealing with sin and the secular world's separation from God? No. As I saw with Allan Fuller's church in Phoenix and IYC in San Antonio, the issues that are tearing apart our communities and families are often dealt with more candidly in these younger ministries than in the more traditional churches. While churches led by the younger generation get pegged as moral relativists in their approach by more traditional churches, the reality is that these churches are doing a pretty good job of identifying, labeling, and confronting the sins that are destroying people in our Christian communities—such as Internet pornography. Radical sin is dealt with in radical ways.

"We had a series called 'LoveSex.' I started the series by standing in front of everyone and saying 'God loves sex.' Behind Pastor Curt, the platform was made to look like a hotel room with a bed, smoke, and neon lights. I shift in my seat as Curt and P. J. relate the scene.[12]

The point of the series was that God is not against sex. He created it for us to enjoy. But our society abuses sex and turns something beautiful into

---

12. On another occasion in a series on "putting things to death," Pastor Curt preached a sermon from a coffin and people wrote down on pieces of paper the destructive things they wanted to kill off in their lives and threw those papers into the coffin. Try as I might, I couldn't help but picture Pastor Curt dressed as Count Dracula lying in the coffin.

something ugly and damaging. It's an Augustinian view of how sin distorts the beautiful and holy and makes it ugly. The approach was controversial. There were neighbors that complained. But not everyone was upset.

P. J. tells me about the reaction of some older ladies who attended that particular Sunday.

"We had three senior citizen ladies in the back watching all of this and they were giggling throughout. They said, 'Half this church is going to go home and have sex today.'"

I am not sure about the extracurricular activities that occurred after the sermon among the happily married couples in the church, but the series was life-changing for many.

"Out of that four-week series came the most significant amount of life-change we have had," P. J. relates. Extramarital affairs were stopped after that series. There are people in the church who have been involved in orgies, who have been raped, whohave struggled with promiscuity, or who are getting ready to attend their first high school prom. Into their most private struggles, God was allowed to speak. But the path for Crosspoint toward exposing sin and reaching new levels of intimacy was not through judgment and condemnation but through a more nuanced discussion of God's plan for sexuality. How could "the unknown God" be better? How could sex be better? Crosspoint is presenting a Christianity that is not about rules and judgment, but rather is about grace and the desire to see our distorted, corrupted lives be purified so that we can achieve God's plan for our lives. "We don't start with condemnation," the young pastor from Vancouver, British Columbia, had said to me regarding his emerging church.. "We start out with the assumption that because of sin, something is broken and something needs to be made right."

> Some Church of God people...are willing to look like oddballs just as they did at the end of the nineteenth century.

"In the nineteenth century, the Church of God was distinctive and there was almost a pride in being distinct. The movement should be the same today," Curt suggests. For Curt and P. J. their radical church is connected to that original Church of God spirit. At the dawn of the twenty-first century, there are some Church of God people who are willing to look like oddballs just as they did at the end of the nineteenth century.

And Crosspoint practices unity. "We pray for the Wesleyan church up the street and the Journey church across the street (which follows a similar approach) and I've prayed with the pastor," Curt tells me. "Extending our hand to every blood-washed one" is something that comes easy for this generation. There's not much ego with Gen-X pastors. They are happy to see others surpass them and they don't feel the need to be the biggest on the block. With Millennials they actually prefer working in groups and shun the idea of the focus being on just one person. This may be a very healthy corrective for the church, which has often been too obsessed with finding dynamic leaders and charismatic personalities which can often lead to the creation of institutions and churches that aren't structured to survive the leader.

The leadership at Crosspoint spends very little time thinking about their church's expansion as an institution and focus mainly on the life-change of the people. "We don't ask people to come to our building. We may never even own a building," Curt says. As with the early Church of God reformers, one gets the sense that nobody here would find it strange if they ended up needing to meet above the feed store as long as people were being liberated by the good news. Although today, the feed store might be an Irish pub playing U2 or a dance club playing Coldplay. The music may be the same at Crosspoint, but the worldview is fundamentally different.

"I was always the person with bad associations with the church," one young lady at Crosspoint said. "Now I'm the one inviting people to church."

The music at Crosspoint may not be traditional hymns, but for many at Crosspoint, the song of their life is finally starting to make sense.

Here Come the Pentecostals!

The Philippines, along with Guatemala, has the largest percentage of Christians that are Pentecostal. This Asian country has ninety million people and 92.6 percent of them are Christian. It is Asia's most Christian nation. Nearly 50 percent of all Christians (Roman Catholic and Protestant) in the Philippines are charismatic and among Protestants, 70 percent identified themselves as charismatic in a recent Pew survey.[13]

---

13. The Pew Forum on Religion and Public Life, *Spirit and Power: A 10 Country Survey of Pentecostals* (Washington, DC: Pew Research Center, 2006), 87. http://pewforum.org/newassets/surveys/pentecostal/pentecostals-08.pdf

If current trends hold up, there will be as many Pentecostals in the world as there are Hindus in the coming decades. Pentecostalism, which now has five hundred million adherents and outnumbers Buddhism, is becoming the dominant form of Christianity in the world and this is coming as a tremendous shock to many, particularly in the West, where many evangelical and fundamentalist Christians reject the emphasis on supernatural gifts of the Spirit. Fundamentalists have tended to believe that speaking in tongues and other supernatural manifestations of the Holy Spirit were unique to the early Christian church and are no longer a part of Christian practice. Many, but not all evangelicals agree.

The early Church of God encountered the issue of speaking in tongues as early as the 1880s.[14] The Church of God, like the Pentecostals, was a Holiness movement that expected God to empower believers and the church through his Spirit. Divine healing was a key part of the early movement and D. S. Warner and others encountered tongues as well, and a significant amount of early believers experienced the gift. Merle Strege reveals that Warner at times seemed to accept it as a part of the Spirit's work and at other times condemned it, but overall he "failed to elaborate on the meaning of the phrase 'speak in tongues.'"[15] Other early leaders, such as J. W. Byers, Jennie Carpenter Rutty, E. E. Byrum, and F. G. Smith, examined the issue and for the most part remained uncomfortable with what had occurred at Azusa. By the early 1920s Strege reports that the Church of God movement leadership had achieved something like a consensus on the question of speaking in tongues. "The consensus was that the phenomenon of "tongues speaking" that had erupted at Azusa Street and beyond was a heterodox movement."[16] The issue was revisited in 1986 by a study committee after it was called for during a General Assembly meeting the previous

---

14. Merle Strege, *I Saw theChurch*, 124.
15. Ibid., 124–25.
16. Ibid., 129.

year.[17] At this time, most in the Church of God do not speak in tongues and are not that comfortable with it, although along my travels I met Church of God people who do speak in tongues in the privacy of their own homes. Among African-American churches in the Church of God movement, however, tongues is accepted as part of the black Holiness-Pentecostal tradition in that community.

When the Church of God formed along with other protest sects on the American frontier, it too was viewed as a potentially dangerous movement that threatened Christianity. If D. S. Warner felt that denominations were outside of the Christian church, the opposite was true as well—those groups viewed the Church of God as a new "dangerous" sect. It's important to remember that at the time, mainline denominations *were* Christianity, and for outside groups like the Church of God to meet on their own, come up with their own theological interpretations, operate their churches in such an ad-hoc fashion, and offer salvation outside of the well-established denominations was both "wrong" and threatening. Groups like the Church of God were often viewed as an embarrassment to mainline denominations. Before that, however, groups such as the Baptists, Quakers, Puritans, Methodists, Pietists, and many others had fled to America because they too were deemed an inappropriate form of Christianity. Prior to that, back in England, the English Reformation had led to a break with the Roman Catholic Church and the newly formed Anglican Church was deemed an inappropriate form of Christianity. Throughout Christian history, any time the church manifested itself into new forms, the older forms of Christianity reacted with disapproval and hostility. Today, much of mainstream Christianity has the same feeling about Pentecostalism, particularly as it is expressed in the non-Western world.

---

17. "Glossolalia and the Church's Life." See Barry Callen (ed.), *Following the Light*, entry 172. As one might expect from the Church of God, a real consensus was not achieved and their wasn't a widespread proclamation issued to all churches around the world on the issue. Merle Strege reports that "Among the areas of agreement were that 1) the believer's quest for the infilling of the Holy Spirit and a holy life is to be encouraged; 2) the gifts of the Spirit are to be understood as primarily intended for service in and to the church that it might be strengthened and made more effective in its mission, 3) a life of love, not glossolalia, is the essential evidence of the infilling of the Holy Spirit; and 4) which gift, or the number of gifts, are not factors in a person's salvation or sanctification (John W. V. Smith and Merle D. Strege, *The Quest for Holiness and Unity*, 2nd ed. [Anderson, IN: Warner Press, 2009], 470). While the lack of consensus can at times be frustrating to us CHOGers, it's worth noting how few serious schisms have erupted in the life of this movement over the years. Perhaps our flexibility has a positive side as well. Many other denominations and movements have had to face far more painful divisions over sensitive issues such as this.

The Pentecostal movement (the name is taken from the Day of Pentecost in Acts 2) is said to have begun on January 1, 1901, when during a worship service led by Charles Fox Parham in Topeka, Kansas, people began to speak-in-tongues.[18] The great modern-day Pentecostal movement is often said to have begun with the Azusa Street Revival, which occurred under the preaching of an African-American man named William J. Seymour. Seymour was influenced by Parham as well as the Church of God. Seymour first experienced sanctification after meeting some "Evening Light Saints," as Church of God people called themselves back then. He was ordained by the Evening Light Saints and took a church in Houston before eventually moving out West.[19] He broke with the Church of God after learning about Parham and of the possibility of attaining the gift of tongues, something the Evening Light Saints did not approve of.

The Azusa Street Revival in 1906 brought widespread notoriety to the movement which, most likely, had been active globally even before Parham's Kansas service.[20] As with many of the Holiness groups, Pentecostalism attracted the poor and disenfranchised and various denominations and movements were born out of it including The Church of God (Cleveland, Tennessee), the Church of God Prophecy, the Church of God Mountain Assembly Inc., the predominantly African-American Church of God in Christ, the Foursquare Church, and the Assemblies of God. Over the next one hundred years Pentecostalism spread to Latin America, Sub-Saharan Africa, South India, Eastern Europe, and East Asia.

Pentecostalism is appealing in much of the world because its supernatural emphasis resonates with people in the non-Western world, where the spiritual realm is taken far more seriously than in the West. Pentecostalism tackles addictions head on, confronts evil regularly, and pushes a real submission to the Holy Spirit in all matters. The result is that many find illnesses gone, addictions gone, commitments to monogamy made, and families restored; and they often become upwardly-mobile. From China to Brazil, Pentecostals often experience real, dramatic change in their lives.

---

18. George M. Marsden, *Religion and American Culture*, 2nd ed. (Fort Worth, TX: Harcourt College Publishers), 166.

19. See Merle Strege, *I Saw the Church: The Life of the Church of God Told Theologically* (Anderson, IN: Warner Press, 2002); James S. Tinney, "William James Seymour: Father of Modern-day Pentecostalism," *Journal of the Interdenominational Theological Center* 4, no. 1 (Fall 1976): 34–44.

20. In reality, charismatic strands of the faith were present in other parts of the world and in other eras of Christian history. *The New International Dictionary of Pentecostal and Charismatic Movements* is a good place to begin to explore this issue further.

"The proof is in our experience," they might say, echoing the early Church of God reformers.[21] In general, Pentecostalism is also very decentralized and very democratic in its insistence that all have access to the Spirit. For people coming from class-based and race-based societies, the idea that the Spirit is dispensed to all without regard for rank or race is very liberating. A woman may see no gender-equality in India, a black may not see racial equality in Brazil, and a Mayan may not see ethnic equality in Guatemala, but when the Spirit speaks through them and they preach in their churches, they have been validated by God.

Pentecostalism's loose organization allows churches to be planted anywhere and everywhere. There is a saying in the dangerous *favelas* (slums) of Brazil, "*when the police move out, the Pentecostals move in.*"[22] Pentecostalism's emphasis on the end-times also resonates with believers around the world who feel very oppressed and long for Christ's return.

Mainstream concerns are with Pentecostalism being prone to division, an extreme emphasis on tongues as evidence of the Holy Spirit, and syncretism (the mixing of Christianity with other religions). While some in the West argue that the age of such supernatural Christianity has passed, Pentecostals point to the works of Jesus and the Apostles, who regularly prayed, fasted, performed healings, and exorcisms and who were told by Jesus that they would do greater things. Pentecostals are often mystified by Western Christianity's ambivalence toward the things Jesus and the Apostles did and promised we would do as well. Some of the things that African Pentecostals do, such as anointing shirts and sending them out, is not much different from what the Church of God did in its early years. In some ways, these African Pentecostals might have more in common with E. E. Byrum than they do with the average leader of a Church of God congregation today.

An example of the expanding—and to many, unnerving—influence of Pentecostalism is another "Church of God," the Redeemed Christian Church of God in Nigeria, which dates back to the 1950s but is only now entering the radar screens of the West. The RCCG (Pentecostal-Holiness) combines Yoruba tribal spirituality with Western-style megachurch organizational principles and preaches the prosperity gospel. The church has absolutely

---

21. And like the Church of God reformers, Pentecostals have been less concerned with theology and doctrine.

22. Pentecostalism does very well among the poor in the non-Western world, but it has also done well in developed nations, such as South Korea and Sweden. It is growing quickly among professionals in China and in Africa.

exploded over the past few decades. The primary auditorium at "Redemption Camp" holds more than five hundred thousand people. Today there are over two thousand RCCG churches in Nigeria, and there are numerous churches throughout Africa and Europe in places as unlikely as County Clare, Ireland. With more than three hundred RCCG churches in North America, the denomination has U.S. headquarters in Dallas, Texas (RCCGNA). [23]

In the same way that Church of God reformers believed that God was restoring his church around the world through them in the American Midwest, today many Pentecostals, such as the Nigerians of the Redeemed Christian Church of God believe that God is establishing his kingdom and modeling a way for the church through them in Nigeria.[24] In fact, many Africans believe that with their humble backgrounds and deep belief in spirituality, God has a special plan for African Christians in finishing global evangelism before Christ's return.

The self-understanding of many of these Pentecostal churches is that they are meant to shake up the entire world.

In the same way that North Americans and Europeans always viewed their church as destined to go global, non-Western churches now believe that they too are meant to be global, not simply remain African or Mexican. Chinese Christians in the "Back to Jerusalem Movement" believe that God has called Chinese Christians to bring Christianity to Muslim Central Asia—a place where Western missionaries cannot easily go. The early Church of God reformers believed that they were uniquely called out to lead the church to the truth. What we often don't realize is that many other groups feel the exact same way—and that even now—130 years later, there are Christian

---

23. In addition to the RCCG, there are many other large Pentecostal churches that have gone global. Many Pentecostal churches are sending out large numbers of non-Western missionaries such as La Luz del Mundo, whose primary church in Guadalajara, Mexico, is a pyramid that seats twelve thousand (four million adherents in forty countries). Another is the Universal Church of the Kingdom of God in Brazil, which is especially controversial (six million adherents in 115 nations).

24. Quite often, these churches are labeled neo-Pentecostal (or charismatic) because they do not require speaking-in-tongues as evidence of the Holy Spirit. They are also more comfortable with modernity and do not have strict creeds. They also emphasize lay leadership (including youth) to an even greater degree than traditional Pentecostal churches. "Pentecostals" typically belong to one of the historic Pentecostal denominations and very much emphasize speaking-in-tongues as proof of baptism in the Holy Spirit. "Charismatic" churches may or may not involve tongues, but there are other supernatural signs. There are charismatic Roman Catholics and mainline Protestants throughout the world. Together the Pentecostals, neo-Pentecostals, or charismatics are also sometimes referred to as "renewalists."

groups from Nigeria to China that feel the exact same way the founders of the Church of God did!

The self-understanding of many of these Pentecostal churches is that they are meant to shake up the entire world. The Embassy of the Blessed Kingdom of God for All Nations in Kiev, Ukraine, has twenty-five thousand people and is the largest church in Europe. It has fifteen services on Sunday in Kiev and 126 satellite churches throughout the rest of the country. Its name is intentionally international, having rejected its original more American-sounding name (Word of Faith Bible Church), and it now has churches in forty countries. It is Europe's largest church, and it is pastored by a Nigerian of Yoruba descent. Sunday Adelaga is the African pastor of a congregation that is 90 percent white and located in a place where atheism and racism still flourish. "God has called us to effect another reformation," he has said, sounding not too different from the early Church of God pioneers."[25] The language of non-Western, non-white Pentecostal movements in the twenty-first century often parallels that of the Church of God reformation movement as it understood itself in the nineteenth century. The emphasis on experience in these movements also resonates with many Western postmoderns as it has historically with the Church of God.

In many places where the Church of God is located, Pentecostalism has created a challenging environment for ministry and growth. Church of God pastors in countries like the Philippines, India, Costa Rica, and perhaps most surprising—Egypt, report of clashes between our churches and the Pentecostals.

The Pentecostal movement has positive aspects and negative aspects. A great amount of good work is being done within this movement of nearly half a billion people and to suggest that this is not the case would be disingenuous. I have a number of very good charismatic and Pentecostal friends who are an inspiration to me. In my limited travels for this book, however, Church of God congregations were often frustrated by the quick growth of the Pentecostal church in their areas and the lack of personal holiness present in the life of the believers. What emerged was a role that Church of God people could play within this greater, global trend.

---

25. J. Kwabena Asamoah-Gyadu. "African Initiated Christianity in Eastern Europe: The Church of the Embassy of God in the Ukraine," *International Bulletin of Missionary Research* 30, no 2 (April 2006): 73–75. See also J. Kwabena Asamoah-Gyadu, "An African Pentecostal on Mission in Eastern Europe: The Church of the 'Embassy of God' in the Ukraine," *Pneuma* 27, no 2 (2005): 297–321).

The Charisma in Manila

In the Philippines, I accompany my newly adopted Philipine sister Marlene Viray into the slums of Manila. We walk through neighborhoods where entire families live in tin and wood shacks no larger than a dog house in North America. Children wander the streets looking dirty, but joyful. Many of the squatter homes have been built in a cemetery. Inside the modest homes, women make rugs that they hope to sell for a few cents. But amid the poverty I meet some of the families supported by the Children of Promise program.

"This was the pilot program," Marlene told me as we stopped by the home of one of the little girls who get money and support for food, health, clothes, and other necessities. Children of Promise has improved the lives of thousands of impoverished children since 1992 and it has consistently been well-managed in the Philippines locations by the regal Felly Viray, her daughter Marlene, and their friends.[26]

Back at the main church in the Tondo section of Manila, I speak with national leader Eddie Viray and a few of the pastors about the situation of the Church of God in the Philippines. Viray is a very spry man whose vigor and dynamism belie his age. With his sense of humor accompanied by a contagious laugh, he is definitely charismatic without actually being a charismatic.

"In 1968, this church was three feet higher than the street," Pastor Viray said as we sat in the main office on a typically muggy day. "Today the church and the street are level. The whole city of Manila is sinking," he tells me. "By 2050, the whole church will be underwater."

In the church with us are two *pastoras* from the church in the Philippines. Pastora Amelia knows all about the flooding in Manila. Every year during the rainy season, the water in her home comes up to her waist, just one inch below her bed. So on days when it's raining, she packs up all her things and puts them high up in her home.

"She's a mermaid!" says Pastor Zorbito with a laugh, another energetic Filipino pastor.

The Church of God in the Philippines is not only being flooded by waters, it is also being flooded by a popular Pentecostal movement. Pastor

---

26. Children of Promise serves over thirty-eight hundred children around the world, as of January 2010. Children receive money for education costs, uniforms, school supplies, meals, medical care, or nutritional supplements. Each country has a national leader or missionary who oversees the program.

Viray estimates that 55 percent of Protestant churches are now Pentecostal. Cathedral of Praise, Foursquare, Assemblies of God, the Hour of Miracle, Jesus Is Lord, and the United Pentecostal Church (UPC) are just a few of the Pentecostal groups growing rapidly throughout the Philippines.

Pastora Soledad who belongs to the First International Church of God in Talanay, Quezon City, joins us in the office. She too works in low-income areas. She often runs across the Pentecostals, but says that they do not engage the poor or care about their needs here. Pastora Soledad paints a picture of a movement that focuses on charismatic worship to the exclusion of expecting maturity and holiness from believers.

"The Philippines," she explained to me, "is a country of performers." There are many media stars. We Filipinos love to sing and dance." The Pentecostal church, in Soledad's opinion, duplicates that atmosphere of entertainment without demanding maturity from the believers. The church is always in danger of easily absorbing too much of the culture. The performance-centered worship pulls people in. It creates a "star culture" in which charismatic leaders are worshiped.

"Many enter the churches because of their leaders and the crowd. They are famous; they are popular. It's a very noisy worship. But the danger is that it's not in the Scripture. When they speak, dance, cry, they shout, they climb the walls. If you are not speaking in tongues, you are not accepted as a member. The Church of God, however, has a value for the Word of God. The members have a conviction, and they live with the Living Word of God. We please God for the glory of God, not the glory of man. There's lots of immorality in the Pentecostal church. If you want to become popular, you become Pentecostal."

It's an interesting twist on the traditional call of the Church of God for holiness. While the early Church of God reformers were calling for a deeper spiritual holiness among the spiritually lukewarm members of denominations in nineteenth-century America, the Filipino Church of God in the twenty-first century is calling for holiness among an energized Pentecostal church embracing superficial charismatic worship.

Another pastora, Amelia Cajayon, sums it up with a call for complete holiness: "We know that Jesus answers all our prayers if we give all our life to him. Jesus can accept loud clapping, but you must feel the way you worship him. Give all your life to him."

There are about twenty-eight Church of God congregations in the Philippines. Most churches have twenty to twenty-five people, with the largest church being the Church of God in Nueva Ecija, which has two hundred people. Some are located in urban centers, and others in rural villages and islands.

Pastor Rodolfo Zurbito knows what it is like to call people to holiness as the pioneers did long ago. He does so within the context of Christian growth and competition in the non-Western world of the twenty-first century. Zurbito lives on the island of Masbate, one of seventy-seven thousand islands with eighty-eight million people that make up the country we call the Philippines. He estimates that his island is 99 percent Catholic. There are five thousand people living there and nine Protestant churches. Eight of them are Pentecostal. Zurbito and his non-Pentecostal Church of God friends are considerably outnumbered.

Zurbito's island is strategically located between many other dialects and cultures. Consequently, Pastor Zurbito speaks eight languages.[27] He spoke to me in the only one of those eight languages I understand: English. "I have seen people who are Pentecostal who are good Christians, but as I see it, only 5 percent are changed. It's just the system. In the Church of God we attract people through salvation. We introduce Christ for salvation. But in Pentecostalism, it's the music and the main thing is the healing. In the outdoors, they will say, 'bring your sick people here,' and if people are healed, they are 'saved.' It's not about Jesus, or changes in their life. It's about healing. You don't hear them talk about coming to Christ for salvation."[28]

Zurbito has also noticed something else that is a common criticism toward Pentecostal groups. "When the groups begin too big, they will fall down and scatter, and varying leaders will emerge. There will be five or seven leaders who will sprout from the church. They will start their own

---

27. Those languages are Cebuano, Ilonggo, Waray, Tagalog, English, Bicol Ringconada, Bicol Sorsogon, and Bicol Naga. It is not uncommon for Christians in the non-Western world (particularly outside of the United States and Latin America) to speak more than one language. Many Africans and Asians put us to shame with their ability to speak five to ten languages. That would certainly make one humble in approaching Scripture.

28. In underdeveloped nations, the church sees a lot more miracles and healing than in the Western world. Why is this? When I visited Zambia I learned that there is one doctor for every 136,000 people. When there are so few doctors, people turn toward the church and it often occurs. These are cultures that believe in spiritual manifestations. This also leads to there being more people claiming to have healing-ministries (witch-doctors or Christian cults), and more of an emphasis on healing as being the thing we need from God. In wealthier nations, we may pray for healing but, basically expect our medical care to be our primary help.

church and they look the same. They keep dividing and have no strong doctrine. They have many different names." So the Church of God reformers' call for unity along with holiness is also relevant within this context.

"People in the Philippines throw stones at the Pentecostal churches. Not because they disagree with the theology, but because they are too noisy! The Pentecostals then say, "Ah, we're being persecuted for our faith." Could the Church of God model holiness and unity in these settings?

Despite the dislike of the noise, many Catholic churches are adapting the Pentecostal style in mass (en masse as well), something that displeases the Vatican, but which wins over the Filipino Catholics. When even the Catholics are becoming like the Pentecostals, the Church of God finds itself in the ironic position of now being viewed as the stodgy, traditional church. The Filipino pastors are asked by other pastors about the 'lack of spiritual dynamism' in the Church of God congregations. But that 'lack of spiritual dynamism' actually seems like a healthy and necessary corrective to the excesses found in some Pentecostal worship around the world. The Church of God offers a theology that emphasizes personal holiness, shows a concern for the poor, and tends to have a decentralized-style of organization that is sceptical of authoritarian leadership. This serves to prevent the formation of a shallow, emotion-based worship reliant on a charismatic personality.

> The Church of God finds itself in the ironic position of now being viewed as the stodgy, traditional church.

Zorbito adds: "Our church worship is very simple. They say it's very professional. But it's not the worship that makes the church strong; it's the doctrine. I am the only member on my island who doesn't practice Pentecostalism, but I have a strong church. I have a member that was forty years in the Four Square church. He said, 'This is not the doctrine I learned from my church, but I can't argue it because it is biblical.' Church of God! The name itself is biblical!"

Pastor Viray would love to see more books of theology produced by the Church of God. "The theologians in Fritzlar (Germany) should write a Church of God book," he says. "We need apologetics, we need to preserve the teachings of the Church of God. How do we feel about eschatology? We could use a treatise on tongues." Pastor Viray is right. As the church engages some old challenges in new settings, there is much a new generation of theologians could write about with their focus on how these old theological and liturgical challenges are re-surfacing amid the rise of non-Western Christianity. A thousand Church of God dissertations could be launched.

In the worship service that Sunday, the Virays lovely daughter Sarah Ann leads us through traditional songs found in the *1971 Hymnal of the Church of God,* such as "Blessed Be the Name," "His Yoke Is Easy," and "Will You Come?" as well as some more contemporary songs. The service, the warm people, and the quick way in which they adopted me into the family reminds me so much of my home in Costa Rica that I'm convinced that the Philippines is really a part of Latin America that somehow broke off the Central American isthmus long ago and ended up in Southeast Asia.

"We love the Church of God," I heard the pastors say over and over. "We would die for the Church of God."

Egypt: Holiness and Unity in the Desert

Two weeks later and I am in a church building that looks about the same age and same size as the Tondo church in Manila; but I am not in the Philippines, but rather in a poor section of Alexandria, Egypt, on the Mediterranean Sea, where the local Church of God is known as "the Red Church" because of the color of the building. The main service is on Sunday night since most everyone works during the day on Sunday (this is an Islamic nation and the day of rest is Friday, not Sunday).

The tune of the hymn was familiar. It was "Draw Me Nearer to Thee," but the music was full of Middle Eastern flare, full of minor keys, the guitar and drums kept a beat that a belly-dancer could keep up with, and a woman with a microphone and a beautiful voice sang louder than all the others. Middle Eastern music has a distinct sound that was formed over centuries. It can sound discordant and mournful to foreign ears that are used to more predictable melodies accompanied by choruses of people in harmony. In Middle Eastern music, their octave is divided into quarter tones rather than half tones as we have in the West. What sounds flat or jarring to foreigners is actually an intentional style of music that is very much a product of the isolation found in Bedouin desert cultures. I've never enjoyed "Draw Me Nearer to Thee" more than I do tonight.

The Church of God in Egypt has had their encounters with Pentecostals as well. They too have found that the emphasis is on miracles and healing with little concern for social issues. The churches are often divisive and don't ferment much loyalty among the members. The call of the Church of God for personal holiness stands out here in Alexandria as well.

But the bigger challenge is not the Pentecostals, but the Orthodox Church (Coptics). Eastern Orthodoxy is one of the three main branches of Protestantism (Roman Catholicism and Protestantism are the other two). Orthodox history is very long. To the Orthodox, the Roman Catholics were the new kids on the block and they split from them in the Great Schism of AD 1045. Everything since then is wrong and not Christian. Many Church of God congregations in predominantly Orthodox regions of the world are viewed as cults. As we in the United States view the Jehovah's Witnesses, this is how our Church of God brethren are viewed in places like Russia and Egypt—as a bizarre, unholy, Protestant cult. Of course, the Orthodox Church had its own internal schisms and it has spent much of its history divided. Alexandria, for instance, is home to the Coptic Church of Alexandria and claims to have been founded by St. Mark in AD 42.

It is difficult to present the truths of the *Gospel Trumpet* to people who think their church's founder *wrote* a gospel. But that is just what "the Red Church" is trying to do. Their pastor, Dr. Latif Ramses, is a pharmacist by trade. But he is overseeing a church that worships and operates very differently than the Coptic churches in the area. Orthodox churches practice an elaborate liturgy and have many rites that are less demanding of the people day to day. Dr. Latif is constantly challenging his non-Orthodox church to model a new way of Christianity—the way of holiness and unity. A deep, personal, transformational Christian faith is something most in this area have not been exposed to in their lifetimes.

"We started with children," Dr. Latif tells me as we had tea and cake in a lower room where my son is playing with some Egyptian children. "God gave us a vision for this area and we started with Sunday school for six children. Their behavior was very bad, they were socially awkward, and we had to teach them how to pray. These children began to love church and the kids brought their friends. The more it increased, the more we did personal work with them. As they grew up, we made a middle school with them. We told them to bring their friends and the numbers grew to seventy-two. Some did not come for church, but came for the girls. We kept praying and witnessing to them and we did a conference and prayed that they would receive Christ. This is exactly what happened."

Now Dr. Latif has a solid core of motivated Christian leaders emerging in the church. "They do technical things, teaching, and they learn some music." They are also exposed to theology. It begins at the age of twelve with basic Christian doctrine. From ages eighteen to twenty-five, kids are immersed in Church of God theology. Families are targeted and discipleship groups are formed wherein those involved are learning how to be leaders. It is a stark contrast to the Coptic churches.

"Orthodox worship is completely different. It's a different type of service. Here there's more freedom, more participation, and there's more time to pray and listen to the Word. We have special meetings for teaching and Bible study and we have youth meetings and ladies meetings, and they are very practical—about living the Christian life."[29]

I asked Dr. Latif if the worship is not only distinct from the Coptic Church, but whether it is also distinct from other evangelical churches.

"It is different. The teaching here is very Bible-centered. Secondly, love! The atmosphere of love! They feel the presence of God. We will not behave as the Pentecostals do. As the Holy Spirit leads us in worship, we will do. We may sing songs and we may clap hands, or we may pray. It's different from time to time, but it is according to what the Holy Spirit leads."

The Church of God in Egypt has big ambitions to reach all of their neighborhoods—modeling wholeness in their Christian life through holiness. This has meant decentralizing; allowing young leaders to emerge and moving away from 'the pastor-must-do-everything approach' that diminishes the role of lay leadership. Speaking with a group of Church of God pastors in Cairo a few days earlier, I learned that there is now a new generation of leadership in the Egyptian churches. "Seven years ago we were few; we only had four or five pastors," the national chairman, Mounir R. Soliman, told me. "Now we have pastors for every church and most of our pastors are young now." They have also achieved financial independence as of 2004, and they have planted churches in new locations. Franco Santonocito, the Italian missionary and evangelist whose work throughout the Mediterranean and Europe has him now based out of Egypt, reported that "most of

29. In Egypt (and Russia), the Church of God engages people and the community in hands-on ways that are very different from the Orthodox church. However, in Lebanon, the Orthodox churches and Roman Catholic churches have learned to imitate the evangelical churches. In Beirut, Joy Mallouh shared with me that "now they have youth groups; they have choirs. They do the things we do, and sometimes they do it better than we do. They say to us, 'You taught us how to do these things; now go your own way.'" This makes it more difficult for evangelical churches and the Church of God to stand out when this is the case.

the existing churches are growing and that the Church of God has good relationships and a good reputation among other evangelical churches."[30] The Church of God has been part of the evangelical fellowship in Egypt since 1919. Furthermore, the church in Egypt now owns all of its property (no small matter in a Muslim country), and they have a new one-year intensive course on Church of God theology for leaders of all churches that they hope to expand throughout the Mediterranean region.

There are challenges. The Church of God in Egypt is at a disadvantage financially as it tries to model a different way of faith than the Coptic Church. The pastors mentioned that they are often surrounded by Coptic churches that are extremely wealthy and offer services for the poor. In some of the village churches in Egypt, Church of God parishioners may work two to three jobs just to make ends meet. Raising funds is not easy. Pastor Ayman Mounir reports that he opened a day care church in his village and the Coptics opened a cheaper one and took three-quarters of the people. Mounir Soliman points out that in Shoubra, they are surrounded by four Coptic churches in their neighborhood. "Other evangelical denominations are supported by big missions from outside."

Despite the fact that the Church of God in Egypt has thirteen churches, six societies, and fifteen hundred people, there are still not enough congregations. When parishioners move, there may not be another Church of God in Egypt that they can attend in their new village or town.

And then there's the discrimination that all Christians face in Egypt if they are not Muslim. Walking past a clothes store in Cairo earlier during my stay, an Egyptian friend pointed out to my wife and me that they had recently put up a sign that said: "Help wanted. Christians need not apply." The prejudice might be something as subtle as a waiter not serving a Christian woman not wearing a headscarf or outright persecution in some parts of Egypt. In Egypt, your religion is listed on your I.D. card.[31]

In thinking about his own church, Dr. Latif cautions that it has taken years to form this healthy dynamic within the church. The church literally had to grow up and adopt a new culture, which is now part of its DNA.

---

30. It was Brother Franco who did the interpreting for me when one of the Egyptian pastors could not speak English.

31. Your name may give you away too. There are not too many Christian Muhammeds and there are not very many Muslims named Georgios (George, as in St. George). Many Christians have a second name that they use.

Dr. Latif tells me a story: "A person came from a very staunch Orthodox background and his wife and kids are in our church. The wife was praying for her husband. From time to time, they would invite him to the church. The wife would talk to him but he said, 'I go to the mother church, the real church, the Orthodox church." One day we had family meetings and he attended with his wife. He found love, and everyone welcomed him. The subject interested him and he became part of the church. Now he brings others to the church. One day he brought a man who said upon hearing his first sermon in the Church of God that it was as if 'God was causing a small child to be born.'"

Jesus told the religious man Nicodemus that he must be born again. Egypt is a very religious society. "People have religious inclinations here," Dr. Latif said. "Even those who don't attend church are happy to listen to the Word of God." But there is a deeper calling upon our lives, and in very religious places such as Egypt and the Philippines—where the rituals are followed by millions, but the Spirit and the meaning behind them is often unknown—the Church of God's message of holiness and unity today is just as revolutionary and just as needed as it was on the farmlands of the Midwest 130 years ago.

how far to the nearest church of god?

The Geographical Challenge
Russia, New Zealand, Prestonsburg, Lebanon, Pennsylvania, Cyberspace

I am in Siberia being beaten with reeds by a naked Russian man. I wish I were kidding, but I am not. Let there be no doubt, cultural differences in this world are huge. In Russia, the men of the Church of God like to disrobe, go into a sauna that's 125 degrees with 100 percent humidity, and eat potato chips and Coke. Every fifteen minutes or so, one of them gets up to pour a bucket of ice water on their bodies. It is my very definition of hell, yet this is a must for any male visitor to this part of the world. It is a regular get-together for the men and a great time to socialize and share. It is called *bania*.

Historically the *bania* used to be the only way of washing yourself. It was like a shower for us today. Every house had to have a *bania*. Today, Russians have water in their homes, but the *bania* remains a time when Russians escape the cold and have fellowship. The only thing unusual about this particular Russian group of men is that when they finish in the *bania*, they do not leave a trail of alcoholic bottles behind as most groups do. As for me, I am given no option about attending this event and I suddenly feel very sorry for my American missionary friend Dwayne Goldman who must undergo this exercise in massive dehydration on a regular basis. Kelley Phillips of Gateway Berlin, who served as a missionary here, loves the

171

bania experience and laughs at my discomfort as I enter the hot room. I did travel to Russia to get to know my Russian Church of God brothers better, but in the *bania,* I feel as if I was getting to know them *far* too well. As early as 1909 members of the German Church of God were spreading the reformation message in Russia, and as I feel myself losing consciousness due to the suffocating heat, I began to wonder to myself if any of them had to undergo the *bania* experience.

There are three pastors in the Church of God congregation in Chelyabinsk, Russia. Pastor Sergei is a man of few words who radiates a priestly countenance. With his large presence and distinguished beard, one can easily picture him as an Orthodox priest. Fortunately for us, he is not. Pastor Andrei is the thirty-something extrovert with flawless English. And last but not least, Pastor Alexei, who is the administrator and a successful entrepreneur, is a master at beating a visitor's skin until it's raw. "Go easy on me. I bruise like a grape," I say to Alexei as I prepare for my therapeutic flogging.

"Just relax, Patrick," he tells me as I feel myself on the brink of passing out. He is obviously taking it easy on me and not giving me the full Russian treatment, but it is still on the brink of killing me. I lie on a wooden bench. The heat coming off of the wood toward my face is almost enough to make me lose my breath and faint. The potato chips and Coke have helped to dehydrate me to the point that I feel like a slug that has had a bucket of salt poured on him. I am convinced that I will never have saliva in my mouth again. I hoped that at the very least I am losing some serious weight so that this experience will be worth it.

"I'm so glad you've had the bania experience," Kelley says to me.

"I've have the bania experience everyday. This is what it feels like everyday in Hong Kong!" I complain recalling the muggy place I call home.

Why people would do this for fun is beyond me.

But the *bania* is an important communal gathering in a country where the weather and geography can create tremendous isolation. During the winter months, the sky is very dark in Chelyabinsk with the sun only shining for four hours a day. In the dead of winter it can get down to 35 degrees below freezing (Celsius). This northern country is so large that it covers eleven time zones, yet unlike the United States, there are very few large cities. Russians live in communities far away from other places and much of their time is spent escaping from the bitter cold. So in conditions that extreme, what's a little nudity and heat among friends?

The Road Map

In this chapter we will start with a geographically isolated church in Russia and discuss how many Church of God congregations have been planted in isolation making it difficult for these churches to reinforce Church of God identity and connection. Another geographical challenge is that in today's world, people are highly mobile making it difficult to build up consistent leadership or to transmit denominational identity. Many in our pews have no history or awareness of the Church of God at all. We will journey to New Zealand to visit a church that has to not only deal with extreme geographical isolation from other Church of God congregations, but which also has the challenge of living in a very transient, multicultural community. We will then stop in rural Kentucky to begin seeing how even within the United States, geographical differences can create different cultures which view the Church of God very differently from other places. We will also get to know our brothers and sisters in the Pastor's Fellowship. In Lebanon, we will see how in some countries geography can mean the difference between a safe place to do ministry and a dangerous place to even exist as a Christian. In Pennsylvania, we will meet some Hispanic pastors whose congregations are made of mostly migrant workers. Finally, we will go into cyberspace, to see how new methods of communication may affect the Church of God.

Geography Matters

One of the least considered challenges to the unity and cohesion of the Church of God has been geography. From the beginning, the pioneers had a desire to share "the evening light" with as many people as possible. Their decentralized style which included mission homes, allowed them to spread the message far and wide. Initially, the Church of God did not even want to inhabit buildings or have pastors who served for long periods of time in churches. But eventually it became clear that churches needed a shepherd and the more traditional model of church emerged.

Ocean travel had become common enough that early reformers were able to sail to Europe and Asia with the message of holiness and unity. Copies of the *Gospel Trumpet* reached far and wide, and to this day, I still meet leaders around the world whose first encounter with the Church of God and their subsequent decision to join the movement was because of this periodical or its successor *Vital Christianity*. The result was that the movement grew quickly, but a unified strategy for keeping new believers and churches connected and accountable did not materialize. Consequently, as the movement has grown geographically, it has always struggled to grow in unity.

The American Midwest was not Siberia, but the pioneer spirit of the early reformers was influenced by their location in other ways. In the late nineteenth century, Ohio, Michigan, and Indiana were a world away from the large, wealthy, urban centers of the East Coast, which were industrializing quickly, creating a class of people who were very different from those on the rural prairies. It was in those older established Eastern areas that denominations had their headquarters. The Holiness movement, on the other hand, often emerged from people of a lower class economically. Geography shapes the church in many ways, and it has challenged the unity of the Church of God.

The Church of God has also not always done a good job of making sure congregations have other Church of God congregations close by to support them. Since movements and denominations have a particular culture, theology and style of organization, it is helpful to have other communities close for interaction, support, and re-affirmation of the particulars of the Church of God. It is also important to have structures and relationships that provide accountability and can assist if churches get into trouble. Many of our churches around the world have not had this and they have suffered from isolation and have difficulties keeping up a strong identification with the Church of God. Europe, for instance, has many churches that were planted far apart and are considerably isolated. One Church of God congregation may represent the whole country and they will speak in a language different from their nearest neighbor in a different country. In Asia, there are a number of examples of churches that exist in isolation. Hong Kong and Taiwan, for instance, were too easily isolated from the Church of God. Even within the United States, there are churches that exist utterly alone and seemingly off the map. No congregation exemplifies this isolation better than our sole congregation in Hawaii.

In the United States, geographic distance has been a factor as many West Coast pastors find it hard to relate to, or feel very disconnected from what takes place in Anderson. In some countries like India, the country is so diverse that the different regions (with different languages, dialects, and cultures) may have a hard time preserving unity. There are many ways that geography can be a challenge, but one way or another geography matters.

Russia: Reaching Out from Isolation

In Russia, geography means not only being far away from other Church of God congregations, but also being surrounded by a Russian Orthodox Church that is hostile toward Protestant Christianity.

My family and I are in Russia to attend a conference of Women of the Church of God. While my wife Jamie and the WCG ladies attend the conference and get to know the Russian women, I am able to get to know the pastors and hear about the challenges of doing ministry in Russia.

We arrive in spring, and the sky is consistently blue, but it remains very cold. Dirty snow piles up on the streets and my breath is visible as we head to the church. We are fortunate to be here at this time of year. In the dead of winter, many people do not leave their homes and cars are often not able to start. But today it is a sultry 28 degrees Fahrenheit outside. Siberian bikini weather! I still manage to slip on the ice covered sidewalk and fall flat on my back, much to the merriment of my son.

The church is meeting at a place called the Palace of the Blind. It belongs to the Blind Society of Russia and is rented out to organizations. Currently, four churches are renting it. According to Russian law, churches cannot rent schools or hospitals or meet in public places. The remaining options are buildings like this and they quickly become overbooked. Most churches here cannot afford to have a building and need to move several times a year because the rent goes up. Consequently, a place like the Palace of the Blind, where the rent is cheap and the location is central, is always busy. At one point the Church of God in Chelyabinsk had to deal with the fact that pornography DVDs were being sold in the foyer of the shared building.

Pastor Andrei, a thirty-something pastor who also teaches English at a local university, tells me more about the challenges of sharing a building. "This place hosts elections, so on those occasions we have to move our services to Saturday. We also cannot have foot-washing or Communion before Easter because the facility is rented by other organizations. For about a year we met in the same hall as the Mormons. For many people there is no difference between us and the Mormons. As soon as they hear that Mormons meet there, your church is branded as a cult of the same kind."

The first great schism in the Church of God (Anderson, Indiana) was the necktie controversy, which, not surprisingly, hasn't made it onto the radar screen of most church historians. But the Great Schism in the universal church of God occurred in AD 1054 when the Eastern church and the Western church divided. Two great powers emerged (Constantinople and Rome), and a debate about the nature of Christ ended up in a division within the Christian world that exists to this day.

Russia became a part of the Eastern Christian sphere, where Christianity has existed for more than a thousand years. To say that aspects of Christianity are deeply imbedded in the Russian psyche is an understatement. It's impossible to understand Russia, its history and her people without understanding the Russian Orthodox Church. To this day, everything else is a sect—heresy.

In the early days of the Church of God, the reformers were also viewed as a sect. They were called "come-outers," challenging people from denominations to become part of the one unified Church of God. We don't do this much anymore, because denominationalism is not much of an issue. My friend Scott, for instance, attends a wonderful church that is not part of the Church of God. There's no reason for me to ask him to "come-out" of his neighborhood church (although I will happily take his money to support my ministry). In Russia, however, the Russian Orthodox Church, much like the old denominations the reformers fought against, stands strongly apart from Church of God ideas.

"The Russian Orthodox Church is the official state religion," Andrei explains. "You have to explain to people that our church is not a cult. They imagine a certain way church is done with a priest, cathedrals, and icons. When they truly want to know something about God, they are surprised that you can hear the gospel in a language in a way they can understand, and they like this."

When the cold war ended, many Western evangelicals moved into Russia to bring in the gospel. It was a time of great openness, but over the years, the environment has become more challenging again. And the Russian Orthodox Church was angered and threatened by the various Protestant sects that emerged throughout the country. Despite the hard feelings, at least in Chelyabinsk, Pastor Andrei still reaches out to the Orthodox church.

"I personally know some of the priests. We're not friends, but we can call each other and talk about things. But we cannot do things together. The patriarch made a comment that Orthodoxy is the official church and other churches should never have the same rights. It caused many journalists to be very surprised. We don't know what he meant, or what that will lead to, but traditionally we are viewed as a cult. It's preached on television, on the radio, in the newspaper, and in any Eastern Orthodox book. 'Salvation is only in the Russian Orthodox Church and all others will parish.'"

As I would see in a number of countries that I visited from Thailand to New Zealand, when there is such hostility against Protestant churches, denominational issues become far less important. Without other Church of God congregations around, the Church of God in Chelyabink reaches out to other evangelical churches in the city. It's part of how Church of God theology is made relevant again in a completely new twenty-first century setting. "Everyone washed in the blood of Christ is our brother," Andrei says, echoing the early reformers. "The practical application of that would be Pastor Sokol and his work meeting with other evangelical pastors. He does this so that we would

Russia...is a place where within a new context the nineteenth-century Church of God message of unity lives on.

get to know each other and see what we are all doing. It has grown into doing things together. We have different projects celebrating Easter and Christmas. If we have some training we invite people from other churches to come. Now evangelical churches at large are not viewed as a gathering of individuals but as churches that have fellowship and the Church of God has been the catalyst." Russia, as in the Philippines, is a place where within a new context the nineteenth-century Church of God message of unity lives on. "The Baptists did not want to deal with the charismatics, but all of them were willing to cooperate with us," Andrei says regarding the unique role the Church of God has been able to play as a force for unity.

The fellowship with churches from other denominations is important, since the Church of God in Chelyabinsk is very isolated from other sister congregations. Which begs the question, "How far to the nearest Church of God, anyway?"

I learn that it is here in Siberia, but about seven hundred miles to the East (on Russian roads). It takes ten hours by train to get to the congregation of eighty people in the Volgograd region. The Church of God in Chelyabinsk has also connected with a church in Pallasovke—a settlement started by a German. They are a very conservative group that consists of the descendents of German immigrants. This small group of twenty people broke away from an even more conservative group. So conservative that—Andrei tells me—initially they were a bit taken aback by the more contemporary worship of the Chelyabinsk church.

"They are conservative in their theology, the way they dress, the songs they sing, and the way they carry on a conversation. When the pastor visited us, he was shocked by seeing women in Russia wearing jewelry and make-up in church and clapping. He couldn't believe his eyes that they were Church of God!" I try to contain my laughter, which is easy because my mouth is frozen shut. My wife is thrilled.

The Pallasovke church now accepts the differences and would like a tighter relationship with the church in Russia and would even like prayer and a visit from brothers and sisters in the United States and other Church of God nations. They crave fellowship. From South America to Central Europe, I would meet Church of God congregations desiring closer connection to other Church of God congregations. One of the reasons breaking the isolation is a positive for the movement is because face-to-face fellowship has a powerful impact on us leading us to drop our preconceptions about each other. This builds unity and it also makes possible more coordinated ministry.

The Russian church also reaches out to churches in the Ukraine, a thousand miles away. It takes thirty-some hours to get there by train, but there are six or seven Church of God congregations in Ukraine, mostly located near Marioupall. The Russians have been meeting with the Ukrainian Church of God for more than twelve years. Getting together over large distances is also hard because most pastors have a day job, which makes it difficult to travel.

Fortunately, numerous churches in the Church of God throughout the world have developed close friendships with the Chelyabinsk church. Chelyabinsk stands out as an excellent example of how important it is for Church of God congregations to be connected to the greater body in order to continue building greater interconnectivity. Connection to other Church of God congregations has been part of the church culture here from the beginning.

Andrei mentions that recently he heard about Church of God believers that he did not know who were praying for Chelyabinsk. "We receive encouragement from Mexico! I was really surprised that there are people in Mexico that know us." In return, the Russians regularly pray for personal requests that come in from the Middle East, Asia, Europe, and North America.

They even take up an offering for Church of God congregations located in areas of persecution.

There are many others that have loved and supported this church as Women of the Church of God from the United States is doing now. "We have had delegations from United States and Germany, and we have established partnerships with many individuals and churches. It does make you feel like a part of the family of the Church of God. I have been fortunate to go to different countries and such experiences are very enriching. I went to India and it was a life-changing experience. They still write letters and we pray for them. We also send money to help churches suffering from persecution. We have sent a Russian couple to the church plant in Gold Coast, Australia, and will be supporting them."

At the Palace of the Blind, we have a spirited worship service. The church is meeting in an auditorium with wooden theatre seats. The music is contemporary, and the people are very warm and friendly. All of us enjoy connecting with our Russian brothers and sisters. The emotional reserve of the Russians, which makes them seem so austere in public, evaporates quickly when in their homes, in the church, or in the bath. We are all charmed.

The church hopes to move from this building relatively soon. They have begun construction on a new building, and all of us visitors head over to the site after church. The unfinished building is two stories and quite large. The grey cement blocks take the shape of the skeleton of a traditional church building.

Building anything in Russia is a very challenging process. There is a great deal of red tape, and bribes are expected in this country where the rule of law is not yet firmly established. As we tour the building we learn that the building is in constant danger of being robbed. Two or three times, people have broken into the building and stolen tools. One time they stole a drill and broke the lock. Sometimes small children break windows on the façade or the tiles. A guard or Pastor Sergei has to watch over the building at all times, even during the brutal winters. There is no heating, and the weather is severe for much of the year. Connecting to central heating has taken three years, but it still cannot be turned on.

Perhaps the most difficult part of the building process has been dealing with inflation, which has been as high as 13 percent annually. This means that all the prices for materials that come from outside of Russia increase

179

significantly. The building permit also stipulates that the building would be completed within two years. Each year that the deadline is not met, the fee for incompletion doubles.[1]

The building process has been very challenging for the church in Chelyabinsk. But it has also served as an example of how important it is for Church of God congregations to have global connections. The obstacles here are significant, but they are made more manageable by the assistance and support of foreign congregations. It's vital that Chelyabinsk be supported because they already are doing such a good job of keeping Church of God congregations in the region connected to the movement. While some may want to argue for isolation and a total lack of dependence from outside help, Russia is a good example of how in some places, the challenges the church faces are so great that the national church is in need of support in a variety of ways from international churches in our movement. We should not be so quick to make general statements about indigenous churches. Strategic support of an isolated church in a foreign country can benefit the whole movement in a variety of ways.

I watch as the Women of the Church of God group gathers on the top floor of the unfinished building to form a circle to pray for protection of the property and completion of the project. As I watch the Russians and the Americans hold hands, I marvel at the distances that have been breached between our two cultures as well as geographically. It's hard to believe that the world was once divided into the Communist East and the Capitalist West. Today, even within our movement, these geographical and ideological barriers have disappeared. The church in Chelyabinsk is being reminded that despite their geographic isolation, they are not alone.

New Zealand: An Island Unto Itself

I am sitting in the worship service at Westside Christian Fellowship trying to sing along in an unfamiliar language:

Ka Koropiko Ahau

Ki to Aroaro

Ma to kororia

---

1. It reached $7,000 U.S. by 2008 before a constant fee was initiated alleviating some of the pressure.

Kite ana to mate

Kotahi atu te inoi, ki a koe e ihowa

Wairua tapu, nau mai ra[2]

It is Māori, the language of the indigenous people of Aotearoa, the land we now call New Zealand. As I listen to Church of God missionary Doug Beasley lead us in worship, I wonder if my new friends Alisa Wolsey and John Kemp are among the only Māoris in the Church of God movement. There can't be many. There are less than eight hundred thousand Māori in the whole world.

Both John and Alisa have interesting stories about how they came to the Lord and found themselves in this Church of God congregation located in the city of Auckland. John spent much of his life living as a homeless person on the streets. He joined his sister Rangi (which means "sky" in Māori) on the cold streets of Auckland at the age of twelve in 1987. It was not for another fourteen years that he finally left the sidewalks of downtown. John remembers that as a homeless person, very few people cared and it left him feeling defeated for many years. But over the years, he kept his ears open to the voice of God and eventually God spoke to him. The Māori, like the Aboriginals of Australia (and some would say the Bible), place a high value on the role of dreams in our lives. And so one day, God used a dream to speak to John, and he told John that he needed to go down the street and meet a saxophone player. John agreed, but proceeded to move toward God "like the Egyptians built the pyramids—inch by inch." A gifted musician, he began using his money to buy music equipment once he was off the streets and employed. One day he bought an amplifier and had to call a taxi to pick him up to transport the new purchase to his home in the section of Auckland called Te Atatu. As the taxi driver dropped him off, he said to John, "by the way, you need to go down the street and meet the saxophone player."

It was startling to say the least. John lived in the neighborhood and remembered the voice of God also telling him about the saxophone player, but he didn't have an address, so he just walked down the street until he stumbled upon a small, traditional Anglican Church building which is where

---

2. "Clothed in your glory, it's your name I see, unto you I surrender, lift my hands to thee, Come Holy Spirit, cover me"

Westside holds their services. Inside, Pastor Chad Davenport was playing his saxophone. John, homeless for so long, found a spiritual home.

Alisa Wolsey, like many Māori, was raised a Catholic. But she found that she didn't know God despite having been raised around the church. At thirty-six, she rededicated herself to the Catholic church, but soon found that she wasn't growing. It was during that time of searching that she struck up a friendship with a woman from the Church of God. Alisa visited the church and felt she had found a home. "I can't even explain to you why I started to shake and cry uncontrollably in that moment. From that moment on I just knew that this church here—this group of people—were going to be the ones I needed to grow with."

Her desire was to be baptized in the ocean. Before the baptism her skeptical husband's heart started giving out and he ended up in the hospital. He was visited by people from the church and Alisa proceeded on her way toward baptism. The day of the baptism, the weather threatened not to cooperate. The tide went out and they had to walk out far into the ocean to get immersed, but before long she was officially baptized.

"As I walked back on the beach, I saw a woman who was singing along with our church. I felt the urge to talk to her. She said to me, 'I hope you don't mind that I stopped to watch. I'm a Christian and I desperately need to be a part of this,' Alisa recounts. The woman shared that she wanted her partner to be baptized. Alisa told her about how she desperately wanted her husband Peter to be baptized as well. At that very moment, she turned around and saw her husband Peter marching out into the water to be baptized. The two women couldn't believe it. Miracles do happen! She encouraged her new friend to call her partner and tell him to come and be baptized. "Are you sure? Will people wait for me?" the woman asked. "Of course," Alisa replied. Not only was her partner baptized that day but another person walking by saw the commotion and asked to be baptized as well.

John and Alisa's conversion is a miracle in more than one way. The South Pacific is the most Christianized region in the world. But New Zealand, an island nation about fifteen hundred miles southeast of Australia, is one of the most secular countries in the world. Among the white population, there is very little interest in Christianity. Even in the more spiritual indigenous Māori culture, there are a lot of negative feelings associated with Christianity due to the actions of misguided missionaries in New Zealand's history. The history of Christianity here can be ugly, but the country certainly isn't.

In 2005, our family took our vacation in New Zealand and drove around the large southern island. The country is so gorgeous, it's difficult to describe. Imagine if Switzerland had beaches, fjords, wine country, and volcanoes all within its borders. It almost seems unfair that one country could possess so much natural beauty. And therein lies one of the biggest challenges for the church. "Kiwis," as New Zealanders are called, prefer to spend their free time sailing, hiking, and doing just about anything other than going to church. In post-Christendom societies, things such as family, recreation, and sports come first—even among Christians in the church.

But another challenge for the whole country is distance. Traveling around the country, I wondered why the whole world hasn't decided to move to New Zealand? A place this nice anywhere else in the world would be completely overpopulated. Their economy is doing well and there's even a low unemployment rate. Instead, New Zealand is a country that has more sheep than people. On the southern island, we never encountered traffic and often didn't even see other cars for miles. The temptation of the open roads proved to be too great and I was pulled over for speeding. Defying the percentages, the police officer happened to be a church-going Christian and gave me a missionary discount. What this says about both the cop and the missionary I will leave to you to decide. Despite the ticket, the country still seemed like the closest thing to heaven I had ever seen. Yet, one-fifth of all New Zealanders choose to live outside of their beautiful country. The reason is because New Zealand is a very isolated place. It takes three hours by plane just to get to the East Coast of Australia—which is itself located about nine hours from the major cities in Asia! It is never cheap and never easy to get here from anywhere.

In the past few decades, many immigrants have arrived on New Zealand's shores. But quite often, people settle in New Zealand only temporarily which means that it is a highly transient population. All of this makes for huge challenges for the Church of God in New Zealand. Our one congregation in the city of Auckland faces a highly secular society, a difficult national Christian past, great distances separating them from other Church of God congregations, and a high turnover rate in the congregation due to people moving away from New Zealand. When I visited in 2005, the church was struggling with these local challenges.

Four years later in 2009, I am back to see how the church is doing. It has grown to about fifty (they say that the effort it takes to grow a church to one hundred thirty-five in the United States will get you about thirty-five in New Zealand), and there is a solid core of committed believers. While it remains multicultural, it is now rooted in a particular neighborhood instead of intentionally structuring itself as an international church. The saxophone-playing pastor is a good friend of mine. Chad Davenport, an American in his mid-thirties, never had any intention of being a senior pastor. He arrived in New Zealand in 2001 as a special assignment missionary sent to teach in local schools at a time when the church was known as Auckland International Church and targeted immigrants. Once the founding pastor, David Ravell, moved on to establish a church on Australia's Gold Coast, Chad was thrust in the role and two years ago the church was rechristened as Westside Christian Fellowship basing itself on a peninsula on Auckland's west side. Ravell's Journey Church in Australia, which is three hours away by plane, is about the closest church to Westside and faces many of the same challenges as the Auckland church. Australia and New Zealand are beautiful and tough. These are resilient pastors.[3]

Despite once being a "Christian nation," today most people in New Zealand have little understanding of Christianity or the church. Even Easter and Christmas don't bring people into the church. Nevertheless, it remains illegal for businesses to be open on Good Friday.

"Christianity is something you can believe in as a kid, like Santa Claus, but once you reach ten, eleven, or twelve, there's this expectation that you will outgrow it," Pastor Chad tells me as we sit in a park watching the planes land at Auckland International Airport. "When I tell people I'm a pastor, people ask, 'so what is that?' And then when I tell them I'm American, a Christian, *and* a pastor that immediately shuts down the conversation."

In a post-Christendom society like New Zealand, not only is there little interest in Christianity but there is deep suspicion. For those of us who grew up in societies where Christianity is still an important part of the cultural

---

3. I had the wonderful opportunity of spending time with the Journey church in Gold Coast, Australia. New Zealand, Holland, Canada, Germany, and France are countries where the Church of God has to wrestle deeply with the post-Christendom, postmodern culture, which is now spreading into many parts of the United States and even wealthier parts of the non-Western world. It takes a lot of resiliency to pastor in countries such as this. We often think of places in Africa or rural Latin America as being tough because they are poor, but the challenge for ministries and pastors in post-Christian settings are many, and we need to remember that re-evangelizing the West is often a discouraging and long-term project that needs just as much support as evangelism into new areas, perhaps more.

landscape, it's hard to imagine that our churches may be viewed as threats. Chad recalls an incident that illustrates the suspicion and discomfort people have with Christianity. "Recently, some kids came into our church and went home and said, 'It felt spooky.' Church, being spiritual and unfamiliar to them, felt evil because it was so foreign." Spooky—the way we might view a Hindu temple or watching an animal sacrifice.

Preserving Church of God identity is not easy in a place where the congregation has over the years consisted of Koreans, Chinese, Japanese, Singaporeans, Malaysians, Australians, Germans, Jordanians, Thais, and secular Kiwis who have little understanding of how Western Christianity has been formed. Very few would respond to an overt attempt to create "Church of God" people. But the Church of God has never been particularly interested in establishing an identity independent of the universal Church of God. Instead, we have extended our hand "to every blood-washed one." Something that, as Chad points out, becomes very important in a setting like New Zealand. Working across denominational lines helps to keep the churches encouraged and, in the case of Westside, gives them support which they are not able to get from geographically distant Church of God congregations.

The youth group currently meets up with an Open Brethren Church youth group. The youth attend a Baptist camp, and the church itself meets in an aging Anglican church that had dwindled down to just a few people. Due to the isolation from the Church of God, Pastor Chad has built up a relationship of accountability with the Nazarene and Wesleyan-Methodist churches. "Does that mean that we no longer care about the Church of God or are no longer Church of God?" Chad asks rhetorically. "No," he answers, "but there is a greater kingdom work that needs to happen in New Zealand."

That is not to say that the church in New Zealand does not feel supported by the greater Church of God. Chad and Diane Davenport and Doug and Danette Beasley are supported by American congregations and were sent to New Zealand by Global Missions. People write them and pray for them regularly. In 2004, our Church of God congregation in Hong Kong linked up with the New Zealand Church of God to do a joint-mission trip in East Asia. We intentionally reached out to New Zealand (and Chelyabink, Russia) because, like Hong Kong, they were geographically distant Church of God congregations. It was our way of proactively connecting ourselves to isolated churches.

Despite the connection, geography and a lack of structure leaves the Church of God in Auckland vulnerable. "If anything were to go wrong here, we would really be in trouble. That is why we are trying to build a relationship with these other denominations because there is not enough accountability." And the only reason anyone would ever know that there was a problem would be if someone was accountable enough in Auckland to raise the red flag to other Church of God congregations and ask for assistance. This doesn't always happen in the Church of God.

> "We don't have to go through a lot of red tape to get things going here. We're trusted to do the right thing."

"We would like for there to be greater interaction between our churches and in the movement as a whole. But there are times when that disconnection gives us freedom. We don't have to go through a lot of red tape to get things going here. We're trusted to do the right thing. If we felt we needed to take the ministry in another way, no one would block it. There's a lot of trust, but that trust comes at a price." The price is something we have often overlooked.

In the Church of God, connection has to be done intentionally. No structure will do it for you. Consequently, it is easy to become an island, like New Zealand, detached from the rest of the world. Accountability and relationship to the Church of God and for the local church ends up falling into the hands of the local leadership. Complete autonomy and disconnection, unfortunately, has occurred too many times in the past. In New Zealand, despite the lack of a helpful structure and great geographical distance, the church is finding its way toward biblical accountability.

Kia ma tonu ai

Kia ora tunu ai

Toku ngakau[4]

---

4. "Purify my heart, sanctify my soul, cover me."

Prestonsburg: The Fellowship of the Church of God

It is 22 degrees and I see the first snow of my two-year trip as I make my way through the mountains of eastern Kentucky. I am visiting Pastor Steve Williams and the Church of God congregation in Prestonsburg, Kentucky; a small town about twenty-five miles as-the-crow-flies from the West Virginia border. This region is known as Appalachia, an area abundant in natural resources, but which has often struggled economically. Prestonsburg has just under four thousand people, which is about one-tenth the population of my apartment complex in Hong Kong. It's big enough to a have a KFC and Taco Bell, as well as a college, but it is mainly a one-street town. This is my first time to visit a church in eastern Kentucky, although I have visited several in West Virginia; also a part of Appalachia. My mother was from Kentucky and is buried not far from here.

Even within the Church of God movement in the United States, geography has produced different cultures. Of all the states I have visited as a speaker, the one that is hands down the friendliest is West Virginia. I have attended the West Virginia Camp Meeting at Rippling Waters two different times and have numerous supporting churches in West Virginia. I am always struck by the incredible friendliness and the warmth of the people. West Virginia is very rural (its largest city has only fifty thousand people) and has traditionally been a very poor state. There are stereotypes about Appalachia, and one of them is that the people from this region are not as educated as those in an area such as New England. Yet I have found that the smartest, most engaging questions that I have ever fielded about my work come from the people of West Virginia. I can always be assured that a trip to this mountainous state will garner me many new friends.

That is why it was surprising to me to hear from a couple of pastors that it is very difficult to win the trust of people in Appalachia. "You tend to always stay an outsider," one minister told me. It was hard to reconcile that with the friendliness and openness that I had always received in this scenic area. But a closer look at the geography and history of the region revealed why trusting strangers might not come so easily to these mountaineers.

West Virginia and eastern Kentucky are very mountainous. In the case of West Virginia, the entire state is within the Appalachian mountain range. Driving across it, I often feel as if the car is either straining to go up a hill, or catching too much speed as I go down. Very mountainous places can often lead to a culture that isolates itself from the non-mountainous places beyond. This is certainly the case in South Korea, for instance, where distrust of outsiders is very striking. South Korea, where I lived for a while, is known as the Hermit Kingdom. West Virginia is known as the Mountain State, with the proudly exclusive motto, "Mountaineers are always free."

After the Civil War, Appalachia was targeted for its coal which was then used to propel the American economy through the Industrial Revolution. As often happens with land that is rich in minerals, outsiders began to descend on the state looking for profit. Surveyors would arrive, buy the mineral rights to the land, and tell the townsfolk that the land would not be used and assured them that they would not be displaced. Before long, however, the Industrial Revolution made its way to their backyards and people were given the choice to comply or be evicted from their land. Coal mining became the new industry with many West Virginia and Kentucky citizens working the dangerous mines and seeing both their money and health disappear as profits were taken outside the region. Prestonsburg's experience has been no different. Country musician Dwight Yoakam mentions Prestonsburg in his song "Readin', Rightin' Route 23" and speaks about the broken promises given to men that cough their life away as the result of their exposure to coal in mines."

Consequently, in this region it has traditionally not been wise to trust outsiders. Tight-knit communities and families became vital to survival and helped one avoid being fleeced. This helps to explain why people in Appalachia can be so good at friendliness and community, yet be distrustful of outsiders. Geography helps to shape our cultures and then Christianity must operate there.

One Church of God pastor told me about how he was referred to as "Preacher Man," as opposed to pastor, for years. "It was a hard transition to move to Appalachia from the Midwest," he said. "When you move into the coal fields, you have to be a long-term pastor. I pastored for ten years and still had one family refer to me as preacher."

At one time, this region was the center of the Church of God organizationally before it moved to Anderson, Indiana. Today, it is still the region that most reveres Church of God heritage. This is obvious to me as I pull up into the church's parking lot and park next to a white trailer with a picture of D. S. Warner on the side. Under the large picture it says "Holiness Reformer: 1842–1895." This trailer belongs to Reformation Publishers, which is keeping important Church of God books on doctrine and history alive for current and future generations.

As I make my way into the sanctuary of the small red brick church built in the 1950s and founded by Church of God pastor Moses Kitchen, the Appalachian friendliness is felt immediately. I am surrounded by seventh-grader Megan, eighth grader Traci, and fourth graders Ashly and Alex, all talking simultaneously. They are interested in the fact that I've come from China. Megan says in her Kentucky-accented English, "I recently saw that China now has the largest shopping mall in the world." She's right! It's about an hour from where I live.

Sunday school starts and Brother Larry leads us in a Bible story that explores the lineage of Jesus as described in Matthew chapter 1. Brother Larry mentions that he has pastors and bootleggers in his family lineage. I've got black ancestors and ancestors that were in the Klan." In the study, he makes a profound point. "Jesus represented all people: King David, the Levites, prostitutes, adulterers, murderers, tricksters—he cared for all people." Even the genes in his physical body demonstrate his inclusive nature. "God was in control at the very beginning," Brother Larry tells us.

The curriculum we used in Sunday school was specifically Church of God (BRIDGES) and other than the Christmas songs (it's December), the songs we sing are Church of God hymns including one by Barney E. Warren. The worship service, which includes a choir, looks exactly like the services of my youth—the style I still prefer. There are no drums and no guitar, although they've just installed a new retractable screen. There are about forty people present on this Sunday.

The sermon begins, and what follows is an unapologetic tour-de-force of Church of God doctrine, a continuation of last's week's message on Babylon as written about in Revelation 18. Brother Steve quotes the *Gospel Trumpet*; preaches against false doctrines, such as the Catholic doctrine of purgatory and the Calvinist idea of eternal security; and decries the use of tongues by Pentecostal groups—of which there are many in this part of the country. "A movement can go from a man, to a movement, to a burden that wanes, which then becomes a machine and ends up a monument," he preaches. "Jesus didn't die on Calvary to start a monument." Pastor Steve actually mentions the 1881 Carson City Resolutions,[5] discusses sanctifica-

---

5. Where D. S. Warner made his opposition against any kind of membership clear to the Indiana State Holiness Association, thus helping to set the stage for his eventual pioneering effort.

tion, quotes Barry Callen, mentions D. S. Warner, discusses the reason for the use of the name "Church of God," challenges the use of institutions in the church, says that we have "no creed but the Bible," and mentions the importance of footwashing. I have heard more Church of God doctrine and history in this one sermon than in all previous sermons combined in the last twenty years. If I am looking for a Church of God congregation that still views our message as unique and relevant, I have come to the right place and the right region. We close with "It Is Truly Wonderful," by Barney E. Warren.

After a carry-in dinner of turkey, mashed potatoes, and gravy, I follow Brother Steve to a building behind the parsonage where *The Reformation Witness* is printed. This publication is produced by the Pastor's Fellowship, a group of pastors in the Church of God that formed in 1973; the group is committed to preaching, teaching, and publishing the doctrines of the Church of God reformation movement to reach the current generation and to pass it down to future generations. As we have seen throughout this book, preserving the identity and message of a denomination or movement is difficult in the twenty-first century. In this sense, the Pastor's Fellowship is playing a very important role for the larger Church of God fellowship.

Like so many pastors in this area, Pastor Williams is bivocational and runs the community-used Williams Printing (which is also Reformation Publishers) out of this rented building, which is owned by the church. Reformation Publishers bills itself as the "world's largest selection of Church of God Literature." It is an on-demand press, printing only as many copies as are needed to prevent expensive, excess overstock. There is a large inventory room, which tries to keep at least ten copies of Church of God works available at all times, as well as rooms filled with fancy machinery, including laminating machines, stamping machines, folding machines, a book-board cutter, perforating number machine, and many others I don't understand.

Are all of these documents relics of a by-gone age? Not according to Jason and Jan Johnson, a married couple that are serving as youth pastors and choir directors. Both of their parents work for the coal mining industry. As far as they are concerned, the real treasures to be mined are found in this building.

"So many gems in here," Jason says as he surveys the various Church of God works on the shelves.

"We keep telling Steve that he's got the Ark of the Covenant in here somewhere," Jan laughs.

Jason and Jan stumbled upon the Church of God after visiting numerous churches. They were attracted to the emphasis of the Church of God away from man-made institutions. They were also disturbed by the pulpit being used for politics or hateful agendas, while ignoring the preaching of Scripture. They were not giving up hope on Christianity, but they were starting to give up hope that church could be a healthy place. Jason—who on his way to work each day drives by five "Church of God" congregations, only one of which is Church of God Anderson, Indiana—complained to friends about the churches he had been visiting. He was then introduced to our movement and its teachings by a good friend. "I saw this church for what it was," he tells me, "the spotless Bride." Jason's anger toward the church dissipated and he began to study the heritage of the Church of God. "These ideas and doctrines really started speaking to me." Twenty-seven year old Jason is wearing a black shirt and jeans. He has a shaved head, wears a thick goatee, and has earrings in both ears. He breaks the stereotype of someone who would be attracted to the Church of God pioneer's early ideas, but he is committed to our movement.

"Church of God people are breaking from the traditionalism, but they are abandoning the doctrine and the heritage as well."

"Church of God people are breaking from the traditionalism, but they are abandoning the doctrine and the heritage as well." Jason sees this as a danger. "Today's youth want truth. What does the Bible say about it? I see a lot of preaching of a self-help doctrine and here in eastern Kentucky I see a lot of the prosperity gospel. But those people come back a few years later because they need more than that."

"The early reformers were not afraid of changing an idea. The Church of God was evolving toward biblical truths. But now, I worry that we are not evolving toward biblical truths. Are we becoming a cheap rip-off of the megachurch movement? Instead of looking at spiritual growth, we are looking at numbers. I love contemporary worship because some of those aspects got me into church and got me started. But there's a lack of doctrine and you see a lot of people who say they are Christian but they don't know what that means."

Jason says that the Pastors' Fellowship meetings that he has attended have been the key to his spiritual growth. There are Reformation Rallies in fifteen places around the country and an annual conference on the first Monday and Tuesday of May each year that draws up to a thousand people. "I personally experience more growth at camp meetings than in a conference setting." But Jason's main concern is that the Church of God is not preaching its unique message.

"We've seen in eastern Kentucky that there are some who are moving toward the contemporary-style, but they are leaving the message behind," Jan interjects. So even in an area where the Church of God heritage is the strongest, there are forces pulling away from that. "We need to teach these truths to young people because there's a part of this reformation movement that we are in danger of losing if we don't teach it and hold it high." Jason believes we have come to a crossroads. "We need to ask ourselves these questions: 'What makes the Church of God important? And am I preaching what is important?' The message is no longer a uniting factor. Our uniting factor is a state office or a central office. Our heritage is not traditionalism. It's biblical truth."

Despite the fact that some churches in eastern Kentucky are moving away from this heightened emphasis on Church of God doctrine, the region remains unusually unified, and one of the reasons is Jeff Justice, whom I meet during my visit to Prestonsburg. Jeff is the East District chairman of the Church of God congregations of eastern Kentucky and visits congregations throughout the region. He receives no salary for his work. Pastor Steve and Jeff started six regional rallies throughout the year which bring over twenty congregations together for one service. This was a grassroots effort to build connectivity and communication between Church of God congregations in the region in the hopes that this would particularly inspire the young generation. There is a youth convention, an e-newsletter, and a ministers' retreat which are building up unity. "We try to preach and practice the doctrine of unity," Jeff tells me. "Out of the sixty-nine churches, 82 percent have bivocational pastors, so there is a lack of communication because of work. So we have our rallies on Sunday nights and we've had 90 percent participation. It's a different culture when you deal with people who work forty-hour-plus jobs; they need time to spend with their families and then for ministry. The majority of our churches are under one hundred people."

I ask Jeff how this region has managed to keep such a unified sense. "The original doctrines have been preached and preserved in this region, and passed on to the next generation."

"This is grassroots. We've watched congregations that had not had fellowship for a hundred years come together. We've watched pastors who have been offended by other pastors for one reason or another now reconcile. It is a great point of unity for all of our congregations."

A few minutes later I am talking with Pastor Steve about the efforts of Pastors' Fellowship to keep the movement's ideas at the forefront, particularly through the *Reformation Witness* periodical, which goes to seven thousand people and relies on donations. "We are a renewal movement. Every movement has got the pendulum working in both directions. Most every group has a conservative group and a more liberal group. Pastors' Fellowship is the conservative group, but everything is relative. You could go to the no neck-tie Church of God people, the restoration movement, which has more of an Amish flavor."[6]

So Pastors' Fellowship stands as a sort of bulwark against the abandonment of some very important Church of God beliefs. "We want to retain what brought us into existence" Steve says. Pastors' Fellowship has at times been misunderstood by the greater movement, which, perhaps, view it as too concerned with past traditions and aims to divide the church.

Steve continues, "In the beginning they thought it was just a political attempt in the Church of God to take control of the General Assembly. When I went to Anderson College, we started a group called Reformation Emphasis Fellowship that was a conservative student group in 1982. Robert Reardon, the president at the time, was convinced that Pastor's Fellowship had talked us into this to extend their political mission in the Church of God. We told him, 'We just love the preaching, and we can't find a church where we are hearing that, so we want to have a conservative student fellowship.' We got the blessing and that's how my relationship with President Reardon began, and Prestonsburg was one of the last places he preached before he passed away."

Brother Steve applauds the current general director of Church of God Ministries, Ron Duncan, for his efforts to reach out to the various groups

---

6. There are other groups that trace their heritage back to D. S. Warner, based in places like Guthrie, Oklahoma; Newark, Ohio; Hagerstown, Maryland; and Kansas City, Missouri.

in the Church of God. "Ron is so open to the diversity that we have in the church. He always answers my e-mails."

This renewal group within the Church of God has spread far and wide, but the majority of the people who support it come from this particular part of the United States "In the Church of God, this area tends to be conservative. Kentucky, West Virginia, Ohio, Tennessee—the Appalachian area—we are very similar as a people," Pastor Steve tells me as he reflects.

It seems Appalachia is a region that has people who are willing to take a stand, even when others choose to stay silent. Southern culture is a protest culture, a culture of tradition and community, and a culture that will mobilize for strongly held beliefs. Pastors' Fellowship seems to have this cultural strain, and Pastor Steve agrees. But this protest culture (which the early pioneers certainly were infused with) does not aim to bring division but unity.

"We are losing our connection with a common mission. We've lost the hymnals; we've lost *Vital Christianity*; a lot of people don't go to camp meetings. We are isolated islands."

Pastors' Fellowship is proactively dealing with a number of strategic issues that challenge the movement: the need for connection, the need for unity, and the transmission of Church of God theology. The meetings, the support of a publication, the grassroots networking, and the preaching, perhaps most of all, help to rebuild those pillars that a movement must retain if it is to keep its identity.

Not every group of people in the Church of God would agree with the Pastors' Fellowship about every issue of doctrine. However, there may be far more points of unity than we might think. Don Neece, who serves as the editor in chief of *Reformation Witness* and pastors in Dublin, Virginia, was part of an effort to bring racial unity in the Church of God in that state. The Church of God in Virginia had two different assemblies: the African-American Virginia Association of the Church of God and the Virginia Assembly of the Church of God (Anglo). The two operated with little interaction.

In a conversation with Pastor Don, he discussed their efforts to live out the doctrine of unity: "We started by praying together as credential committees. We found that we were on the same page doctrinally and that we were both facing the same issues: 'how do we do credentials, how do we raise up leaders?' We started talking about doctrine issues and saw that we have far more in common than we thought." The two organizations became one, and the first chair was an African-American leader. "We took the emphasis from properties and boundaries and put it on our theology." Women in ministry and racial unity re-emerged as core pillars of belief. "I've seen what can happen when we get together on our theology. God has not released us from preaching that message of unity in the kingdom."

Pastors' Fellowship feels called to remind us, rightly I believe, that there is still a role for our message of holiness and unity. Driving down the highway through the mountains of Appalachia, I notice that the snow has begun to melt.

Lebanon: Real Counterterrorism

Nowhere is the impact of geography and land more obvious than in the Middle East. From Genesis to Revelation, land is an important character in the great act of redemption chronicled in the Bible. Associating geography with particular tribes, religions, and moments in history is par for the course in the Middle East and nowhere more-so than in "the Holy Lands." Even the location of "the Holy Lands" can be interpreted differently. Western Christians assume that we are always referring to those geographic locations located within the borders of modern day Israel. But modern-day Israel's borders were first established in 1948, and many of the events chronicled in the Bible occur in a geographic area wider than those borders.

For instance, I am currently standing in the Bekaa Valley, Lebanon, which is mentioned in the Bible (Numbers 13:23–24) and is thus part of the Holy Lands. In the Bible, this part of the land of Canaan goes by an older name, "Eschol." Jesus' parables about fig trees and vineyards take on a richer meaning in this part of the world, where traditions, customs, and geography depicted in the Bible still exist. This is the agricultural heartland of the country of Lebanon—a country so small that it's a two-hour drive from the capital city of Beirut on modest, slow-going roads to the northern, southern, and eastern borders. Beirut is a beautiful, cosmopolitan city on the Mediterranean filled with swank cafés, American chain restaurants, and cosmetically altered, glamorous-looking people. But in the Bekaa, life is much closer to centuries past.

I am standing by a road in the Bekaa meeting with a former member of Al-Qaeda who is now a Christian. It's a beautiful cloudless day with a perfect temperature as we meet up with two new Muslim converts, "Peter" and "Jonathan."

Peter is from Syria and his parents are fanatical Muslims who forced him to study the Koran. He refused to obey his parents and lived a life of debauchery. As his life was spiraling out of control, he started to feel suicidal. Peter was then confronted by members of Al-Qaeda who told him that he was on the road to hell. They encouraged Peter to join them, study the Koran, and become a suicide bomber so that he could go to paradise. For one year, he studied with them and planned to do a suicide mission in Iraq that would kill American soldiers and Iraqi soldiers.

One day, Peter heard a Christian pastor based in the Bekaa Valley who had a show on the radio. The pastor invited people to learn about Jesus Christ and receive a copy of the Bible. Peter listened intently and went on a journey to find a pastor. The radio speaker introduced Peter to "Joseph," a Church of God pastor in Lebanon. It has been two years since Joseph began teaching Peter about Christ, and Peter is now an excited Christian. Peter began sharing about his conversion from prospective suicide bomber to follower of Christ, and now other Muslims in Bekaa have converted as well. Today he works somewhere in the valley for a Christian boss.

Although Lebanon is technically a sovereign state, parts of the country are under the control of the terrorist group Hezbollah. In this area where I am currently, Hezbollah has control, and Al-Qaeda's presence can be felt as well. We are just a stone's throw away from the Syrian border. In this region, Christians doing evangelism face great danger, as they do in India, China, and many other locations around the world. In some geographical locations of the world such as Orissa, India, or Qom, Iran, it is no small decision to accept Christ. And even though some Christians might raise their eyebrows at the fact that Peter still smokes and Jonathan, another recent convert, has two wives, down from four (what does the Bible say about a person who becomes a Christian who already has multiple wives?), Peter and Jonathan are taking risks for Christ that few of us will ever be called to do. Peter and Jonathan don't know anything about Martin Luther or D. S. Warner, or how to speak "evangelicalese," but they know Christ has changed their lives, and they are willing to risk their lives to share the good news with others.

Church of God pastor Joseph takes those risks as well. In one of Joseph's congregations, there are about ten people from Al-Qaeda and Hezbollah in the congregation. There are also rival families. Ancient family feuds that make the Hatfields and McCoys of Appalachia look like Tom and Jerry still exist in this part of the world. Despite those kinds of ancient divisions, Pastor Joseph is seeing feuding families, former terrorists, and pious Muslims accepting Christ and joining his church. Pastor Joseph has even struck up a relationship with a local imam (Islamic religious leader).

In various areas throughout the Bekaa, Pastor Joseph is seeing great success in winning Muslims to Christ. He has a big vision to expand his ministries in this part of Lebanon, a large valley that has been significantly underevangelized. But the more success this Church of God pastor has, the greater the chance that he could lose his life. A Church of God located here is not in the position to do many of the things that foster denominational identity (e.g., conferences, publications, discourses on theology), but the Church of God is expanding in the unlikeliest of places.

While most of us turn on the news to hear stories of suicide bombers, troop surges, and war, the story that we are missing is that God is at work in the Middle East—even within our own movement.

We always tend to watch the news of the world through the eyes of our own nationality first. But perhaps it is time to look at the world as citizens of the kingdom of God. The next time we watch images of a suicide bombing on the nightly newscast, perhaps we could stop and pray for the Church of God. Why? Because amid the carnage and chaos of the tensions that perpetually grip the Middle East, our Church of God family is growing.

It's dangerous for Peter, Joseph, and Jonathan. Standing by the side of the road for our quick, secret rendezvous, I am prepared for just a handshake, but Peter, the would-be-Al-Qaeda suicide-bomber, extends both arms and gives me a big hug. I marvel at this miracle. Instead of killing the American, he is hugging his brother in Christ. Counterterrorism indeed!

Pennsylvania: Resident Aliens

Once again, I am in a clandestine meeting. Instead of a highway in the Middle East, I am in a Denny's-like diner in Pennsylvania run by Mexicans. Everyone is speaking Spanish in here, including Pastor Jorge and Pastor "Luis." Pastor Luis is not a legal resident of the United States. He comes from Central America and joins the 11.2 million immigrants living illegally in the United States.[7] As in other places in the world, such as Germany, Saudi Arabia, and South Korea, the vast majority of immigrants and migrant workers

---

7. This number is now in decline due to the recession. The development of the Mexican economy is reducing these numbers as well (Emily Bazar, "Study: Illegal Residents Decline," *USA Today*, July 30, 2008. http://www.usatoday.com/news/nation/2008-07-30-immigration_N.htm

do difficult, menial jobs that the locals no longer want to do. Globalization has ushered in a new wave of migration around the world, even in unlikely places. In fact, the country with the largest immigrant population is not the United States but Russia. The influx of foreigners can create tensions.

In any country where there are illegal aliens, a debate arises about whether the immigrants serve a healthy boost to the economy or whether they threaten locals' job opportunities. The life of an illegal immigrant in most countries is tough. They are often involved in back-breaking labor for wages that are very low. The work hours are long and the living conditions are often very unpleasant. There is the constant fear of being caught and the pressure of supporting dependents and extended family back in the home country. There is also a considerable amount of homesickness. All of these pressures can come together to make immigrant communities places of great pain and dislocation. But immigrants are people with souls too, and so amid the trials and tribulations of living a life of sweat and tears, comes the search for the One who can fill the soul: Jesus Christ.

Pastor Jorge and Pastor Luis are pastors in this area of eastern Pennsylvania. There are five Latino Church of God congregations in the immediate area, made up mostly of Mexicans and Guatemalans. Eighty-percent of the congregants are illegal aliens. These churches are part of the Hispanic Council of the Church of God (*Concilio*), which aims to plant new churches that reach first-generation Spanish-speaking individuals as well as bilinguals who still feel more comfortable in churches with the Spanish language and culture. The Concilio also runs a Hispanic Bible Institute that trains leaders, prepares them for the credentialing process, and teaches Church of God theology and doctrine. The Concilio also maintains fellowship among the Spanish churches as well as with the larger church through Anderson.

Pastor Jorge, who is a United States citizen but is originally from El Salvador, moved to this area in 2001 and took over a church that had fifteen people. They visited apartments in the area sharing Christ and inviting people to church and soon the church grew because there were so many Latinos in need. Today there are two hundred in the church. Pastor Jorge began producing leaders, and Luis became a pastor and eventually started his own church despite not being in the country legally.

"When people don't have documents, they seek God. That same thirst for a better economic life makes them seek a better life in the Lord," Pastor Jorge tells me. Most of the people in their churches work long hours, often having to drive an hour or more to their difficult jobs in construction or in the agricultural fields. "I have people who have to drive to New York each day," he tells me. In the wintertime, the work decreases and there is little money for food and rent. Conflicts can arise in the community.

"We get emergency calls to help people in conflict. Right now we have a woman in our house who was physically abused. She went to the church and felt protected by the church. She's staying at Pastor Jorge's house at the moment," Pastor Luis tells me.

This particular part of Pennsylvania has a high population of Spanish-speaking people from the U.S. territory of Puerto Rico who are here legally. They have been able to integrate well, but the Church of God congregations here are mostly reaching out to migrant workers, many of which never intended to stay long-term. Pastor Luis is one such case: "I came to work, pay off my debts, and I thought that as soon as I did that I would go back. But what happened is that I got called by God and when God calls you, you can't run."

Like many Concilio pastors, Luis is a product of a lot of in-house training. Many of these Hispanic churches fit into the Book of Acts world that I described in chapter 4. The people are theologically conservative and produce leadership from within. They are often ineligible to receive formal institutional training from a seminary in the United States. Instead they are mentored by their pastors and soon begin doing evangelism and planting new churches. The Concilio, which was originally centered in California, Arizona, Texas and Florida, has seen dramatic growth in the past ten years with more than one hundred churches now in the fellowship. The goal is to have at least one church in every state. Thus far, Concilio churches are in thirty states.

The level of commitment is high, Luis shares. "We tell people about opportunities for ministry and that they need to have call. We have people who were once shy and afraid to go to the altar who can now preach. If we tell them that we need to pray at 4:00 AM, they will arrive at the church at 4:00 AM. It's not about fame and fortune. You suffer, you have to leave comfort, and you don't depend on work, but on what God gives you." When the hard-working, risk-taking ethos of the immigrant gets channeled into the church, it produces dynamic Christian communities.

With the dynamism come administrative realities, such as dealing with finances. "We have a finance committee that administers and signs checks with the pastor, and there are more people involved to ensure accountability, Pastor Jorge tells me. "In Latin American countries, there is a problem with financial accountability."

Complications also begin to arise when the children of immigrant parents become acculturated more quickly than the parents. "The kids are the ones who learn English because they were raised here. So we start to have youth who don't think of Spanish as their primary language. That means we have to have bilingual teachers in Sunday school, which is not easy, Luis explains. "I did a baptism class yesterday and there was a girl who understood English perfectly but couldn't speak Spanish. So we had to explain the details to her in English. Kids like her would probably feel better in an Anglo church. We try and encourage the parents to help the kids retain their Spanish."

"Jesus never asked for a green card."

It is also difficult for the undocumented teenagers when their peers in school start to drive and go to college. They came to the United States because of their parents, but are now in a country that they love and understand, but which has not yet made them legal residents.

Living and integrating in a country illegally leads to a lot of complications for the families and pastors. The biggest question that lingers is, What are we to make of pastors in the Church of God who are illegal aliens?

I posed this question to Jim Johnman. Johnman, who is the Hispanic Promoter of the Church of God and Director of New Works and Evangelism in the Concilio, had an answer for me because it is a question he has been asked a lot.

"Many of the new churches are comprised of illegal immigrants. Our primary emphasis, though, is to reach the lost for Christ. Jesus said, 'Whosoever will, let him take the water of life freely.' Jesus never asked for a green card."

That being said, the Concilio does not ordain illegal immigrants. But they will do whatever it takes to get the paperwork for the pastors. Handling the immigration process is Johnman's job. "We submit two hundred or three hundred pages of documents to the government for our pastors. So far we have not lost a case," he reports.

In actuality, the U.S. government has responded positively because these illegals are working hard; they are starting churches and going into ministry. These are the kind of citizens that we want in the country and in the kingdom. The illegal aliens have been turned into "Resident Aliens,"to use a phrase coined by Stanley Hauerwas and William Willamon signifying Christians being a community set apart in a fallen world."

Pastor Jorge's church, like many immigrant churches, does not have a building. A local Episcopalian church has opened up their building to this Concilio church. Quite often, these are churches that have seen their numbers decline steeply and are now opening up their buildings to make ends meet. These older Anglo churches steeped in the traditional world take notice of these new dynamic Christian communities. "Most are older, adult churches," Pastor Jorge says. "They don't have young people and kids. They ask us, 'Why do you Latinos have so many children?' They notice that we get married young and have children at a young age. These churches are sad that they are in such steep decline."The Episcopal church that shares the building with Jorge lost thirty people in one year and is now down to a total of ninety."Most of them are fifty-five and over. One gentleman said to me that our Spanish church looked like his did fifty years ago."

While Christianity in the Anglo community is in decline, particularly among the traditional world, immigrants are bringing in fresh dynamism and rapid growth in a Book of Acts style. It would be ironic if those within the traditional church became hostile toward immigrants when it is these very immigrants who not only propagate the values and theology of the traditional world but live out the Book of Acts in their churches.

Cyberspace: The Church of God Is Only a Click Away

If geography can play such a huge part in challenging our unity, then we should be grateful for the recent microchip revolution which has made this world interconnected through our computers. With fewer books written on the movement, lower attendance at camp meetings, and no World Conference, it's easy to get the impression that important issues regarding the future of the movement are not being discussed. There is a place, however, where dialogues continue to take place daily: cyberspace.

I visit the Web site of Lloyd Moritz, who is the executive director for the Pacific Northwest Association, which encompasses most of Washington, northern Idaho, and northeastern Oregon.[8] He hails originally from Canada, but today you can find him anywhere that you have access to a computer. He is the creator of a Web site called CHOG Blog.

Pastor Lloyd has a technical background, having been a bivocational church planter. He was a computer network analyst at the time, and this has given him an understanding of technology and its potential. CHOG Blog is a site where Pastor Lloyd writes about issues related to the theology and mission of the Church of God. As I peruse the Web site while I write this, he currently has a post about his trip to the Annual Western Area Regional Ministerium in Arizona, another one on the need for dialogue in the Church of God, and one appropriately on the role that geography has on our identity.

From my home in Hong Kong, I click on a button and use Skype to connect to Lloyd in Yakima, Washington. If only the plane flights were this quick! I asked him about his reasons for starting this blog.

"Part of my motivation has been to contribute to ongoing discussion within the Church of God. I think we are at a place in our history where we are trying to discover our identity. We know who we are from the past, but we don't know who we are today. We are no longer just a Midwestern phenomenon." Lloyd comes in crystal clear on my computer monitor in more ways then one.

A blog, like the one Lloyd has, is a Web site created by an individual that allows them to put up regular commentary about their lives or things that they find interesting. They are often great forums for discussion. I have had one for the past seven years.

"A lot of people don't know what to do with blogs. For many people they are a strange entity. Most people don't know how to use them effectively. I'm one of those early adopters when it comes to technology. I have been watching and following blogs for a long time. "

I had assumed that this kind of interaction over the computer is a pretty recent thing, but Lloyd tells me that this kind of communication has been going on for years in the Church of God.

Here is an online forum that has evolved and changed names and has been going on at least sixteen years. This was back even before the Internet was hot. There was a group of pastors connected to Ecunet through Compuserve before the public Internet and we were connected. Today it's called Chogtalk, and it is a Yahoo group. You can only get on by having one

---

8. CHOG Blog can be found at http://chogblog.blogspot.com/.

of the facilitators let you on. Sometimes the discussions get pretty heated and they have to pull the plug for a few weeks to cool things down. This type of a setting has generated a lot of discussion.

Lloyd's preference is for blogging, however.

"Blogging offers a new way of doing it. Instead of having a free-for-all discussion, it allows someone to set up a place where they can blog and state positions and state views, and there's a place for comments and interaction. But the real value is not your own blog and the comments that happen but the network of blogs that develop. You follow other people who are blogging, and it becomes a ring of blogs that are going in the same direction. It's unwieldy and modern, but I saw it as a way that I could be one voice among many others and to keep the conversation going in some way."

As I look at his Web site, I see that CHOG Blog is linked to many other Web sites, including those of other pastors. It is also linked to the Church of God Ministries official Web site.[9] This inter-connectivity can only be a good thing. Pastor Lloyd understands how difficult unity can be when geography and the different cultures it produces are taken into account. He originally comes from Canada, and that alone has given him a different perspective about the Church of God and helps him see cultural blind spots that the American church possesses.

"We have to move out of our narrow views, and it has to start within our own diversity in the country here. Our district is one of the most diverse. We have Hispanic, Native American churches, ultra-urban Seattle churches, rural churches in eastern Washington and northern Idaho, so it all goes back to dealing with diversity. It's all part of the role for those of us in leadership at the district or national level—to draw us together despite that diversity and to celebrate that diversity and to see that it's part of God's vision for the kingdom and for the church.

"We are great proponents of unity in the Church of God. As I see it, the unity of the church is not going to happen organizationally or even through events, and this has caused a lot of frustration in the church. Because of globalization, and the communication that surrounds this, we are having trouble knowing what to do with all this diversity. In the past, we have taken these events like Anderson Camp Meeting as rallying points where we can come and celebrate; we've been a relational movement from the beginning, and that's how we have expressed our unity, rather than through doctrine

---

9. http://www.chog.org

and institutions. Now people are not wanting to connect at those types of relational events. The relational connectivity is not there. We believe in Christian unity and we believe that the church needs to be drawn together, but it's going to be difficult to express our unity in real ways. We are having a hard time finding practical ways to express that."

So is the answer simply a stronger central organization, or large events, or theological statements?

"Unity is not going to come through formal structures. We have to unite around our mission and we have been very weak in this area. Having a mis-sional driven unity is, I think, the way that we will need to go if we are to work together, if we can get past the worship wars and cultural differences and see that God is working in different styles and through our mission, if we could see that it is through our common mission that we can find our unity. Because unity is one of our core distinctives and we have got to come to terms with that. We have an opportunity to experience that and express that within the larger Christian community."

So can cyberspace help us as we communicate, do mission, and re-discover our identity? Lloyd certainly thinks so, but he cautions against using the Internet with the expectation that it can somehow centralize the movement.

"I think the potential of computers in general, and the Internet specifi-cally, is allowing everyone to participate. There's a certain level of democ-ratization in the Internet and you want to encourage that in the best way possible. I see the potential of how technology can be harnessed to com-municate and do all these wonderful things. But if we approach it from a modern mindset that says 'we have to centralize things,' we need to realize that people on the Internet do not function on the Internet in an orderly fashion. The future is going to be that of networking and that is going to be at a whole range of different levels; through e-mails, social networking, twitter, and blogs. All this stuff may be very un-orderly and may seem cha-otic at times but it is drawing people together. We need to encourage that to happen and facilitate it, but as soon as we try to rein it in and put a fence around it, I think we kill it. The secret is to encourage it, but not stifle it."

Lloyd's point is well-taken. The Internet with its diversity and decen-tralized system is a reflection of our global, interconnected world. It is this world that denominations and movements have to navigate in breaching challenges such as geographic and cultural unity. Trying to bring unity in the twenty-first century does not necessarily mean homogeny. It is paradoxical, but the freedom to be ourselves in our own creative ways can strengthen the overall movement. The Internet is a great example since its decentralized nature has made it appealing and greatly expanded its influence.

Like the Internet, the Church of God over the years has created a broad, decentralized network that allows people all over the world to be the church in a variety of ways. Diversity and decentralization have been part of our appeal and our success. But unlike the Internet, we are a Christian movement with the purpose to expand the Christian kingdom in holiness and unity. If mission, diversity, and decentralization are keys to regenerating our movement, what is the glue (the broadband?) that holds us together? We must break the geographic barriers and tackle the issues together.

what language do we speak?

The Multicultural Challenge
Albuquerque, Corpus Christi, London, Paris, Torrance, El Cajon

The history of race relations in the Church of God is mixed. On one hand, we can be proud of the fact that long before the Civil Rights Act of the 1960s, the Church of God was multicultural, consisting of Germans, Greeks, Scandinavians, Slavic people, African Americans, Latinos, and many others. Early yearbooks included the languages spoken by pastors, and Church of God pioneers took the message of unity seriously and refused to segregate blacks from whites during services. Despite the fact that today many Church of God congregations are located in rural areas, the early pioneers established churches and missionary homes in large multicultural urban centers such as Chicago, New York, St. Louis, and Pittsburgh, the latter of which was led by African American R. J. Smith.[1] And very early on, there was an effort to transmit the message of holiness and unity internationally.

But sadly, after a promising start, racial tensions—particularly between Caucasians and African Americans—began to increase. Pastors were registered by color and African Americans were made to feel unwelcome in a variety of ways. This included pressure to have African Americans worship separately from whites at Anderson Camp Meeting. According to historian

---

1. Merle Strege reports that R. J. Smith was shot at after one particularly challenging sermon in the South (*Tell Me the Tale* [Anderson, IN: Warner Press, 1991], 69–72).

John W. V. Smith, by 1915 numerous congregations had split over the issue of race.[2] By 1917, a campground was established in West Middlesex, Pennsylvania, that was indisputably open to interracial worship. Out of that, the National Association of the Church of God was established by African Americans, and parallel organizations emerged in the Church of God even though a separate new black movement never arose.

Nearly one hundred years later, a more complicated picture is emerging. While predominantly white congregations and predominantly black congregations in the Church of God in America remain mostly distant, the racial landscape around both groups is changing at a dramatic speed. Both white and black congregations are finding themselves in neighborhoods that are increasingly becoming more interracial and multicultural. Bicultural marriages and newly emerging ethnic groups, as well as a youth culture accustomed to diversity, are rendering the old black–white divide less potent.

Furthermore, as with so many other denominations originating in Europe and North America, the fastest growing segment of the Church of God today involves people of color in Asia, Africa, and Latin America. Whites are not only becoming a minority within denominations but within Christianity as a whole. While many of us (even outside of the West) still tend to think of the Church of God as a primarily white movement, the reality is that today the Church of God is a multiracial movement because so many people around the world are accepting Christ. Nobody I know has a problem with that. Quite the contrary, the movement is filled with churches investing people and resources into non-Western and non-white ministries.

Racism and prejudice do exist in the Church of God, as they do in all societies, and that should not be tolerated. But this is not just an American phenomenon. In fact, within the global context, the racial prejudice in America of Anglos against Latinos and African Americans is far less of a problem than it is in a great number of regions in the world that I have visited. I say this as someone with dark skin who has traveled to more than sixty countries on six continents. On a scale of one to ten, with ten being the worst, I would give America a four as far as its racism is concerned. I have been in countries that I would give a ten, and the difference is that in those countries, racism and prejudice are perfectly acceptable culturally-speaking. Racism is the unchallenged norm. The United States appears to

---

2. John W. V. Smith, *A Brief History of the Church of God Reformation Movement* (Anderson, IN: Warner Press, 2006), 122.

have a terrible race problem primarily because we talk about it all the time. It is also because there is an underlying Judeo-Christian cultural assumption that racism is wrong. Martin Luther King appealed to that Judeo-Christian worldview in his prophetic calls for equality and justice. His words, rooted as they were in Scripture, haunt our racial tendencies. There are Church of God congregations in regions of the world where racism and prejudice is *encouraged* within their cultural worldview. There have never been any Martin Luther Kings speaking in those cultures. Believing in racial or tribal superiority is simply the way it is and has been for centuries in some of these nations.

There are Church of God congregations that are in countries that have endured thousands of years of foreign invasions for example, so prejudice and distrust of foreigners is deeply engrained in the culture. There are also Church of God congregations in countries where the population is so homogenous that racial purity is held up as nonnegotiable despite the racist, non-Christian implications, and there are Church of God congregations where everyone is from the same civilization background and has brown skin but those with dark brown skin instead of lighter brown skin are considered inferior. In other places, people may share the same brown skin, but because some of the people have indigenous blood and darker skin instead of mestizo blood and lighter brown skin, they are viewed as inferior. Racism and prejudice have plagued the country where the Church of God reformation movement began, but some of the largest struggles against racism and prejudice occur beyond the shores of America. Hopefully, Church of God believers in all nations break out of those worldviews, but we can be assured that all do not.

My first encounter with racism was at the age of twenty at a Church of God school. Prior to that, I had never been treated differently by anyone because of the color of my skin. Yet I was studying with Christian young people who felt I was not equal. The racial comments stung, and once it happens it leaves a mark, despite your best efforts. I soon found myself wondering at job interviews or when meeting people for the first time if they were thinking about my skin color. I was never ashamed of my Latin heritage, and I did not begin to assume everyone was maliciously racist, but I marveled at how quickly I began to be conscious of the fact that the color of my skin might be an issue. I've always viewed racism as the result of ignorance and of a lack of experience with the cultural diversity of the world, but it does hurt when it happens.

Despite the racism I encountered at a Church of God school, I have been amazed at the lack of prejudice I have experienced in Church of God congregations throughout the United States. My wife and I are a biracial couple with an ethnically mixed child, and yet we have been deeply loved and supported as missionaries in every part of the country. From the "hollers" of West Virginia to the coastal towns of Washington, we have been made to feel at home. I believe that for the vast majority of Church of God people, racial unity is understood to be nonnegotiable.

In fact, it was not until I was halfway into writing this book that I realized I have spent my life in four ethnically different Church of God congregations (one Latin, one African American, one middle-class white, and one Chinese). How wonderful that I never noticed and that it was never pointed out to me!

What I have seen in the Church of God (and other denominations and organizations) is that people of different races often have different church cultures. Some cultures prefer long services with very long sermons. Others demand a high level of commitment daily and encourage "groupthink" or you are viewed as lukewarm. Other cultures think it is fine for people and children to be talking and running around during the pastor's sermon. Some cultures want a sixty-minute service that ends right on time, while others expect the worship to be open, fluid, and perhaps filled with dancing. From India to China, El Salvador to inner-city DC, to central Kansas, we have different preferences for structuring our churches, organizations, and worship—and we have very different expectations. It is doubtful many African Americans would want to structure their church as the Koreans do. Or that whites from the Midwest would not find some of the services in Central America very distracting. And a mission team from Germany may operate very differently than one from West Africa. Consequently, working together can be challenging. In my career as a missionary, I have brought people from different countries and cultures together to embark on particular projects. Yet I always say, "a mission team of Germans, West Africans, Americans, and Koreans would be a catastrophe." I say it tongue in cheek, but not entirely. Cultural differences are real, and Christianity does not entirely erase them.

If there is one thing I have learned in my travels, it is that culture runs deep. It is very difficult for anyone to leave behind the worldview in which they were brought up. Jesus transcended all cultures with his "good news," yet he was deeply rooted in Jewish culture. The paradox for us as Christians is that we are called to universal love yet are bound to local places and cultures in this lifetime.

Fortunately, more and more of us are learning to leave our comfort zones. Globalization is bringing the world to our doorsteps, whether we live in China or Iowa, and it is pressing us to learn to relate to different cultures. I spoke at a Church of God camp meeting to an overwhelmingly white audience recently and mentioned to them that more and more the world is coming to the neighborhood where our Church of God congregations are located. An elderly white gentleman came up to me afterward and said, "It's not just to our neighborhoods. My *family* now has people from all over the world in it!" It was music to my ears. More and more Anglo Americans have families with biracial marriages or adopted children from Asia or Eastern Europe. Today, Latinos, not African Americans, are the primary minority in the United States. In fact, America will soon be a majority minority nation, meaning that more than 50 percent of the country will be non-white, but no one group (African American, Latino, Asian) will have a clear majority.[3]

> It is very difficult for anyone to leave behind the worldview in which they were brought up.

The Road Map

In this chapter we will go to Albuquerque to hear about Richard Mansfield's experience as a Latino pastor in the Church of God. Pastors like Mansfield, Gilbert Davila, and Luz Gonzales paved the way for guys like me. But with Richard Mansfield we will also see a pastor who takes risks to engage his community wherever they are. Risk-taking is something we too often shy away from in the Church of God. We will then visit a predominantly black church, not in the United States, but in London, England. Then we will cross the English Channel to visit the Church of God in Paris. Both of these churches are ethnic churches in multiethnic, global cities that epitomize

3. Sheryl McCarthy, "The Nation's Changing Complexion," *USA Today*, October 15, 2008. http://www.usatoday.com/printedition/news/20081015/opledewednesday.art.htm

the new global landscape. In Los Angeles, we will meet a truly multiethnic church staff wrestling with issues not just of race, but of class. And we will end with the surprising story of a female pastor ministering in a foreign culture traditionally hostile toward women in ministry.

The New Multicultural Challenge

In 1892, when Benjamin Elliott and his son sailed to Ensenada, Mexico, after having received a pamphlet from D. S. Warner, none of them could have imagined that a century later the Church of God would be still spreading its message with much of the most dynamic evangelism occurring outside of the United States in languages other than English. By 1990, a century later, there were more Church of God people and congregations outside of North America than within.

Traditionally, when we have thought about the multicultural challenge in the Church of God, we have thought about the often tense relationship between African Americans and Anglos in the Church of God. But today the multicultural challenge is much more complicated than this. It is also about churches that were once established in a primarily white or black area dealing with the fact that their communities are now filled with Vietnamese, or Arabs, or Russians. Then there is the reality that every church must now be global and thanks to the ease of travel and communications can engage in global ministry on a scale not possible before. Then there is the issue of people in churches constantly moving, now that we are more prone to relocating frequently. Another consideration is that even in a white church in a white neighborhood, the church may find that the "Christian" culture is being replaced by a postmodern culture that knows nothing about Christianity or a Book of Acts culture that wears its spirituality on its sleeve. So the multicultural challenge is no longer simply about race; it's about migration, immigration, secularism, and globalization.

Trying to preserve a particular "Church of God identity" in the midst of such challenges is not easy. The challenges of a new, mobile, global world are redefining the multicultural challenges in the Church of God. While I was writing this book, Barack Obama was elected president of the United States. While racism and prejudice remain, there is a sense that the ball has been moved forward as far as race is concerned. In my own experience traveling around the Church of God, I see that race has become less of an issue particularly for the younger generations. But I have come along at a good time, and there are others who have had to struggle far more than I have in my time. I visited one such person in the American Southwest.

Albuquerque: The Desert Father

The city of Albuquerque sits at five thousand feet on the Southwest desert floor with the beautiful Sandia Mountains providing a stunning backdrop. Albuquerque is a tough town. It is New Mexico's largest city, with a population of five hundred thousand, and it sits at the intersection of the state's two freeways I-20 and I-45. The Rio Grande snakes its way around the city, as does the famous Route 66. In addition to being the commercial center of the state, it is also a center for drug trafficking. There is a considerable amount of crime and poverty in the city. But it is also a fast-growing city, filling up with young, urban professionals. Up to 44 percent of the citizens are Hispanic, while Caucasians, African Americans, Asians, and Native Americans make up the rest of the mix.

The rough nature of the city can easily mask the fact that the city and the state is actually quite spiritual. Founded more than three hundred years ago as part of the Spanish empire in New Spain, the Catholic church downtown has had services since 1706. The conquistadores allowed the Indians (mostly Navaho and Pueblo) to keep some of their religious traditional *kivas*, and sweatboxes, but they built their altar over the kivas. In addition to the Roman Catholic and Native American spirituality that shaped this land, the state has also become a bastion of new age spirituality.

Amid this challenging environment is the New Beginnings Church pastored by Richard Mansfield, a first generation Mexican-American who has become a beloved speaker in the Church of God and an inspiration to Latino pastors—myself included. Mansfield is known for his engaging sermons and self-depreciating sense of humor, which is pretty unforgettable. He exudes a love of life and a love for the Lord.

His great passion is for the lost. A lot of pastors say that, but Richard Mansfield walks the talk. One of his congregations was shot at three times, his family has been robbed, there have been five drive-by shootings near his house, and he has collected three guns from people who planned to kill him but accepted Christ instead.

No one could have imagined that Richard Mansfield would become a well-known preacher in the Church of God. He was born a Catholic in El Paso, Texas, graduated with a business degree from the University of Texas

(El Paso) by the age of nineteen and soon found himself in the life insurance business. He was introduced to Christ by Pentecostals but found their worship too overwhelming given his Roman Catholic background. Eventually, he met someone from Pastor Gilbert Davila's church and was sold on the Church of God after hearing a bilingual prayer for the offering in the worship service. Richard Mansfield had found a home.

It was in the late 1970s that the Jim Jones cult tragedy occurred in Guyana and was making news around the world. This unsettled Mansfield, so before even possessing a Bible, he enrolled in Bible college to find out what he had gotten himself into. Pastor Davila and eight other brothers from the church joined Mansfield in his Bible class. After that Pastor Davila led the men from the Iglesia de Dios in a time of processing everything they had learned. A month later, Mansfield was visiting jails as part of the church's prison ministry. It was during the prison meetings that Mansfield began to realize how he had just narrowly avoided a life of emptiness and sin, having previously struggled with alcoholism.

It was also in the prison that Mansfield spoke for the first time. His first sermon as a young Christian was less than spectacular as far as technique and form were concerned. The text was from 1 John and dealt with sin being lawlessness. It went something like this: "Sin is sin. Sin is sin. Sin is sin. When you don't obey the law, it's sin! When you don't do what's right, it is sin! Sin is sin. It's sin! You've sinned; I've sinned; we've all sinned! Sin is sin!" Twenty people were saved.

Today, his preaching gifts have improved considerably, and it is a well-established fact that he has touched many lives. Somewhere in a village in Africa, an African found Mansfield's sermons online, and now there is a group of two hundred people who huddle around a computer listening to Richard preach. A church without a pastor in New Mexico began to listen to his sermons and grow. People pass CDs of his sermons around Albuquerque and people get saved. Kids load his sermons on their iPods. His preaching has been featured on radio and on the Trinity Broadcast Network. And there are soldiers in Iraq and Afghanistan regularly listening to his messages.

The signs that God had anointed him for a special preaching ministry came early. By July 7, 1982, Pastor Mansfield, his wife, and his six-month-old son were on their way to take a pastorate in Albuquerque—a city, Mansfield said, that "didn't have an inner city like Chicago but had inner-city dynamics." He moved into the *barrio*, which was the most gang-infested, drug-infested part of the city. Three to four nights of the week, gunshots echoed throughout the neighborhood, and right behind the church, addicts were shooting up with needles, drinking, and selling drugs. After praying together in their new home, the family began the process of unpacking boxes.

"One Wednesday night as I was unlocking the front door of the church, I heard a drive-by shooting, and I ran over toward the shooting. Someone had just shot a four-year-old boy and a six-month-old baby. The father was a gang member who jumped under the car to hide. They were aiming for the father, but they said, 'If we can't get you, we'll get your children.' I ran over and helped the mother and father get their children into the car, and I had blood on my hands. I said, 'God what are we doing? We are playing church! I'm going to go into church tonight, and they're going to sing "This Is the Day That the Lord Has Made" and they are shooting kids thirty yards from our church! What kind of joke is this? I'm not making a difference in my neighborhood.'"

That night he told the church, "I am going to reach these gangs." The church thought he was nuts. Many had children who were in gangs and knew of their power. Nevertheless, they prayed as Mansfield set about befriending gang members over the next few months. At the time the congregation had a "Day of Prayer for the Lost." On that day, fifty gang members showed up at the church, and twenty accepted Christ. "Aren't we a funny people?" Mansfield asks. "We ask for miracles and when it comes we can't believe it!" Many gang members began to join Mansfield in cleaning up the community. A peace treaty was signed between a couple of gangs. But there was always resistance, including drive-by shootings at the church.

Perhaps the toughest shots fired at Mansfield in his career as a Church of God pastor, however, have not been from gang members but from Church of God people who have been prejudiced against Mansfield because he is Latino. The wounds of racism can run deep and leave a mark. It's not something that Pastor Richard dwells on. "A chip on your shoulder is indication of wood," he says regarding keeping grudges against people with racist attitudes. "I don't want to be a blockhead."

On one occasion Mansfield was having a successful week of preaching at a camp meeting in the Midwest. Toward the end of the week, he felt led to say something he had never said before: "God wants to do a work in some of you, but the reason he can't do a work in you is because this week, you have had a problem with the fact that these sermons have been preached to you by a Hispanic."

After the service a man came up and said, "My daughter married one of your kind."

"Is he a no good, dirty, lazy Mexican who beats your daughter?" Mansfield asked.

"Far from it," the man replied. "He's a deacon in the church, he's an engineer, and he just built her a three-thousand-square-foot home, they have two beautiful children, and he treats her like a queen."

"I see," Mansfield said. "You prayed that God would give your daughter a man who would love the Lord, love your daughter and their children, work hard, and provide for them, but you forgot to say, 'Make sure he's not a Mexican.'"

And the man, oblivious to the irony, said, "Exactly!"

The night ended with the man calling his daughter and son-in-law to ask for forgiveness from them and from God.

Some of the racism has been clear. There were times when the Latino brothers and sisters in Albuquerque were told by other Church of God folks to "stay on their side of the river." In one case, they were not allowed to use the baptistery in a Church of God building. But there have been other more subtle challenges.

Mansfield notes, "There has been the overlooking of some great Latino and African-American leaders because of a lack of understanding. It may not be race. But they may see that you are a Latino and assume you don't have a college education. All Latinos are not dishwashers. I have a Latino friend with five degrees, but he has an accent. Just because a person has an accent doesn't mean he thinks with one. And we think they do! So we treat them differently."

In a time when there's a shortage of pastors and an increase in multiculturalism in neighborhoods across America, churches are not making their staffs as multicultural as they probably should. There may be the assumption that because you speak Spanish, you could never serve English-speaking people even if you are bilingual. There are many empty pulpits in Church of God congregations that could be filled by Latino pastors who speak English. There are also churches in multicultural settings that could be hiring associate pastors or worship leaders who are Latino or African-American. "Why not bring them on staff, instead of just giving Latinos a room and saying start a Spanish ministry?" Manfield asks. Mansfield practices what he preaches. He has an Anglo associate pastor. This multicultural stretching is not just for white churches; it is for *all* churches. "A church should be reaching out to the neighborhood. Some of us have lost that. They are still committed to the Church of God and their congregation, but not to the people outside their congregation."

The current church in Albuquerque is the outcome of an Anglo church closing. The primarily Anglo Montgomery Place Church of God closed its doors because of dwindling numbers. As the congregation found itself down to only twenty people, they felt led by God to give their property to the predominantly Latino Southside Church of God, where Mansfield was the pastor. The Montgomery Place Church was not always a place so open to their Latino Church of God brothers and sisters on the south side of town, and much of the racism was aimed directly at Mansfield. There was considerable irony that the Church of God on the north side of town that had rejected him was now going to become the building that his ministry and church would call home. But home it became. Today there are not only Anglos and Latinos in the church, but there are many mixed couples as well: Anglos with Latinos, Latinos with African Americans, African Americans with Anglos, Latinos with Native Americans, and Native Americans with Anglos.

The transition was handled gingerly. The twenty remaining members of Montgomery Place were invited to stay to continue worshiping in their own building. Fourteen stayed on in what became a predominantly Hispanic congregation. Instead of Southside just taking over Montgomery Place's old building, the decision was made to start a new church, and a competition was held to rename the church. The result was New Beginnings, and it opened on Mother's Day in 2004 on the second busiest corner in Albuquerque.

"Snake, Will You Lead Us in Prayer?"

New Beginnings is a church that is willing to take huge risks to meet people where they are at in life. The entire Church of God could take a lesson from this Albuquerque church because they put it all on the line. The sad truth is that many churches and many pastors dream of courting a particularly prosperous demographic. Too many churches dream of having a large, upper-middle-class church with a considerable amount of tithers instead of being willing to go into those areas we know are full of darkness with little to offer to the creation of an organization. Of course this is not expressed openly, but rarely have I heard pastors say *"I want a church full of drug dealers striving to kick the habit for Jesus."* Instead, the unspoken goal is to create a church that will look stable and prosperous. In other words, we want a church that's safe for us and looks like us and which we will be able to develop into something larger and more successful.

Richard Mansfield's church is exactly the opposite. He is leading a church that is safe *for the wounded*. It is reaching out to real people with real problems who have nothing much to give in return. New Beginnings is not courting the elite, the middle class, the "respectable" demographical groups. Instead, they are opening their doors to those in need in their neighborhood and their city. This is not a church in pursuit of safety. Its mission matches its name. It is offering nothing less than new beginnings.

Take Snake (yes, that is his real name), for instance, who while giving his testimony pulled out a machine gun and pointed it at the congregation.

> **Richard Mansfield's church... is reaching out to real people with real problems who have nothing much to give in return.**

"We lost families over that one," Mansfield tells me in all seriousness as I laugh out loud. Apparently, there were a few Anglos who worried about a shooting in the church. "I had to explain that Chicanos won't shoot in a church. In the parking lot, on the street yeah, but Chicanos have too much respect for the church to shoot inside," Mansfield says.

I laugh because he's right. It's a cultural thing. The people left anyway.

This is not a sign of chaos in New Beginnings. It's a sign that this is a church that meets people where they are at. All of us, myself included, have a long way to go before we are consistent in our walk with Christ. "So many people call this their church home," Mansfield says of the many new Christians in the church. "They may show up once every month, but as far as they're concerned they are going to church. You have to understand these are people who only went to church on Christmas and Easter if they went at all."

As I hear Richard speak I think of Jesus' ministry. Perhaps there were occasional "questionable" followers of Jesus who truly felt as if they were committed to him. Perhaps Jesus called those people down from a tree where they were hiding and dined at their house. Perhaps?

There are not any tax collectors in the church, but there are ex-prostitutes, ex-heroin addicts, ex-gang members, attorneys, even judges. "When you see a bank vice president and an ex-gang member become best friends and share their lives with each other, that is the power of God! Our whole model is healing and restoring lives in the name of Jesus Christ."

As far as he's concerned, the church should be reaching out to anyone who is hurting, and issues of race or class are utterly beside the point. Opening the church doors to people who are fighting serious battles in their lives means that superficial piety is not an option. We all struggle with sin and this fallen world. Maturing as a Christian takes time. The New Beginnings church has people who smoke and has ashtrays outside, for example. This is something that might offend the piety of many in our conservative holiness movement. But some of the smokers in the church are the kinds of people who have broken twenty-year addictions to heroin after accepting Christ. Quitting heroin is no minor thing. And that means going on a journey with people as they become new creatures. "I believe that sanctification is a process." Mansfield says. "We have become a religious people. Jesus was persecuted for eating with notorious sinners. I believe that if Jesus was here on earth today and he went to a restaurant and they asked, "Preference of table?" I believe Jesus would say 'in the smoking section by the bar.' Not because he would want to be contaminated but because he would want to save sinners."

For those of us who are Latinos, we owe a great debt of gratitude to Latino Church of God pastors like Richard Mansfield, Gilbert Davila and many others. As I left Richard, I was so conscious of the many "bullets" that have been fired at him long before I came along. He has paved the way and I have not had to endure nearly as many blows as he had. I felt deeply inspired by my time with Pastor Mansfield aware that we will never fully know the burden he has carried as a Latino evangelist in our movement.

But that is not the recognition that Mansfield craves. He wants people to recognize that Jesus is Lord. And in the process of proclaiming this truth, many people who have never had a father have found a spiritual father in Richard Mansfield. He is a reflection of our Holy Father in the life of many people in the spiritual desert of New Mexico. He has achieved something even more difficult than presidential recognition. He is trusted by the kind of people who don't trust anyone.

Corpus Christi: Motorcycle Man and the Lazarus Church

I heard about a church in Texas that died but, like Lazarus, came back to life in an amazing way. I have come to Corpus Christi to see it. I want to know if it is possible for a church to die gracefully and be reborn as something new, a community that reaches out to all regardless of race or class or socioeconomic status?.

As I walk down Leopard Street, I can tell that I am not exactly on the right side of the tracks. On a 100-degree summer's day, I pass by an indigent man in a wheelchair drooling on himself and a prostitute standing in front of Alma's Bail Bonds. Alma's Bail Bonds is located next door to Casa Rez Bail Bonds. Across the street is Amy's Bail Bonds, which has on its roof a mannequin in pin stripes incarcerated behind bars. My eye scans below the incarcerated mannequin and to the right of Amy's, where I see Gracepoint Church. Fortunately, there is no creepy mannequin on top of it.

I'm not sure what I will find inside the church. Instead of finding a sanctuary or offices, I walk into a ballroom with a large chandelier overhead. There is a dance floor, a mezzanine, numerous tables, and a very large bar. It looks like Club Tropicana. I'm expecting Ricky Ricardo to come out and sing "Babalu." Jumping up quickly from one of the tables is twenty-nine-year-old Brent Doster, who comes at me with a big smile, big blue eyes, and a bald head. He's the pastor.

"Welcome. Have a seat! Want something to drink?" he asks as I scan the bar and lounge, which take up the rear half of the building.

We sit down at one of the many four-person tables scattered around the sanctuary. Brent is in a great mood, although he has every right to feel discouraged. The roof above the ballroom stage collapsed while he was attending the North American Convention in Anderson, and now plastic sheeting covers part of the stage. They had also been visiting Brent's sick father in Indiana. On their way back, the car's $3,500 transmission completely died—leaving Brent, his wife, and their three daughters (two of them baby twins) stranded in a small Missouri town of 780 people. For a pastor with a wife and three children to feed, $3,500 is a lot of money.

As for the collapsed roof, it wasn't clear whether insurance would pay for it. "The church had to meet in the bar area that Sunday," he explains. (It should be noted that the bar doesn't serve alcohol.)

This is no new, trendy church that suddenly sprang up. Gracepoint is the product of Parkside Church of God, one of the oldest Church of God congregations in Corpus Christi. In the 1970s and 1980s, the oil boom brought a lot of growth to the inner city, but as the city and the economy changed, people moved away and the church went into decline. It's a common story in churches across America. What is uncommon about Parkside Church was that the twelve or fifteen people remaining were still committed to reaching the city, although they didn't know how to do it. With numbers decreasing, finances dwindling, and the church property in decline, they called the Church of God offices in Anderson and asked them to send someone to help.

Anderson sent John Newton to talk to the remaining members. He suggested a radical idea: "What about a complete rebirth?"

The remaining members wanted to change, but they knew they wouldn't be able to do it in the same building with all its familiar trappings and sentimental connections with their beloved Parkside Church of God. So they moved to the deserted cinema.

Newton then contacted Brent Doster. Brent said, "No way am I going to Corpus Christi." But he and his lovely wife Aurora decided to pray about it. They resolved not to discuss the matter with each other as they sought counsel from the Lord. He spoke to both of them. Six months later, as Brent describes it, they were "driving a U-haul from a city where nine out of every ten people are white or some variation thereof to a place where nine out of every ten people are brown or some variation thereof." They knew that Aurora's experience as a former employee of Global Missions was going to come in handy.

With a median age of sixty-five, the remaining members of Parkside bravely decided to become an entirely new congregation. Brent was upfront about how this was going to involve radical change. But he also wisely allowed the members to grieve for Parkside. There was none of the impatient spirit that often callously encourages congregations to kill off ineffective ministries, close their buildings, and get on with their lives. Instead, Brent and the Parkside congregation shared their favorite memories and celebrated the lives that had been changed. Some of them had erected their former church building with their very own hands! It would be a painful good-bye. Brent encouraged honesty.

"The hardest thing about this sort of transition is walking people through a healthy process of grief so that they don't bring disease into the new body," Brent tells me. "That was really hard."

So how did it go?

"It was difficult. When the doors opened on the first Sunday, several new Hispanic and African-American families appeared. It was hard to keep reminding the Parkside people that we are building a church that looks like the kingdom of God, not one that looks like ourselves."

In addition to the new demographics, they were worshiping in a movie theatre, with projection screens and a live band. Several families decided to leave, and Brent assisted them in finding a new church home. He made clear that their decision left him with no hard feelings. His grace-filled and realistic approach is worth noting.

While some of the original group decided to stay with the new re-birthed church, a house church was started by one of the remaining members of Parkside. In addition, the former Parkside building was occupied by a Hispanic congregation. Out of one dying church came three.

Parkside was reborn as Gracepoint, but three and a half months into the new ministry, God challenged Brent to restructure the plans again. A lot of specialized ministries in the heart of the city gave food or shelter to the homeless, but there wasn't a place for street people to associate with one another. God called Brent to leave the theatre behind and go right into the heart of Corpus Christi's decaying downtown.

God also made Brent conscious of the fact that they were attracting a lot of new people but not necessarily creating disciples. "We needed to connect disconnected people to God and become followers of Christ," Brent says. "We needed to be a disciple-making factory."

This meant another dramatic change, and the ministry itself had to quickly recalibrate. The congregation's willingness to reexamine themselves constantly was key. Their focus had been too worship-centered. They needed to become more missional. Pastor Brent lays out how radically different the vision became.

"It meant that we would not grow as fast as we could have, but our goal was not to grow quickly. It was to connect the disconnected. We could try to start an instant church that would grow quickly and then figure out later how to help people have relationships. Or we could grow relationships first, take the people out of a consumer mindset, and give them a missional mindset. So our dream is to plant the next Gracepoint church in three years. When that time comes, we are going to have a healthy core of believers who will replicate their lives in others instead of trying to move fifty consumer-based Christians from a place they enjoy to a new place. So even in our infancy we have done a radical shift in our way of doing ministry."

Not everyone in the church liked the prospect of moving so close to the center of seedy nightlife. One senior in the church asked Brent, "Do you really want a church where businessmen and homeless people worship together?"

After mulling it over, Brent replied, "That's the only kind of church I want to pastor."

Outside the church, a sign reads, "Encounter Jesus." On Sunday morning, you see young people, African-American people, Hispanic people, and homeless people mingling together. There is even a fellow who used to deal drugs out of the ballroom bar that is now the Gracepoint building. The owner of the building became a Christian and so did a tattooed tow-truck driver who was baptized in the nearby bay. There have been quite a lot of new converts as well as rededications.

Not all of the older people could handle the change, but some have.

One of the older members said, "I have been a believer for over fifty years, but this is the first time in my life I have felt truly alive."

"It hasn't been painless, but it's been rewarding," Brent tells me. "There's a fine line between awesome and terrifying."

Things are always in flux in ministry. That's a lesson for the whole Church of God. A church planter's slogan is never far from Brent's mind: "You work hard on Plan A, you pray for Plan B, you attempt to make Plan C happen, but most often Plan D is what you are stuck with." It should be no surprise if Gracepoint looks completely different in a couple of years.

Currently, Gracepoint is located immediately off of a section of I-37 between an African-American neighborhood and a Hispanic neighborhood, just a few short blocks from the downtown business center with modest skyscrapers. Due to its proximity to the Mexican border, many Hispanics are wary of any white man, including Brent. Many of them are legal residents but do not necessarily feel safe. The only way Brent reaches them is through Hispanic people in his church, who vouch for him as a good guy.

Brent is also reaching upwardly mobile young people who live in the suburbs but come downtown to party. In much of America, the inner city is being revitalized by younger professionals who not only socialize downtown but increasingly want to live there as well. Many churches would be ahead of the population curve if they decided to head back into the heart of their cities. We are still laboring under the belief that inner cities are in decay and the suburbs will boom forever, but the exact opposite is happening in many places across the country. There's new social life downtown, so there should be more opportunities for a new life spiritually. This trend is seen in Corpus Christi.

"Many of the young people are conflicted about living in the suburbs, so they come downtown to hit the clubs and restaurants," Brent tells me. So now at Gracepoint there is a Saturday night service. As a young, white bald guy with a motorcycle, Brent catches the attention of Yuppies partying downtown, who call him the Motorcycle Man. They are shocked to find out that he is a pastor. As for his bike, it is well-protected by Richard and "Railroad," guys from the streets who were drawn increasingly to their pastor and ultimately to Christ.

"I'm not just here to feed you, preach to you, and put you out on the streets," Brent says to the many street people who pass through the doors. "Come to Gracepoint to be with someone who cares for your life."

"Most of these guys are called 'Bum,' 'Deadbeat,' 'Old-Timer,'—everything but the name God gave them. But here we call them by name!" He speaks with passion.

"Yes, I want to share the message of Jesus with them and lead them to wholeness in Christ. But first I want to call them by name and allow them to feel a sense of hope, dignity, and peace. Then they will know this church is different."

If a church ministering to the homeless seems a bit unnerving, keep in mind that this is exactly how the Church of God operated when it moved to urban environments in the 1920s.

The doors on Sunday morning open at 8:15, and people show up to church early and sit at the tables and bars and talk long before the actual church service starts. There are chairs on the ballroom floor facing the stage as they would in any church, but here the people seem to prefer the tables and the bar stools. Instead of gin and tonics in this former bar, there are donuts and coffee. There are actually two mezzanines above the sanctuary/ballroom/bar, which will be turned into lounges. One of them is for family worship. Once a month, families sit in the mezzanine together during the whole service. There is also a children's room.

The owner of the building had only been to church three times in his life. Now he has become a Christian and has started to count the number of consecutive Sundays that he is in church. Amazing! Sometimes they hand out sack lunches on the streets. It ends up costing the church only a few cents per meal.

Lest you think that Gracepoint is just trying to be some new, out-of-the-box paradigm-busting church, Brent will set you straight. This is not the story of a church following a trend or trying to create a new one. It's the story of a church that decided to die and then be reborn as a church that is committed to producing people who die to themselves daily. This is not a new model.

Not every church that is struggling needs to die like Gracepoint; nor should a struggling church fear that they will end up on their own corner of I-37. Instead, Gracepoint illustrates that God may have a whole new journey for a struggling church. Anytime we submit our will to Christ's will, we are in for a challenging ride. But we must be willing to allow God to move us and mold us.

"We're not trying to be the biggest or coolest church in town," Pastor Brent tells me as he finishes his diet soda. "We did not want to be cool, hip, relevant, or unique, but we wanted to be different because Christ calls us beyond 'business as usual.'"

Before Corpus Christi, Brent says, he spent "ten years trying to be Mr. Church of God." He knew the history and theology of the movement. He even pastored a church in Mecca (Anderson). He says he became a "radical, rabid" Church of God person. "The emphasis on movement and not on structure and organization—I just ate it up," he says.

But despite his love for all those traditions and the institutions that have arisen out of them, God called Brent Doster to something totally different, and the Holy Spirit led him to something he never would have thought of on his own. Despite the fact that he finds himself in a setting unlike what we have traditionally known, he is still a Church of God minister. Pastor Brent and his people are true Church of God reformers because they have allowed their hearts and their church to be re-formed by the Holy Spirit and they have fought to preserve their unity through the challenging process of saying good-bye to the Parkside church. The quest for holiness and unity, indeed!

The thing that strikes me about Brent is that he has taken on himself all of the challenges he has asked of his congregation. He walks the talk. The church had to be willing to accept a new culture, but so did Brent. He left his home in Indiana, even though he didn't want to go to a new location and a new culture. In the same way that he asked his congregation to re-imagine themselves, God asked Brent to re-imagine his vision for the church. His thirty-five pages of church planting ideas went out the window. God asked both Brent and Parkside Church of God to get out of their comfort zone and allow him to shape them into something totally different. That requires a faith that takes Jesus seriously.

I say good-bye to Brent Doster and the Gracepoint church. As I walk outside, I pass by Alma's Bail Bonds, Casa Rez Bail Bonds and Amy's Bail Bonds. The mannequin is still imprisoned behind the bars above Amy's—and looking as creepy as ever—but at the church on the corner, people are set free all the time.

London: A Global Mission Field

It is hard to find a more multicultural city than London. London has always been a large global city, but in today's United Kingdom, anyone from a European Union (EU) nation has the right to settle here and look for a job. These new European immigrants join the large Pakistani, Indian, Caribbean, and African communities that settled here years ago. In this highly multicultural city, it is hard to find a more diverse community than Tottenham, where the largest Church of God congregation in England is located.

Seven Sisters Road takes you past Polski Slep, the Polish Delicatessen; El Shaddai's Afro-European unisex salon; and Shukran, the kebob place, before you arrive at St. Ann's Road, where the Community Church of God is housed in a thirty-year-old red-brick building with a blue roof. The church itself is fifty years old; the Church of God presence, which began in Liverpool, is more than a century old.

Worship is lively in Tottenham, the people are friendly, and the Spirit is clearly present. It's been almost fifteen years since I first visited the church, and over the years, it has grown considerably. They have even planted a new church in Gwodmays, a community just outside of London. The church is pastored by Mickel Mascall, a Trinidadian in his early forties who graduated from West Indies Theological College, the Church of God college in the Caribbean. Church of God congregations in the U.K. have an arrangement with WITC that each year, the top third-year student comes to Britain to work in the four churches for three months. The idea is that putting the students in a different cultural setting and allowing them to learn and serve will better prepare them for ministry.

Pastor Mickel Mascall graduated at the top of his class, and after graduation he came to Britain to work in the churches. The Tottenham church had been in need of a pastor for two years, and Mickel answered the call. That was six years ago.

Pastor Mascall and I met in his office on an unusually warm March evening. I ask Pastor Mascall what was the most difficult thing to adjust to after the move. "The weather," he answers without hesitation as we sit in his office. "And adjusting to dampness and the coldness." It's something I completely understand. For me in Hong Kong, it was the other way around. After years of enjoying a cool, cloudy climate, it was an unpleasant shock to live in constant humidity and sun. Sun makes me grouchy. "I should probably switch places with Pastor Mascall," I think to myself.

Even the way the sun rises and sets took adjustment for Pastor Mascall. During the summer months, it is light at four o'clock in the morning, and at half past nine in the evening, it is just beginning to get dark. Then in winter, at eight o'clock, it's still dark, and then by four o'clock, it is dark again.

Then there's the English food, which doesn't usually win rave reviews outside the U.K., or even within the U.K. The most popular food is Indian curry. For Caribbean people, typical English food lacks spice.

Then there's the fact that the English are more reserved than the average Caribbean person. "The friendliness you would be accustomed to back home you don't get here in the British culture. If you say, 'Good morning,' some will stare at you in the face and they won't answer you. They think you are strange or up to something. As you walk the streets, everyone is minding his or her own business. In Trinidad, you walk into a public bus and you say, 'Good morning.' And everyone says, 'Good morning' back to you. Here they might not even answer."

My wife and I experienced the same thing going from the United States to Hong Kong. But had we moved to Trinidad, we would have been coming from the "colder" culture to the "warmer" culture. There are huge cultural variances around the world even in expectations about basic greetings. Cultural differences run deep.

The Tottenham Community Church is primarily made up of people from the Caribbean. It is not intentionally that way, but that is how it is. The people come from Trinidad, Jamaica, Barbados, Guyana, and a few other places. With so many Caribbean people, one would think that finding a common culture would be easy, but that is not the case. There are considerable differences between Jamaicans and Trinidadians, for instance, just as there are enormous differences between Koreans, Japanese, and Chinese people, although to outsiders they all seem to have some very similar East Asian cultural traits. What this means is that navigating cultural differences is always a challenge, even when the people are from one race and one particular region on the globe.

The cultural differences are celebrated in the Tottenham church. Every two years, there is an international evening when all the different cultures set up stalls with their different foods. Each country puts on a drama and uses the speech and slang of their country.

As we sit in his office sipping tea English-style, Pastor Mascall tells me that Tottenham is one of the deprived areas in London. Although there are many ethnic groups, it is primarily black.

"People are basically friendly but still hard to reach spiritually. The crime rate is pretty high, but we are making some headway. It is lowering. There is a problem with antisocial behavior among the young people." I would later encounter this as I headed back toward central London and saw a lot of evidence of Britain's huge club scene and binge-drinking culture. Women lay passed out on the streets.

> Navigating cultural differences is always a challenge, even when the people are from one race and one particular region on the globe.

"For young people, one of the pressures you have is gang wars. If young people from this area go into another community, they have to be careful with their cell phones. Other gangs will be aggressive. You have a lot of peer pressure with young people getting money from degrading means and fraudulent practices. It's hard on our young people who are growing in their faith."

In many immigrant communities the parents or grandparents may come with a strong connection to religion, but the younger generation raised in a different, more secular country may struggle to see the relevance of faith the way their parents do. For those coming from nations like the ones found in the Caribbean where Christianity is dominant, the challenge is to keep the young people in church and to help them have an actual connection to Jesus Christ as opposed to an affiliation by way of their parents.

Pastor Mascall finds that holiness, understanding that Christianity is about a transformed life, is an important teaching for the young in his community.

Christian immigrants to Western Europe face the challenge of living not just in a highly secular culture but in one that is unapologetically antagonistic toward Christianity. Pastor Mickel tells me about the challenge of doing evangelism in a culture like this.

"Going out to the homes is far more common in the West Indies. People are more open to the gospel there. But here, hand in hand with the multicultural background you have a multifaith setting: you have Muslims and Hindus and Buddhists and those who do not believe in God. In the universities here, they do not believe God even exists. Preaching the gospel or trying to reach people for Christ is a greater challenge.

"Back in the West Indies you knock on doors and speak to people. But here people can be less receptive. What we practice here is that we slip flyers in their doors and you still do not get much response when you invite people to special meetings.

"It is almost a "godless" society. You know the historical background, The British spread Christianity into the West Indies and so many parts of the world, but the society has gone away from that. Recently, there were signs on the London buses that said, 'Probably, there is no God.' The teaching of evolution is strong here."

I recalled that as I walked through the London underground, I saw a museum advertising a Darwin symposium. Even the advertisements seemed hostile toward religion.

"Friendship evangelism on a one-to-one basis is something we are doing presently. We also do cell groups. Groups meet in homes and we rotate the venues. We encourage our people to invite friends. The cell groups are not as rigid as the main service. It is more casual. In the Caribbean, you would be able to have a person with a microphone and a group behind preaching in public. But in London it is very politically incorrect, and you are treading on dangerous grounds if you proclaim, 'Jesus is Lord,' and, 'He is the way.' It can come across very negatively. You cannot proclaim God or Jesus in that way."

With a society so skeptical about the message of Jesus, it becomes vital that the church engage the community and Tottenham does that. Britain doesn't value Christianity much, but they do value the role that communities of faith can play in keeping the peace—particularly in areas like Tottenham.

"What is quite good here is the security services (police), which in this borough are quite willing to work with ministers and church leaders for the community's sake in the fight against crime, promoting peace and that sort of thing. There are projects ongoing where the different faiths come together to discuss how we can best promote peace in this society. The officers are willing to come to speak to the young people in the church. We have something called street pastors where ministers of the gospel will be out late in the night ministering to people, trying to sustain peace, ministering to people that are hurt, frustrated, or drunk on alcohol. They say it has helped with the reduction in crime."

Multifaith cooperation is strong in Britain and France, but it has become increasingly evident that one religion gets devalued more than any others (Christianity), and another one is catered to more than the others (Islam). "Avenues are being shut against Christianity, although this country is basically a Christian country in principle. All of this has contributed to the godlessness of society where the Christian principles are being shut out and the Christian practices are being discontinued. Islam is pressing its way in, and they fight for their rights. They seem to be making headway. They have more rights and privileges than the Christians even though this is a Christian-based country."

Very multicultural cities in the West (e.g., Paris, London, Toronto, Sydney) find that promoting multiculturalism and tolerance means validating various religious communities. For religions that primarily stay within their ethnic communities (Taoism, Buddhism, Islam, Judaism), this works well enough. Christianity, however, is not so easily bound to any one ethnic group. It is quite the opposite in fact. Consequently, the Christian desire to take the gospel to all the nations collides with the multicultural ethos that promotes the idea that all religions are of equal value. Multicultural cities are difficult places for the Christian church.

On top of that challenge is the fact that even within a cultural community (the black Caribbean culture, for instance), there may be great diversity. Yet, bringing in people from other ethnicities is not as easy as it looks. "How do we bring people from different races into our church?" sister Janelle Xavier at Tottenham asked me after the Sunday service. "My first instinct is to only invite Caribbean friends because I know that they will be more comfortable," she said.

I don't have any good answers for her, because the truth is that a Korean would most likely be more comfortable in a Korean church and an Anglo could easily prefer an Anglo church—not for racist reasons but because of all the subtle ways that a particular culture shapes the church. I tell her that the power of culture is very strong and it may be that Caribbean people will always be more likely to join a church like Tottenham than Anglos, Asians, or Latinos. But one way or another, a church probably needs to always stretch itself beyond its own ethnic and cultural community. It's up to God whether a diverse group ends up joining the church. We must not limit ourselves to one culture, yet paradoxically, our own culture limits our ability to transcend cultures consistently. The Bible is filled with this tension among God's people.

It would be easy to be discouraged in such a secular and hostile place as modern-day, multicultural London. But Pastor Mascall is not discouraged and he believes a life of personal holiness is paramount in a location such as this.

"When I came to this church, I said to them before I took the position, my greatest aim and focus as a minister of the gospel is that I lead those who I lead in a life that is pleasing to God that in the end, the Lord can say, 'Well done, my good and faithful servant. Enter into the joy of the Lord.' In other words, you are fit. You are presented before God worthy after his grace into the kingdom."

Amen.

Paris: A Ray of Light in the City of Lights

A mere three hours away from London by high-speed train is the Church of God in Paris. As a joke, I e-mail a picture to my friends of the famous Notre Dame cathedral and label it "The Church of God in Paris." When I show up, however, the joke turns out to not be as funny as I expected. The Church of God in Paris is located in the heart of Paris, a mere kilometer from Notre Dame. It takes me less than ten minutes to walk from Notre Dame on the Ile-de-Cite past the magnificent Hôtel de Ville and onto the Rue Lobau to their meeting place, a stone's throw from the Seine. Furthermore, the building where the worship is held is a five-hundred-year-old historic landmark itself, a Lutheran Evangelical Cathedral with a gorgeous stone façade.

It is mind-boggling that the church in Paris is so close to the heart of one of the world's most visited cities, yet the vast majority of people in the Church of God are not even aware that we have a congregation in France. How many Church of God people have visited "the City of Lights" as tourists and remained oblivious to the fact that we have a church here? In eight visits, this is my first time at the church having only learned about its existence a year earlier. It's another sign of how disconnected the movement is at this point in time. It's possible for churches and entire countries to fly under the radar.

I make my way into the beautiful building and find a modestly-sized group of people preparing for worship. Paris, like London, is a highly multicultural society with a large African and Middle-Eastern population in particular. Outside of the church the day before, I had a conversation with a homeless French man who speaks perfect Spanish. Even the indigent people are multilingual in Paris! Inside, the service is in French and Arabic. The Lebanese pastor's fourteen-year-old daughter Rebecca speaks French, Italian, and Arabic. Their twelve-year-old son Mikey speaks Arabic, French, and Spanish. And the parents, Pastor Michel Fegali and his wife Frida, speak a number of languages including English.

Like Pastor Mickel in London, Pastor Michel and Frida are graduates of a Church of God school who are now pastoring in a different country from where they grew up. Michel and Frida were the first graduates of the Mediterranean Bible College in Beirut, Lebanon, back in 1985. In 1989, the Fegalis relocated to Paris, where they have a subcontracting company. Upon arrival, they were challenged by well-known Lebanese leader Fouad Melki to start a church in Paris among the Arabic-speaking population. They began by meeting in a house, and the people came from a variety of cultures and religious backgrounds. There were Baptists, Coptics, Pentecostals, Bretheren, and others. Pastor Michel himself is originally from a Pentecostal background.

I am speaking with them in their beautiful home in the eastern suburb of Villemomble. They have a considerable plot of land on a hillside behind their home where Michel is constructing a green house and where they have chickens and rabbits. A prophecy was given to them by a visiting pastor from Cameroon that land would be given to the Fegalis. Since then, their property has grown. But Pastor Michel says that as soon as they moved into this lovely home, God reminded him to not get too attached to it, that it belonged to him and that he may have a special purpose for it.

After a great Lebanese meal in which I eat more vegetables than I have in ten years combined—and a birthday party for their ten-year-old nephew—we sit down in their office and talk about the Church of God in Paris.

"People would ask me what we are, and I would say Church of God. I am from a Pentecostal background, but I studied at MBC. The theology and inclusiveness of the Church of God is nearest to all of these backgrounds. We are a Christian church that believes in the unity of all believers. There's only one church in the world, the Church of God. Everyone is a member if he is in Christ and is born again. Many people came to our church because of the name 'Church of God.'"

As I would find time and time again in my travels, many people originally came to the Church of God because of that spirit of inclusivity. In a multicultural setting where people may come from backgrounds as diverse as Baptist and Coptic, the emphasis on believing in Jesus as the only requirement for belonging is a useful thing. Once again, in its doctrine, the Church of God is situated well for the multicultural challenges of places like Paris, Toronto, and London.

As in London however, just because most of the congregants are of Middle-Eastern background does not mean that their cultures are all the same. Cultural differences between Egyptians and Lebanese, for instance, became apparent early on in the life of the church, and there were many people who had a problem with the Church of God belief that women can be in ministry. Even women leading worship was deemed too much for some from cultures where women are still viewed as inferior to men. The Fegalis were very patient, and today it is a nonissue, but as Frida tells me, "It took ten years."

As I sit in the service, I follow the words on the screen as we sing. They are in French; the words then shift to Arabic. It would be easy for the Church of God in Paris to just focus on Arab communities, but everything in this church is translated into French as well. Frida explains the reasoning.

"This church is a historical monument," she says of the gorgeous church. "People come from all over to visit this building. If we speak French, then perhaps someone can be saved. We translate everything. Maybe someone comes in and they are contemplating suicide. We don't know how this could affect them." And the day I visited, a Caucasian French woman visited the service—one of a few non-Arabs present in the church.

But translating everything takes a very long time, and the bulk of the work falls upon Frida's shoulders. Both she and Michel work full time in addition to running the church. "I may translate more than one hundred things during the week, but this is the vision God gave me. We need to help people on the outside, especially the French community!"

Then there's the multicultural nature of marriages in today's society, which is a new factor churches have to deal with. "We have Middle Eastern-ers married to French people," Frida adds. "They will leave the church if it is not in French."

As in much of Western Europe, it is very easy for congregations to be passive, just showing up at church when nobody else in society does is enough to make one feel active in the Christian life. But as with Pastor Mascall in London, Pastor Fegali is challenging his congregation to take more ownership in the church and become more involved in reaching out to their community. It is difficult. Paris is one of the world's most expensive cities. An issue as basic as finding a place to park and paying the exorbitant parking fees can be an obstacle to growth here.

"One month ago," Pastor Fegali relates, "I asked them, the principal leaders in the church, do you really want to serve God in this church? If the Church of God in Paris is your church in which you are proud and in which you take a decision with God, then you have to write down your name, date, and how you want to serve God. And give me the paper. Keep a copy for yourself, and I want to work with those people who are really proud of this church.

"I received many responses from people accepting that challenge. We have many things to do, evangelize, visits, and to go out and do ministry and give reports afterward. I want every three months or twice a year to see what each person has done with the group and to give reports about our ministry. I was very patient over the years, but we wasted a lot of time. Now it's time to go to a new phase.

"Five months ago, I took Nehemiah and explained it in detail. I said we have to be like Nehemiah. If you want to build the wall, you have to be active in your place. If this church is your place, we have to work to-gether. Somebody came after that and said, 'I think God will do many things with us.'"

I can see that the Fegalis have labored long and hard in a very difficult region that presents complex challenges for a Church of God congregation. I wonder if they get discouraged.

"The only thing that I look at is Jesus," Frida says. "Keep your eyes on Jesus. We need the spirit of challenge. When you are facing a problem, you don't say, 'I will retreat.' Jesus didn't say to the storms, 'I will go back.' Jesus went to the storm. When there seems to be no hope, he will come to help."

The Paris church exists in considerable isolation, both within a very secular nation and as part of the Church of God movement. It's an unhealthy kind of autonomy that is widespread in our movement among churches and pastors.

"We don't want to be independent in this way," Frida says. "We want to speak about our problems, share with others, and take advice from people. We want to have a relationship with a church in the United States; to have exchanges and encourage us. We need new ideas, and we need people who can evangelize. We need people with a spirit for evangelism."

The Church of God's rejection of institutionalism would play well in Europe if it were understood.

They also need a piano player. I can think of worse gigs than playing the piano in Paris as a ministry. "Perhaps the French-speaking people in the Church of God in Canada could help out?" Michel suggests. I like the idea. It's this kind of global interconnectivity in dealing with mutual challenges that is sorely lacking in the Church of God movement precisely at a time when global interconnectivity has never been easier.

What about the notoriously secular French government? "They mostly leave the churches alone. Even the Satanists!" Frida tells me. But they do send government officials to spy as they do in other countries, such as Egypt and China. As in the U.K., the French government does a lot of work trying to create an environment of multicultural religious tolerance. Their work in Marseilles using interfaith dialogue to address common citywide concerns has been a model for other parts of Europe and may eventually be copied in the United States. But on the whole, people in France are not interested in Christianity.

"They think of it as an institution. They endured the wars of religion between Protestants and Catholics, and they don't want to listen," Michel tells me. It is helpful to remember that one-third of Europe was wiped out in the seventeenth century and that the numbers of wars that took place would fill up this entire page if listed side by side. Christendom, the age of institutional Christianity, was hugely destructive to Europe, while in North America, religion has been largely beneficial thanks to the separation of church and state. The Church of God's rejection of institutionalism would play well in Europe if it were understood by the Europeans.

Despite the secular environment, there are occasional breakthroughs. When one of the ethnically French sisters was baptized in the church, the father refused to go and said he would not recognize her as his daughter anymore. Their family was Catholic. But her mother did come to the baptism and wept. A little while later the father ended up in the hospital and the church brothers and sisters visited him. They prayed for him and he then told his daughter he would come to church.

"He came, and he had tears in his eyes," Michel tells me. "The man said, 'I was surprised because you speak about love, not about religion. It's not about 'You have to'; it's about 'I love to.'"

"We are a church that expresses love, and I thank God for this," says Pastor Michel. "I pray that God will rebuild this church in France to live for him and that Christ will be the winner. We need to watch how we act and do good things, but first of all, we need to ask for the mercy of God. Because he is the one who built the church. If he doesn't build the church, nobody can do it."

Los Angeles: Three Worlds, One Church

It's a perfectly gorgeous day in Los Angeles, and I am sitting at Alondra Park in Torrance with the Adwalpalker family having a Subway sandwich. Warner, Byrum, Smith, Adwalpalker. The name doesn't sound like an old traditional Church of God name, but that was then and this is now. Adwalpalker is an Indian name, and Pastor Darren has dark skin and preaches in Spanish and English. His father was a brilliant student from India who immigrated to the United States. They originally hail from Goa, but Darren is from New York and grew up in the Assemblies of God. He married Amy, a California girl from Orange County. Their three-year-old son Josiah Sanjay has red hair and looks like Huck Finn. Their baby daughter Hannah has dark skin and dark hair and looks like a little Indian princess. They now serve in a church with a Guatemalan associate pastor, an African-American youth pastor, and a Chinese children's minister. The congregation is mostly Latino and Anglo. If you are confused, welcome to their church!

As with so many Church of God congregations, fifty years ago this diversity was not the case. The church in North America was traditionally in a white, middle-class community and was very traditional. Today, throughout the continent, neighborhoods are getting more racially and culturally complex. This makes church much more complicated.

In chapter 3, I described the three worlds of the Church of God: the traditional world, the post-Christendom world, and the Book of Acts world. The Church of God in Torrance is unique (for now) in that it actually has all three worlds in one church. Amy Adwalpalker gives me an example as she prepares Josiah Sanjay's lunch:

"If we sing 'God Bless America,' you'll get flack from the young generation who will say, "Why are we singing that in church?" The traditional older adults will say 'Why don't you do that more often? It's about time!' And the Spanish-speakers will say, "Look out! Immigration is going to deport us!' We get three totally different responses to the same action." I can't help but laugh. Imagine navigating that as a pastor.

South Bay Church of God is on the border of Torrance and Lawndale. On one street it is an urban neighborhood where the population density doubles and you can find bulletproof glass at Taco Bell. But just down the street, it is predominantly Anglo, with upscale shopping malls where non-Anglos don't bother to go. "People coexist but don't crossover," Amy observes. "Church is one of the only places where you might get people together who live a half a mile from each other but live in totally different worlds. You will get guys with minuteman militia bumper stickers on their cars and illegal immigrants in the same building. There's a tension there, but there's a beauty there."

These kinds of extremes seem pretty strange for those of us who have been raised in more traditional settings. It's different for today's youth, according to Amy.

"The youth don't think it's weird that it's diverse. We're two-thirds Latino in our youth group. But we are encountering all of these new kinds of issues. We went on a train trip that only cost $20, but they didn't have $20 because a lot of these families have three youths, which makes it $60 for all the children to go; and they may have a single mom who is unemployed and is probably illegal. So we had to create a scholarship program, and we give them opportunities to work at the church and earn their money. So when we look at an event like the International Youth Convention, it's going to cost $1,000 a kid. If we make that the priority of our ministry, the whole youth group does a fundraiser, and only four Anglo kids get to go, because they are the only ones who can really afford it. I am seeing this split and we need to rethink everything. Some of these forms are for the traditional church, and they don't work for the low-income, cross-cultural setting."

In multicultural locations, the church is often affected as much by socioeconomic class issues as they are by issues of race. This can mean the way they process the faith is entirely different.

"There are different education levels, which affects how kids think and process the faith. Some kids are home-schooled kids, have parents that are doctors and engineers, and think abstractly," Amy says, referring to those that live a middle-class or upper-class existence. "But other kids have parents with a third-grade education, they don't speak English, they can't read the NIV out loud, they don't know their own address, and they spell their own name wrong."

Even the use of the Bible becomes an issue. "The NIV is incomprehensible for our group. The New Living is better, but even that is tough. How do we make the gospel acceptable to a group that is so diverse?" Amy asks rhetorically.

The biggest challenge with the youth is not race (they are comfortable with a multicultural world); it is class. Amy provides an illustration: "We did a game called Two Truths and a Lie. One kid may say, 'I've been to Europe, I have a varsity letter in football, and I swam twenty miles.' The object of the game is to discern which one is a lie. In our church, one kid said, 'I live in a home, I can write, and I killed someone.' We were hoping that the third one was the lie," Amy jokes making me spit out my sandwich.

Darren and Amy are Wheaton graduates just entering their thirties. Darren studied sociology, and Amy studied ancient languages. They then both got master's degrees at Biola University in multicultural studies and applied linguistics. "We've always had a desire to be bridge people," she says, as her son Josiah flies circles around us with his new toy airplane.

"In the old pictures of this church, you see one African American girl and about eighty Anglos. You see women in housedresses and a very neat legacy. But it doesn't resonate with the current people, and to the young it seems like *Leave It to Beaver*. It sounds harsh, and I don't mean it that way, because it's a gift and an inheritance. But for instance, this community used to have a bus ministry that went around and picked kids up. Well, today, you could go to prison for that."

Many churches would like to have a multicultural church and many are doing so by necessity. There's a lot of naiveté out there, however. It's not as easy as just getting people into the same room. Cultural differences are huge and affect theology and worship. For example, Pastor Darren Adwal-palker preaches differently to the Latinos than he does the Anglos.

"Our nine o'clock service is Spanish, and eleven o'clock is English. The style and applications are very different, even if I preach the same text. With Spanish, my balance is more on inspiration because that is what moves the Latin heart. If they hear just an informational sermon, they will feel cheated. If the Anglos get a purely inspirational service, *they* will feel cheated. In Spanish, it's more *del corazon* [of the heart], and for the Anglos, it's more about breaking through the strongholds of the mind [rational arguments].

"If there's no emotion with Latinos, then they assume your sermon isn't important," Amy interjects. "Because if it were important, there would be more passion. They will think you are *frio* [cold]. It's been a challenge for the Latinos to understand the Anglo worship because to them it doesn't look like they are doing anything."

"A key for us," Darren adds, "is the concept of bridge people. It is some-one who is firmly connected to both sides and both cultures and then gets walked on." I chuckle at the appropriate metaphor, having been walked on a few times myself.

Darren continues, "Even if the Anglo person cannot be a full bridge, then the Latino minister has to have a bridge back. Because what happens is that islands of ministry are created where the two ministries do not con-nect and you have a Spanish service and a Caucasian service. That's more of a multicongregational approach. That way is easier. It's like being married and not seeing each other. You can have a marriage, but is there intimacy? If you want to dance closely, then you will be stepping on people's toes. Bridge people need to be your key leaders in both ministries so that they can understand the motivations of the ethnic groups. People often interpret their experience through their own lens. But you have to have people mak-ing an effort, like the way a male must understand a female in a marriage even if he can never be a female. It's not culture A or culture B; its culture C—a synergistic creation."

Basically, Darren and Amy Adwalkpalker are cross-cultural missionaries. They just happen to live in the United States; but increasingly, that is what it takes to pastor in the twenty-first century. A minister may need to enter into a variety of cultures (e.g., African American, Latino, Vietnamese) and worlds (e.g., traditional, post-Christendom, Book of Acts). The skills that Darren and Amy possess are not easy to find. The younger generation—having grown up in the era of Tiger Woods, Barack Obama, and Shakira (whose music is just as popular in Kenya and Singapore as it is in Colombia and Lebanon, where her family is from)—feels comfortable in this environment and excels at forming multicultural friendships. This is good news.

Amy reflects on how this experience of multicultural ministry has affected her. "I've learned a lot. It's been a lot of running into doors. I've been amazed at the cultural differences. We say, 'We all want relationship; we all want love; we all want connection,' but I am amazed at how different we give it, the expectations, the pain and resentment that can occur and the complexity of it. It has been fascinating."

"Even making appointments can be challenging. With an Anglo, appointments are made as far out as possible, but with a Spanish speaker it's a good two-week window with constant reminders." Amy jokes, "In American culture you tell them six months out if you are staying for three days, and with Latinos they'll give you three days warning that someone is coming for six months."

A couple of hours later I find myself in a board meeting at South Bay Church of God. Darren has asked me to share a little bit about the book. I mention the three worlds of the Church of God that I have found in my travels and tell them how amazing it is that all three of those worlds can be found in South Bay. The men gathered seem interested as they have never thought of their congregation that way.

One of the men shares that as the church's racial makeup changed, a former member spoke about his concern, expressing disgust: "If you keep doing what you are doing, this church could be run by non-whites." Today the church is run by nonwhites! "We couldn't have hired you fifteen years ago," one of the men says to Darren. It's a remarkable comment because it is obvious that this is a church that has turned a corner. Cultural differences exist, racial differences exist, but no one culture has exclusive claim to Christ here. That is well understood. We decide to pray together, and as we do, I have a vision of Darren in my head: an Indian-American with a red-headed boy preaching in Spanish and English. That is the Church of God.

El Cajon: Thinking Outside of the Box

I am feeling quite encouraged as I make my way down Southern California's freeways toward the San Diego area. I am on my way to the town of El Cajon, which means "the big box" in Spanish. I've heard about a woman pastor who has an interesting multicultural story to share. I don't know the story; I just know that everyone promises it will be worth the trip.

Driving past the brown hills and beautiful homes of this idyllic Southern California paradise, I make my way toward the church. I am taken aback by the sign in front of the Hillside church. It is in English and Arabic! I had noticed something different in **I am taken aback by the sign in front of the Hillside church. It is in English and Arabic!** this community as I got off of Interstate 8. There are a lot of women with their heads covered in this town. Is this the San Vincente Freeway or the road from Baghdad to Tikrit? It turns out that El Cajon, with its Spanish name and white suburban homes, has the second largest Arabic-speaking population in the United States, behind Dearborn, Michigan. Last year alone, ten thousand refugees poured into this town to find a home.

A bit confused, I enter the church and meet Donna Rothenberger. Donna originally hails from central Indiana, and she radiates friendliness and warmth as she welcomes me into her church. She retains a bit of an Indiana accent and has the demeanor of someone who always faces life's challenges with a smile. Perhaps it's that can-do Midwestern spirit.

Donna grew up a Baptist in the little town of Brownsburg, Indiana, and married a hometown boy. "It was a Mayberry experience," she says of the quaint, rural town in Hendricks County that according to the 2000 census is still 97 percent white. Six years ago, she was called to pastor a church of twenty-seven people here in El Cajon, California. Hillside, which was predominantly an Anglo Church of God, was the kind of small church that people might suspect had seen its better days. Since Donna Rothenberger arrived however, the church has grown 500 percent and now has three services.

Donna begins to explain the neighborhood that I have just driven through. "Only 2 percent of Middle Easterners are born-again Christians. While 98 percent arrive here in El Cajon as Muslims or Catholics, 2 percent arrive looking for a Protestant-style church that teaches Jesus Christ." As Donna wondered where to begin in her new ministry, she made a key decision. "We don't have many Arabic churches here, so when I first got here, I looked at the demographics and saw this increase. I thought, 'We can't do what we want. We gotta see what God is doing and join him.' We immediately began to ask, 'How does an American congregation serve an Arabic community?' We were open heartwise to whatever God wanted to do. This church is full of humble servants. We all wondered, 'What does this mean? 'What will happen to us?' But it has been a wonderful, remarkable experience."

So for Donna and the others at Hillside, the needs of the community dictated the course for the future. Shortly thereafter, they met Kamal Boktor, who had started an Arabic-speaking Bible study in his home. Once the house church got to twenty-five or so, they asked Kamal if his church would like to use the facilities at Hillside.

The addition of Arabic-speaking people into Hillside did not go unnoticed. The community is still predominantly Anglo, and many found the large number of Middle Easterners disconcerting. In this post-9/11 world, no ethnic group undergoes suspicion and scrutiny like Middle Easterners. "People are not aware that there are Christian Arabic-speaking people," Donna relates. The church began to get hate mail because they were "taking in terrorists." "People asked, 'Why are you taking in towelheads?'"

Despite the critics, before long they were seeing their youth program grow as well as an adult woman's Bible study and other groups. The result was that there is now a diverse Sunday morning service, followed by an Arabic-speaking service at noon with Pastor Kamal, as well as a Wednesday night service run by the youth.

"We operate a little independently from the Arabic service and the church because of the cultural differences," Donna explains. "For instance, as a female, I would never go calling or evangelizing or street witnessing with Pastor Kamal. That would be viewed as totally inappropriate by Arabic-speaking people. We had to figure out how to do this. So he and his leaders evangelize in the ways that fit their culture best."

As I learned with the Adwalpalkers, navigating the cultural differences is a significant challenge. Some people suggested to Donna that she not even bother trying.[4] "You need to get control of that church and everyone should be on the same page and everyone needs to do the same thing," they said to her. But Donna felt that the cultural differences required flexibility. Donna felt that with forty thousand Arabic-speaking people in her community, mainly centered around the church's immediate neighborhood, this culture within a culture needed to be taken seriously on its own ground.

That's not to say that they don't occasionally challenge the culture. As a female pastor in the Church of God, there are times when Donna has felt resistance from within the Church of God by those who do not feel women should be pastors. It was even more difficult in the Baptist church where she started. At least in the Church of God, it was made clear to her that the Church of God ordains women. But as hard as those challenges have been, the Arab world is even harder on women regarding issues of leadership. At Hillside, however, Pastor Kamal refers to Donna as his senior pastor, and their working relationship has educated those who carried negative preconceptions. The balance between acquiescing to culture and challenging culture when it goes against Scripture is always difficult, but it is one that both Donna and Kamal deal with in healthy ways.

Sometimes the Hillside congregations have a pitch-in dinner (as well as unity services) where the Westerners and the Middle Easterners share their food and worship time with each other. "It is one of the most moving experiences you have ever been a part of to hear English-speaking people and Arabic-speaking people singing the same songs, especially at this time in our country's history, especially when our country is so divided about these wars in the Middle East. It's so exciting. We have a chance to show our neighbors that Middle-Eastern people and American people can coexist and worship the Lord together. It is so powerful!" That is an excellent

---

4. It is important to note that it is not only Anglo churches that struggle with the reality that their neighborhood is changing racially and become apprehensive about reaching out. Throughout America, African-American churches are finding that their neighborhoods now are filled with Koreans. Hispanic neighborhoods are being inundated with Russians and Vietnamese, and so on. All of them find it difficult to change their direction to reach out to the new ethnic groups in their neighborhood. Ethnic churches filled with first-generation immigrants are often pretty poor at being multicultural themselves, preferring to only deal with their own. While making this book, I met a sharp young couple in their late twenties frustrated by their church's lack of desire to reach out to the different ethnic groups in their neighborhood. The couple was Korean, thinking of leaving their inward-looking Korean church.

example of the church challenging the current assumptions of our North American culture.

As in Torrance, socioeconomic class affects the church greatly. "This part of El Cajon is a low-income area, and 80 percent of our congregation don't own a car, don't own a computer, and often they don't have a cell phone—or their phone has been shut off because they can't pay their bills." It alters the way that Pastor Donna does ministry on a daily basis. "I can't just whip off an e-mail. I have to go to their house and then come back to the office. The meaning of community in a place where so few drive and everyone relies on mass transit, well, the meaning of community changes a lot. Those with cars are expected to help with rides. Those with a home big enough are the ones that host small groups. Those that have a means to connect with people are expected to do so. It changes the nature of community compared to a rural community where everyone owns a car or a church off the freeway where people just drive in from miles away."

It has economic consequences for the church as well. "A lot of our single moms are Section 8 moms (H.U.D. Housing Choice Voucher Program), and they get $800 a month. That's not a lot for tithes, so this church just depends on the Lord. I used to live in the parsonage next door, but after a year, I suggested we sell the parsonage. It was bought the year before for $200,000, and we sold it for $500,000 at the peak of the market. But we are going to come to the end of that money here in the next year. We'll have to be open to the Lord. We just keep putting one foot in front of the other, and I haven't missed a paycheck yet." The recent economic downturn is making the future of this church even more precarious. Nevertheless, Donna doesn't regret for one minute that her church has reached out to those that are not part of the wealthy class.

"We have kids that have come out of gang life. We have parents and grandparents that have taken on single moms and their kids to love and cherish as their own kids; those who have share with those who have not."

The church finds many ways of sharing their blessings. "A lot of cooking goes on in the church thanks to the Kitchen Ladies, Donna tells me. This is a group of women that is always baking something for the church. As Donna shares, it is surprising how the smallest things can have a giant impact in places of great brokenness. For instance, at Hillside, just the smell of chocolate chip cookies in the church make kids feel at home. "These are smells that most of our kids never get to smell," Donna explains. "If you only have one parent and they work a lot, you can't afford those kinds of luxuries."

She continues her analysis on the differences between economic classes: "In the middle class, we find things that make a difference: education, money. I did a sermon on what God thinks about poor people. I spent the whole message talking about how endeared he is to those that have nothing, because they have tried everything. They are closer to finding the authentic God than the rest of us. And when you've tried everything, you find out he is faithful and he is true and he is loyal and he is loving and he is willing to forgive. He is the lifter of my head; he eradicates my shame and guilt and is willing for me to draw close. My ladies love that."

The church is doing very well in such a challenging environment. But there was no master plan. "This has not been a paint-by-numbers experience," Donna insists. "You think black and white is hard, you should try black, white, Arab, and Hispanic. Everything we've done goes against what the great mentors told us. We had no other choice though. People said, 'Don't do this; the people are too poor.' 'Don't do this; the ethnic variety will never give you a good, solid congregation. 'Don't do this because Southern California is expensive', and 'Don't do this, because there are so many megachurches.' But I said, 'I don't want people from the megachurches. I want people that are living day to day, and people that are doing drugs and alcohol to survive day to day."

"You gotta know the people," she continues. "You have to get in their lives and get in their homes. Whether they have fleas jumping on your ankles or ten people living in one apartment, you have to know the people around your church. Church of God doctrine is still intact, but church has had to look really different here. It hasn't been easy, but it's been cool. We have thousands of stories."

Donna is investing heavily in mentoring youth. Out of a group of fifty to seventy kids, there are now about twelve strong, mentored leaders in the group. Her daughter is one of the young leaders in the church who not only plays in two bands but also trains junior-high students to be musicians in the church. "We are big on empowerment here and giving young people opportunities."

In working to raise up youth, Donna noticed that not a lot was happening in the Church of God for college students. So she decided to start a college camp, and twelve students came: five men and seven women ranging in age from seventeen to twenty-six. She called it Doxa Camp. No cell phones, no TV, no computers for a whole week. A letter and registration form went out to every Church of God pastor in Southern California. "I brought in pastors from all over the state to preach and teach from morning until night. In the morning, we did discipleship; at night, we did leadership material. Every day, they had to participate in a physical experience. They had to climb a mountain with a partner on Monday and couldn't leave the trail without their partner. On Tuesday, they took surfing lessons, and they had one hour to get on the board and surf. On Wednesday, they took water polo lessons. On Friday, we went to a horse ranch and my friend used horses to teach us about leadership. Horses are led from internal leading and not external leading," she explains to me. "So if you chase them with a bridle they will run away. But if you communicate with them internally, make it clear that you are in charge and are not going to hurt them, they will follow. Some of our kids had never seen a horse before. The week was unbelievable, and as soon as we finished that week, we went straight to Mexico to build a house for a week. The state coordinator, Dave Winn, said, 'If you can get college kids to pay the fee for the camp, we will pay for their fees for Mexico."

Recently the Board at Hillside met together to discuss the financial challenges. The financial situation looks grim. There may not be money left eight months from now. Donna said to the board members; "We've got two choices: we can try and hoard everything and stretch it to sixteen months and wait for the Grim Reaper. Or we can go out in eight months with the biggest bang and shout of glory. I want to go out with my boots on. I'll be the last one out if they lock the doors, but by golly, those kids are going to be eating chocolate chip cookies, and people are going to be getting healed. And what if God gives us a miracle and we pull it out at the last minute? What if he wants to see if we will be faithful?"

Donna reflects on her out-of-the-box experience in the big box of El Cajon. "If you had told me I would have been pastoring a church like this one, I would have gone running for the hills of Indiana and Kentucky. I never thought I'd have the stamina to pastor in a place like this—in a male dominated society." But along with the cultural challenges has come the beauty of being exposed to Christ through new cultural lenses.

"Nobody can discern Scripture better than people from the Middle East. I can't believe I worship with the descendents of Abraham. That is so cool!" she says as tears roll down her cheeks. "Every church is meant to have a unique experience and ours certainly fits that bill. Our church is what the Church of God looks like when you bring all the children together, red and yellow, black and white." She's got me crying now too.

It strikes me that anytime you decide to do multicultural ministry, you are embarking on a massive learning experience that will make sure that your journey of faith is constantly filled with challenging new insights. When Donna's Baptist parents came out from Indiana and saw the church, they said, "We can't deny what's going on. There's got to be something about this that we don't understand." In his Georgia, southern-drawl, her father said: "The Lord says his ways are mightier and higher than ours. I'm thinking this is one of those cases." I couldn't agree more.

As I leave El Cajon and drive along the Southern California shoreline, I marvel at how much the Church of God has changed since Abraham Nachtigall joined this movement in the nineteenth century. Looking out across the Pacific I think about the Church of God congregations on the other side of the ocean. Memories come flooding back of the pastors and pastoras in the Philippines. I think about the Church of God in Australia, the pastors laboring in the difficult country of Chile, and the challenges facing the fellowship in Zambia. I'm overwhelmed by all I have seen in the past two years. The more the message of the Church of God has spread, the more complicated it has become. But it is precisely because this message has touched so many lives that we now find that our movement encompasses Arabic-speaking people in Lebanon, Egypt, Paris, and El Cajon. Old Abraham is proud, and so is his Spanish-speaking great-grandson.

8
epilogue

A Homecoming of Sorts
South Dakota

I am standing on a windswept hill in South Dakota looking at a tombstone with my name on it. It is a cold winter day with a grey-domed sky surrounding thousands of acres of highly fertile but currently frozen farmland. These are the flatlands of the Great Plains of America, but there are occasional white rises in the horizon due to a fresh blanket of snow. The temperature is in the twenties, there is a bitter wind, and the day feels frigid. It is the kind of day that makes you want to find shelter as the sun remains hidden and the wind chill factor cuts you to the bone. But on this particular day, I am not thinking about death but rather contemplating life, my own life and the life of the Church of God reformation movement that I love.

My journey across the Church of God is over. It was a long journey filled with wonderful moments, disappointments, disillusionment, sadness, and hope. My body is tired, and it takes effort to remain standing when the gusts of wind hit my thick winter coat. I am standing next to the snow-covered tombstones of my ancestors at the Church of God cemetery. The small white wooden church still sits adjacent. My son is examining the names on the headstones and pondering his future and the future of the Church of God that he loves as I once did long ago right here in this very spot.

He's in his forties now and is a healthy, strappingly handsome man despite the fact that he too is slowing down. Neither of us can keep up with my grandson, whose energy seems to know no bounds. He was not very interested in making this trip and ignored much of our discussion as we made our way to the place where it all began for our family 170 years ago.

My son is reflecting on that book I wrote long ago when I made a journey around the world to see the Church of God.

"It must have been amazing to go all over the world and see the Church of God in all its different forms," he says as another gust of cold wind strikes us.

"It was amazing." I say. "The worship services were so diverse, the people's personalities were so different, and each culture was so unique. Yet despite all of that, the Christian message was being proclaimed, and people's lives were being changed."

"What an adventure!" he says enviously.

"Yeah, I was robbed in Kenya." I pause and then decide to tell him something I have never shared with anyone. "And one time I was in a poor, dangerous neighborhood in Africa and two thugs chased me. My taxi driver and I had to run back to the taxi, and the motor wouldn't start! So he's turning the key and the engine won't turn on just like you see in the movies! Finally at the last possible moment, just as the bad guy put his hand through my window to open the door and pull me out to beat me and rob me, the car started and we sped off! It was incredible!"

"You never told Mom and me that part!" my son says with a look of disapproval.

"Yeah, I didn't want to worry your mother." I respond sheepishly. "It was a close call, but the whole time I kept thinking, 'Wow, this will be great for the book!' My eighty-year-old body feels pain as I laugh at the memory.

"But you didn't put it in the book, Dad."

"I know. It was a good story, but I could never figure out how to get it in there."

We both laugh. We've always enjoyed each other's company. The wind is making a whistling sound, and the temperature seems to be dropping. We can both feel it as we give each other a look signifying that we might not be able to take this exposure to the cold much longer. The headstones are visible despite the snow, but the tombstones are not, buried as they are by a foot of snow.

"Actually, I was depressed the whole time I was making the book," I confess.

"What?!" my son says, startled.

"Yes. It was a bleak couple of years. A lot of it was sad." I pause before I decide to speak further. "Parts of the journey were very discouraging and disappointing. It took its toll on me seeing the setbacks, the obstacles, and the divisions. We aspire to make the church representative of God's kingdom, yet so often we fail and our humanity makes us not much different than the rest of the world. It's painful to see the disparity between what we strive to be and what we actually are, which is a group of people who often miss the mark."

I catch my breath and pause before continuing: "I would go to some church somewhere in the world and I would hear all these bad things about Brother Tom or Pastor Jones. I'd hear about the bad ways that they were configuring their ministry or about how they hurt the church somewhere, somehow or how they really aren't Church of God. I would hear many negative things about them. Then I would go down the road to the next church and they would ask me, 'Do you know Brother Tom or Pastor Jones? They saved my life! If it weren't for them, I wouldn't be a Christian today. We love Brother Tom and Pastor Jones!'"

My son laughs. "That must have been confusing."

"It was depressing. Replay this a hundred times over and over, and that is what the experience was like for two years. There were times I could barely keep my head up. Those were probably the two most unhappy years of my life."

"So people really didn't like each other," my son asks as he directly faces me and looks into my eyes.

"No, it was more complicated than that. It was about the fact that our humanity inevitably surfaces no matter how hard we are working for the kingdom of God. As soon as Jesus built his church around those disciples, he opened the door for the church to be both human and divine. When those disciples engaged in that first footwashing, they were certainly engaging in something deeply holy, mystical, and profound. Their running away from Jesus a few hours later, however, was not so inspirational. Yet these are the people Jesus chose to carry his message." I look over at the little old white wooden church adjacent to the cemetery and notice that there are snow flurries.

My son looks over at my grandson to make sure that he is still okay. He is having a conversation with a friend in Tokyo on his watch. He wonders why we are even here and happily tunes us out as he straddles the fence close to the old church.

"And so this message of salvation gets transmitted despite our weaknesses," my son says knowing this paradox to be true.

"Yes, but the strange thing is that we know our own limitations but seem to have no patience or grace for the limitations of others." I respond.

"What do you mean Dad?"

"It's like Peter. He fails Christ by denying him three times. Later Jesus reinstates him and makes it clear that he will continue to use Peter to feed his sheep despite his previous fall. You would think that Peter would have learned the lesson that Jesus can use anybody. But later, Peter won't eat meat with the Hellenized Jews. He's afraid of being seen associating with them, and he gets reprimanded by Paul."

"So, what's your point, Dad?"

"My point is that we are so quick to judge others in the church. On one hand, we preach grace, and on the other hand, we in the church will be the first to take each other down. We need everything as defined and concrete as possible. We crave certainty and legalism despite our dependence on grace. There's something in all of us that wants to build a very large marker that clearly proclaims our understanding is right and anything else is wrong. For a people so dependent on grace, we sure have a funny way of showing it."

My journey around the world taught me that the Christian church is made to take on different shapes and forms.

"Well, we need to have absolutes," my son says firmly. This is a sore spot for him. His generation has reacted to the theological laxness of the previous generations by ushering in an unabashedly Bible-centered movement that demands a well-defined theology. It's the inevitable correction and overcorrection to the failings of the older generation, in this case, my own.

"Yes," I respond, "but my journey around the world taught me that the Christian church is made to take on different shapes and forms. Its leaders all have limitations, and each culture both strengthens the church and weakens it. God seems to allow this. He designed it this way. And a part of us resents that he uses what we don't like or understand. It would have been more comfortable for Peter if the church had adhered to the older understandings, but Paul makes it clear that this movement is growing and must become more inclusive."

"We all fall short of the glory of God, right Dad?"

"I sure do," I say as I look down at the ground. "I am the chief of sinners."

"So, where does our hostility toward each other come from, Dad?"

The snow is coming down steadily now.

"I honestly think it comes from fear, Son. Fear that if people don't subscribe to the exact vision that we have of the church, that the church will fall apart. We imagine ourselves as the last great line of defense before Satan takes over the church and destroys Christianity. But what's under threat is not the Christian church itself, rather it's our understanding of how the church should look."

"There is such a thing as heresy, you know." To my ears, my son's generation can sound so militant about theology and the church.

I affirm him. "Your generation came along at the right time. We did go to an extreme in the 2020s and 2030s. There is heresy, and I'm glad your generation stood up. You guys could have picked a better name for your movement than the New Medievalists, however."

"If you weren't getting so old and frail, I'd give you a quick punch like I used to Dad."

I chuckle. "I remember those punches. And I know you are right about heresy. It exists. But Jesus said to that very human guy Peter: 'I tell you that you are Peter, and on this rock I will build my church and the gates of hell will not overcome it.'"

"Go on," my son says as he zips up his coat.

"Going around the world all my life taught me that it is very hard to defeat the Christian church. Yes, we make mistakes, we enter periods of decline, and we divide at times, but the church continues. Whether I'm in Korea or Nigeria or Australia or Egypt, the message will not be denied. It does not come back void. Despite the brokenness of the world and the limitations of the people in the seats—and despite our bad theology, the bloody persecution, or even our lack of literacy and education—the church perseveres. Because, as Jesus told Peter, 'the gates of hell will not overcome it.'"

"Amen! That's good news! Preach it, old man!"

"Yeah, but apparently it's not such good news to us all the time. We sometimes think that this Christianity is too unwieldy and getting too far out of control, and if we don't rein it in, hell will prevail against us. We seem to think Christianity is far weaker than it is and that God is extremely dependent on us to extend his grace and his kingdom. And so we start retracting grace from each other, all in the name of defending the church, that helpless, hopeless, weak, fragile thing called Christianity."

"I'm listening," he says.

The memories of the faces I saw on my journey so long ago start flashing through my mind. "Half the people had something nice to say about Brother Tom and Pastor Jones. And the other half had something negative to say about Brother Tom and Pastor Jones. But the reality is that God chose to use them both despite their weaknesses, and all glory goes to God who is willing to love the church despite our human limitations and weaknesses."

"I know you think our generation is too militant," my son says self-conscious and frustrated at the same time. He thinks I'm rebuking him, but I'm not.

"And your generation thinks we old-timers are too lax." I put my frail hands on his shoulders. Nowadays, it hurts to raise up my arms past my waist; I miss touching my son's face and shoulders. "And old Abe Nachtigall would have thought both of us were completely apostate!"

"To him, we're Babylon!" my son says as we both laugh.

"He might have used harsher words than that. It was the nineteenth century after all," I say.

"I'll bet old Abraham doesn't think that now," my son says as he scrapes some snow off of old Abe's headstone, "because he can see how our efforts here are but a shadow, a glimpse of the kingdom in its fully realized form. There must be great humility from his current vantage point."

A sharp pain goes through my old broken body as I lift my hands up to his cheeks the way I did when he was younger.

"It's funny; I used to want the church to be one thing, static, never changing. I would get frustrated that we could not say who we are as the Church of God. Yet when I look back on my life, Son, I see that I've been many things in my life. There were times when I was a rebel and a charismatic and an intellectual. Sometimes, I went through phases where I had a very rational, analytical faith. Then difficult times would arrive and I would find myself asking for God's intervention. There would be mystical, unexplainable experiences and I became a mystic. At other times, my faith would get more emotional. I never seemed to be the same person for very long, yet I always stayed in the Church of God, and there was always room for me. Looking back now, I'm glad the Church of God was so diverse because my own faith journey became so complicated. It seems that the Church of God is a journey church, a movement that allows us to meet God in many ways, a church that need not fear that the gates of hell are encroaching upon it."

"It's kind of like the name, right, Dad? 'Church of God.' It's God's church! We need not fear. 'Fear is the enemy of mission,' as you always used to say, old man."

"Yes. Church of God is a good name. It certainly beats 'Church-of-a-weak-God-whose-message-will-get-utterly-ruined-unless-we-personally-somehow-intervene-with-our-super-awesome-wisdom,'" I say with my usual sarcasm.

"Yeah, Dad, that would require a long sign on the front lawn. You could call it COAWGWMWGURUWPSIWOSAW for short!"

We both laugh. My son and I think we are hilarious, but nobody else agrees, especially my grandson, who continues to ignore us as he talks on his watch to his friend in Japan. They are composing some song together at this very moment. It sounds terrible.

I take my hands away from my son's face, but as I do, I run my hands through his hair as I did when he was a child. "I don't know how many more times I will get to do that in my life," I think to myself as I feel his curls against my fingers.

"I'm worried about the future, Dad. It seems as if we really don't tolerate each other's opinions anymore. I think the Church of God could split. The church in Asia is so strong, and they have their own ideas. And those African theologians have introduced so many new ideas, and they seem so different from the strong Church of God congregations in Western Europe. I grew up on all that African theology, but now there are splits in the camps there, and it is challenging us. It's a mess. The second half of this new century looks like it might be rough."

As my arms go straight again, I feel the ravages of time course through my body and wince. "The church will enter another winter season. That's what happens. Things aren't good now. We have hit another rough patch. We panic, we flail, we criticize, we struggle—and the two-thousand-year-old message will continue to be transmitted despite our poor understanding of each other."

"But how do we go forward, Dad?"

"With the prayer, humility, and grace that comes with the knowledge that this really is the Church of God."

This time my son moves toward me and speaks: "When I was younger, I didn't think that you knew anything Dad. But maybe you do know quite a bit." His teenage years go flashing through my mind as he gives me that smirk I know so well.

Another gust of wind strikes.

"No, I don't know much, son. The older I get, the less I know. I know that God loves us. And I know that God loves our church and that he allows us to go through struggles. Perhaps that is when he challenges us to bestow the grace to others that he has bestowed upon us."

The snow comes down more heavily, and the temperature seems to take yet another drop.

"I don't know much at all, Son. I do know that I love you. And I love your mother."

"I know Dad," he says. This time, he puts his hand on my craggy face.

"You know," I say to him as I feel his hands on my face, "there is nothing that you could ever do that would stop me from loving you."

"I know that, Dad."

"And there's nothing that we can ever do that will stop Jesus from loving us."

My son nods.

"He loves us because we are the church. We are his people, his children."

My son removes his hands from my face, and I speak again: "I don't understand why we have such little grace and patience for each other in the church. Why is it that Jesus will lay his life down for the church, yet we cannot extend grace to our fellow human beings in the church? That question haunts me."

"It should haunt all of us," my son adds.

We stare silently at the ground. His boots squeak as he twists his foot on the snow. My son then offers a possible explanation. "Maybe it's because we all love the church so much that we want to hold onto it with all our might in our own little way. Maybe the problem, ironically, is love. But not *agape*-love. Instead, it's a fear-based love of self-protection.

"You get your wisdom from your father," I say. We both laugh knowing that it has to have come from his mother. Making my son laugh has always been my greatest joy.

"Maybe this is why it is so important to be a people that repent," I say as I stroke the back of his head. Even though he's well into middle age, I still see him as my baby, the one I'm so proud of. "If we repent, it reminds us how little we know. How far away from good we are in and of ourselves. Maybe a church that repents is one that always surrenders to the will of God, no matter how scary that may be."

"Are we going to make it through this challenging time, Dad? I grew up in the Church of God, but will my son's son have a Church of God to go to when he grows up?"

"I don't know. It depends on how well we love each other. But I know he will love us through our weaknesses. A baby who is a savior, a carpenter who is a king, a crucified man that is God. From within the weakness of humanity, God chooses to speak."

We are both suddenly startled by a shout.

"Can we go? It's freezing out here!" my grandson yells as he stands next to the gate of the cemetery.

My son and I look at each other and laugh at his obliviousness to our existential queries. If it's not a song, a girl, or a sport, he has no time for it.

"Are you sure you want to put the church in his generation's hands?" My son says, laughing.

I pause dramatically with a look of total fear to make my son laugh more. "Actually," I say, "I would have it no other way."

We leave behind the Church of God cemetery on the plains of South Dakota and close the metal gates behind us. The tracks that we left behind will soon disappear as a fresh layer of snow falls from the sky. There will be little evidence that we were ever here. But the church on the little hill will remain standing. Praise God. Through it all, the church will remain standing.

appendix

Framing the Mosaic
Q & A

"**I**s the Church of God reformation movement finished?" At the beginning of this book, I was at a Church of God cemetery pondering the future of this movement I love. It wasn't at all clear that the Church of God (Anderson, Indiana) could survive the changing landscape of Christianity away from the cultural, theological, and organizational identity that movements and denominations rely on to maintain their cohesion. The forces of decentralization seemed too strong. Now, after spending a few years on the road visiting the Church of God, the task still seems daunting. There is a way forward, however, but there is little time to choose it. The survival of the Church of God (Anderson, Indiana) as a relevant movement will be determined in the next decade.

The Church of God has never had a strong adhesive glue holding it together in comparison to mainline denominations, but in this current era of decentralization, our lack of connectivity combined with our habitual passivity threaten to be our undoing.

When I set out on my journey, I did not intend to write a book that would tell the Church of God what it needs to do in the future. Instead, I set out to listen to as many people as I could, do some research, talk to experts, and through that journey give us a macro-perspective on where we are as a movement at this particular time.

In this appendix, I do not presume to tell a whole movement what to do. I committed in the introduction to making this book descriptive as opposed to prescriptive. Instead, I am offering my opinion of what we need to consider and discuss together if we are to remain a dynamic, relevant movement in the future. In other words, I am trying to establish a platform upon which dialogue can begin and trying to set up some *realistic parameters* for that conversation. I will do this through a Q & A format divided into three sections: (1) Framing the Challenge, (2) Framing the Potential Dangers Ahead, and (3) Final Thoughts.

I. Framing the Challenge

Q: What was it like to take a journey across the Church of God?

It was the journey of a lifetime. The Church of God is filled with wonderful people who are doing God's work amid very challenging circumstances. Everywhere I went, I was awed and humbled by what people are navigating in order to do ministry in the twenty-first century. It's easy to criticize people's approaches from the outside—youth pastors, administrators, traditional churches, megachurches, missionaries, people from different cultures. But once you see the realities that they are grappling with, it makes you very humble. God needs all types of people and all kinds of approaches. Christianity was made for this. It is odd that we look for conformity in the church when what makes Christianity unique among all world religions is its amazing ability to take radically different shapes in this thing we call the church.

Q: Is the Church of God movement finished?

The Church of God reformation movement is not necessarily finished, but it is in crisis, and we need to be realistic about the size and scope of this challenge. We've often thought too simplistically about what the problems with the Church of God have been. This book highlights the myriad challenges movements like ours are facing at the moment. And while a sense of crisis has been with us for most of the last one hundred years because of our unease with institutions and man-made organizations, this time we really are in a fight for our lives. What faces us now is not a slow decline, but rather disintegration. There has always been stormy weather for us, but now a perfect storm has formed.

That perfect storm consists of a few *ultra*-macro-trends that are coming together at one time. These include: **(1) A postmodern rejection of organized religion.** The hostility to institutions and organizations in postmodern cultures and particularly among the younger generations is leading them away from organized religion. **(2) A shift away from centralization to decentralization.** The outdated centralized modes of organizations are being rejected at local, state, and national levels throughout the religious world. **(3) Excessive individualism and excessive autonomy in religious practice.** Societies in both the Western and non-Western worlds are becoming increasingly atomized and individualistic. The wealthier and more urban the world becomes, the more individualistic it becomes. Overly personalized religion can lead to weak, extremely loose, disconnected, and unaccountable relationships between churches, regions, and countries, as well as to a breakdown in community. **(4) Explosive religious growth in the non-Western world.** While the explosive growth of Christianity in Latin America, Africa, and Asia is wonderful, it is also bringing its fair share of heresy and false gospels (many originating in America). They are not necessarily immersed in Christendom's models of organizing the church, and while this can be good, it means groups rooted in Christendom must adjust to this. In addition to these four *ultra*-macro trends are many other macro trends that have weakened the influence of denominations and movements like ours.

Q: What did you find to be the biggest internal challenges facing the Church of God specifically?

The Church of God is not alone in its struggle, but it does have some unique weaknesses that have exacerbated the problem. One of the first is the spirit of excessive autonomy. The Church of God started as a protest movement against divisive denominations that were perceived to care more about building up institutional membership than they did spreading the gospel. The Church of God charted a new "missional" path that emphasized our need to allow the Holy Spirit to guide us and to focus primarily on the gospel message—as opposed to building up institutions and bureaucracies. They believed that their efforts would restore the Church of God to holiness and unity. The message grew and continued to attract people, forcing new levels of organization. While the need for more structures, organizations, and institutions grew, our willingness to find a balance between the need for organization and autonomy shrank. A reactionary posture against institutions and organization arose instead of a more mature healthy skepticism. It is the nature of human beings to go to extremes. Upon seeing the damage that denominations and hierarchical structures can cause to the church, the Church of God went to the other extreme, failing to see that there would be a high cost to this excessive spirit of autonomy. The stage was set for division between numerous camps in the Church of God who would fail to communicate with each other or take each other seriously as partners in the kingdom. This autonomous spirit has spread far from North America to other parts of the world.

The radical individualism of the nineteenth century American frontier entered into the DNA of the Church of God and grew stronger over time, eventually getting transmitted throughout the world. This excessive individualism has even spread to Church of God congregations that have cultures that are highly communal and that culturally reject radical individualism. This is very unfortunate, but it's a testimony to the power of movements and denominations to affect people even in negative ways.

Q: Don't all denominations and movements have divisions within them?

Yes, but without creeds or concrete organizational structures empowered to hold us together, it has been easy for the Church of God to separate into numerous camps with little to pull us back together. Perhaps this would have happened in any denomination or movement, but once again, we have little to fall back on due to our aversion to creeds and organization. Many regions now are quite disconnected from the rest of the global Church of God. Some countries are only too happy to exist completely on their own with little concern or awareness of the greater body. In one country, I met pastors in a wealthy first-world city who had no idea that the Church of God existed outside of their continent. There are countries that try to proactively reach out to their Church of God neighbors and do so in effective ways, but in general, we are not very connected globally. The Church of God went international early. We've always been good at being international. We have not always been good at being global. Those are two different things. We have the DNA of tribalism in our system. We are weaker when we are divided as a body and unaccountable to each other. We are fortunate that we have avoided some of the very serious schisms that other denominations are facing. I would argue that's because we are too divided to divide.

Q: We have valued local church autonomy and avoided creeds and a centralized leadership of the church for good reason! Are these not legitimate concerns?

Yes, but not to the extent that they were in the nineteenth century and early twentieth century. In our earlier history, the Church of God leaders feared man-rule by a central organization. The twentieth century, however, has made excessive centralization by Protestant groups impossible. The danger today is not that Anderson will take over the local church. We have seen in this book very clearly that we have entered a new age of extreme decentralization, and the center or religious organizations (e.g., Anderson, Louisville, Salt Lake City, Rome) are not capable of this kind of autocracy that we were so afraid of back then. It is a highly democratic age now, and even the most successful centralized religious organization (the Roman Catholic Church) is struggling to retain its authority. It flies in the face of everything that has happened in the past sixty years (since denominations peaked) to be so fearful of "man-rule." In many countries, the Church of God has to be linked to a denomination in order to exist or even receive missionaries. These are the kinds of twenty-first century realities that the reformers didn't have to deal with, but we do.

We have a central organization, but it is no more possible for Anderson to become a center of oppressive, hierarchical, man-rule for the entire movement than it is for the city of Anderson to supplant New York City as "the city that never sleeps." It won't happen. The much bigger danger is that we hang onto irrational fears of man-rule while failing to see that we are embracing autonomy past the point of no return. So our organizational weakness (inability to define how we are concretely connected and then remain united) has led to excessive autonomy, which then leads us to be weak in our other core area of emphasis, unity.

Q: So we are not doing well in our key area of unity?

It's been widely recognized for a long time that unity has been hard to come by in the Church of God. Even in the very early years, there was a lot of disagreement and intolerance—even more than now, although the numbers were smaller. But today there is far less name-calling and more widespread detachment. There are a number of linchpins that helped to hold the movement together over the decades that are now gone, for instance the *Gospel Trumpet/Vital Christianity*, the World Conference, the widespread use of Church of God hymnody, and the use of Church of God curricula, to name a few. All of these things have eroded quite a bit. In order to counter this, there will need to be an intentional effort to create new ways (or resuscitating old ways) of transmitting Church of God unity in our relationships, structures, and theology. As a fellowship, the pursuit of unity for unity's sake (devoid of a concrete missional effort), just leads to stagnation as you try to appease every group possible. So we need more strategic unity as opposed to nonstrategic unity.

Q: If the Church of God is made up of "every blood-washed one," why do we even need to worry about the Church of God (Anderson, Indiana)? Perhaps this movement has had its day?

I don't think the issue is whether we need to save our movement because we have an exclusive understanding of Christian truth and salvation. The Church of God was never intended to be a denomination, so we do not all need to rally for the sake of a denomination. But over decades, a relationship evolved and we became a unique family. New works were started, investments made in institutions, and relationships built between countries through work camps; there's property to be managed and pensions to be delivered. We did become this specific part of the greater church body. We also come from the same theological, cultural, organizational DNA. The issue at hand is whether we care about preserving this family that we call the Church of God (Anderson, Indiana) and go on a mission together by using our unique experiences and gifts to strengthen the greater Christian church.

As I traveled around the world, I was surprised by how emphatically people do want to preserve this relationship! Many people are anxiously waiting for something to mobilize us so that we can use our specific gifts as the Church of God to enrich the greater kingdom and save souls. A much smaller group of people say that they don't care, but I have found that they do care; they just feel frustrated at not being part of the conversation or feel as if nothing is happening. I believe the Church of God brings some specific gifts that could enrich the world in the twenty-first century, but we have to identify them and mobilize in unity.

Q: What could be the specific purpose of the Church of God in the twenty-first century? Did the trip yield insights?

The biggest discovery of my journey was that in many ways we are more relevant today than in the nineteenth century; we just don't see it. We have the potential to bring ideas to the greater church that will be vital in the twenty-first century. Let me explain.

First of all, while other denominations and branches of Christendom are struggling with decentralization, we are in a unique position in that we already value the local church and come from a movement that has operated in a decentralized style. In the post-Christendom West, our disinterest in institutionalism makes us very appealing to postmodern people. The ideas of Warner and the reformers are given new life within this twenty-first century context of decentralization. In the non-Western world, Christianity is expanding more rapidly among groups that show flexibility as the Church of God does. We are a decentralized movement for a decentralized world. This is tremendous news for us. Our identity is not wrapped up in an institution the way it is for the Roman Catholic Church. We are positioned perfectly for this era. Look at the way that the young pastors in Fishers and Phoenix (chapter 5) spoke with high regard for the decentralized nature of the Church of God.

Second, the message of holiness is one that is now more relevant than ever. In both the non-Western and Western worlds, we are seeing the growth of false gospels that do not emphasize a holy life but rather focus on things such as materialism and transactional, utilitarian Christianity, a Christianity that's not about having the Holy Spirit transform our lives and community but simply about getting things from God. Christianity becomes a means to an end instead of a journey upon which we take holiness in all aspects of our church life and individual life seriously. The growth of Christianity in the non-Western world is a triumph, but it is also messy and occasionally heretical. The Church of God congregations I visited in Latin America, Africa, Asia, and throughout the non-Western world were unique in their settings because they proclaim an internal change in our daily life—not money or growth or showy worship. In many cases, they are voices crying out in the wilderness. They are very important voices! Think of the role played by Pastor Zurbito on the Philippine island of Masbate or Dr. Latif's church in Alexandria, Egypt (chapter 5).

As for holiness in the Western world—particularly the post-Christendom world—churches will be structured to be less concerned with our old pieties. They will try to be more inclusive of people and will be even less dogmatic than the Baby Boomer churches for at least a generation. However, throughout this movement, there will be a need for a renewed emphasis on holiness as dogma-free churches come close to excessive leniency in the personal realm. Holiness will be a helpful corrector here as long as it doesn't fall into legalism, which is, admittedly, tricky. Holiness is deeply relevant in the twenty-first century. This was perhaps the most striking (and encouraging) thing I saw in my two years of travel.

A third emphasis of ours that is now very relevant as we enter the twenty-first century is unity. We do a poor job of unity within our own movement, and frankly, we need to repent. But time and time again on the road I saw that it is the local Church of God congregation that does the best job of interacting with people of other denominations and movements, as we saw in Russia (chapter 6). This was especially true in the non-Western world. Non-Western Christianity has a tendency to be very fragmented, (although it is not prone to the explosive wars that Western Christianity had during its expansion phase). The Church of God can be a force for peace among Christian churches through strategic endeavors. Furthermore, in many countries, because of various kinds of persecution that are occurring now and will occur in this new century, it is very important that Protestant churches stay connected in places like Russia, Myanmar, Egypt, India, and China—places where all churches concerned with evangelism are linked and maligned by the government. Once again, we can fill a very serious role for the greater Christian church. We are actually more needed in the twenty-first century than in the nineteenth. I firmly believe that! We just haven't seen it and haven't embraced it as a united body.

Q: This sounds exciting, but how do we mobilize ourselves if we have "a reactionary posture against institutions and organizations?"

First, we would have to admit that we have often had an unrealistic view of the need for organizations, structures, and accountability. This inevitably set the stage for problems in the Church of God further down the line. The institutional growth phase in the Church of God coincided with boom times in the American economy. The weak structures of the movement were not necessarily exposed as fast as they might have been because our movement (and all others) was entering a period of rapid expansion.

Hierarchical organizations can be abused and inefficient, and the Church of God was never destined to be one; however, hierarchical organizations also have the potential to create safeguards for the unity of the church by having clear lines of authority, channels of communication on important matters, and structures that clearly reveal who is accountable to whom. Expectations are made clearer, ordination standards are more uniform, and when problems arise, the potential is there for the buck to stop somewhere. Clearly, I am not suggesting that the Church of God should have been a hierarchical church or should now become one. This is not even possible at this late stage in this present era. However, we need to be honest in looking at the upsides and the downsides of the road taken.

In the Church of God, a failure to create structures that value the autonomy of the local church and local pastor but which also *clearly* call for accountability in fellowship have left us very unsure about who is accountable to whom and what being a Church of God congregation even means. In many regions of the Church of God, churches and leaders cut off people in other regions because of disagreements. Proper behavior becomes too subjective. In some countries, little fiefdoms have emerged with each region claiming authority. At times, dangerous leadership has emerged in local or national churches, and there has been no way to deal with it. While it sounds nice in theory to say that every church should just follow the Holy Spirit and be autonomous in regard to other churches, the reality is that as a fellowship we are interconnected, and when problems emerge in one part of the body, they have the potential to infect the whole body.

Q: What do you mean by "clearly call for accountability in fellowship?" You're making me nervous.

What we can do is have a sophisticated discussion on our body of Christ theology. The Church of God does have a rich history of discussions on the matter of ecclesiology, but we have not put that at the forefront in the past few decades. Perhaps it is time to revisit these discussions, and it is most certainly time to renew the discussions about our relationship to one another. General Director Ron Duncan has recently begun discussing what a covenantal relationship looks like. This seems very promising. *Agape*-based discussions on covenantal relationships could be aimed at examining how we could seek our neighbor's highest good through an accountable relationship within the Church of God as opposed to protecting our own turf out of a false sense of oppression by higher powers. It may offend our sensibilities to think about covenants or statements of relationship and accountability, but the past 130 years have shown that in this fallen world, we often need the safeguards that community provides more than we need independence and autonomy. Once again, this is something the world's cultures have long understood (including the Jewish culture in the time of Jesus). The need for concrete community has been a basic supposition of human beings for millennia. We are highly unusual in our extreme aversion to this. Is it biblical?

Q: So the answer is man-made creeds? How dare you!

Not at all! I value my life too much to suggest such a thing. What I am suggesting is that a complete lack of understanding about what fellowship entails in the Church of God is dangerous at this moment in history. It has already led to much disconnection and has the possibility of getting far worse in the atomized environment of this new century. To have a Church of God reformation movement in the twenty-first century is to be able to articulate who we are and how and why we are on a mission together. Holiness and unity, as I discussed above, help us define the who and the why. We believe God put our Wesleyan-Holiness movement together for a reason and our message is an important part of the greater Christian movement at this moment in time. But the how will require a much clearer understanding of how we are related to each other. It may involve a covenant, it may involve an international commitment, or it may involve being much more intentional in defining our new works and old partnerships in the future. It could be all three or something else, but one way or another, we need a far greater level of interconnectivity and accountability to survive.

Q: Doesn't this fly in the face of us being a decentralized movement in a decentralized world? Would we be contradicting ourselves?

No. We mustn't make the same mistake as we have made in the past, which is to assume that the church will function fine without some human coordination. This was proven wrong, and that is how we began the process of institutionalizing in a haphazard and divisive way. The Holy Spirit will always guide the work of the church. But the business of the church requires human involvement. We must not be gnostic about this! We are not talking about centralizing and bureaucratizing. I have already made it clear that this will not work in this era we are now living in. It is more about developing networks and making sure that each region of the Church of God (Anderson, districts, countries, continents) are proactively doing things that help strengthen the core pillars needed for the movement to do mission as a church body with a specific theology and culture. Each region and church needs to be proactive in connecting to the greater body. A renewed emphasis on Church of God theology would need to take place. An understanding of what we specifically have to offer as a movement needs to be articulated. A clearer understanding of our ecclesiology for the sake of mission needs to be embraced.

Q: But there are many voices in the Church of God. What are these voices saying?

There are many voices around the world with very different points of view. This is one of the reasons why I wrote the book—to give them a forum to speak. But we can't be oblivious to the complexity of the challenges before us. That is also why I wrote the book, to take pictures of how turbulent and challenging the environment is when you factor in the whole world—not just our little corner of the Church of God.

In general, the voices I have heard can be divided into five categories:

1. **The renewalists:** These Church of God people want to call us back to our Church of God roots and think the key to bringing dynamism in the movement is focusing on and rearticulating our beliefs as they were understood at the end of the nineteenth century and the beginning and middle of the twentieth century. The strength of this view is that it calls us to take our

movement's theology and culture seriously, which we must do. The potential pitfall is that it can unwittingly frame things in ways that are very rooted in Christendom and that makes sense for the traditional world but that are hard to understand in the post-Christendom and Book of Acts worlds that now exist in the twenty-first century. It can fail to realize that no church exists in a cultural and historical vacuum, not even the churches in the Book of Acts. God doesn't remove us from human history and culture. Quite the opposite. He himself intentionally entered into it and works through the limitations.

2. **Bible and theology proponents:** These Church of God people say we need to simply go back to preaching the Word (forget about the bells and whistles and seeker-sensitive approaches to presenting the gospel) and be unabashedly clear and unapologetic about Christian theological absolutes. The strength of this view is that it seizes upon the truth that the Bible needs to be at the forefront of all we do and that to some extent, the world will always be hostile toward us when we embrace Christian truth. It challenges us to not get overwhelmed by culture in our efforts to do evangelism. The potential pitfall is that it underestimates how inherently diverse Christianity is as a faith. Acts 2 opened the door for Christian truth to be presented in many ways through many different cultures. All of us having the same version of the Bible will not lead a Korean, a Nigerian, an Iowan, and a Seattle Starbucks employee to construct the church or process the faith in the same way. That flexibility is Christianity's great strength, but it means that just having the right theology or biblical interpretation will not yield uniformity. There is orthodoxy in Christianity, but there is no such thing as total uniformity.

3. **The revivalists:** These Church of God people say that what the church needs is to simply pray for revival and a new movement will sweep us up and usher in a new day. They see a lack of dynamism and purpose in the Church of God and believe a fresh wave of inspiration from the Holy Spirit must overtake us. The strength of this view is that it understands that people,

churches, and organizations need a vision from the Lord. We need a specific calling to get our attention and mobilize us for ministry. The potential pitfall is that it underestimates how difficult it is to mobilize such a large, disparate group of people and how it is the nature of movements that they eventually die or go dormant. Movements are easier to usher in when you have a small group of people and a narrow cause everyone can relate to in a concrete way.

4. **The anti-institutionalists:** These Church of God people think that we should really go back to the original Church of God by going forward into the noninstitutional, post-Christendom paradigm where there is no interest in preserving institutions, songs, or anything else. Instead, we simply are a community of believers meeting in houses with no concern for buildings or Church of God (Anderson, Indiana) connections. The Church of God is the whole church, so why worry specifically about our movement? The strength of this view is that it reminds us that we are not meant to be a group of people committed to propping up our man-made institutions. It also introduces flexibility in presenting the gospel and reconfiguring our churches, which may be very necessary in the twenty-first century, particularly in the post-Christendom world and the Book of Acts world. The potential pitfall is that Church of God history shows what happens to loosely knit groups. They either fall apart or institutionalize eventually. It also does not deal with the fact that we have relationships, institutions, property, pension plans, and many other things that are valuable and will not disappear. There are 130 years of experiences and relationships that are still relevant to many people, not to mention the experience of the larger historic church. "There's nothing new under the sun." Living disconnected from everything else is not easy.

5. **The intentionally missional:** These Church of God people, like the revivalists, believe we need to embark on a specific mission. It doesn't necessarily have to be one specific, divinely inspired purpose, but our efforts need to have focus and a clear purpose as opposed to being about "building up our denomina-

tion" or having an inward, self-protective, institutional stance. Forget who we are or who we were and focus on what we are doing now. The strength of this view is that it reminds us that people will not mobilize around an institution (or denomination) that is just interested in self-preservation. Loyalty to a denomination will not just form over time, because too many other organizations mobilize people for kingdom ministry without demanding loyalty. We can't confuse loyalty to the Church of God with loyalty to Jesus. It also strongly reminds us that our purpose is to expand the kingdom and change the world. The potential pitfall is that, as with the anti-institutionalists, they can underestimate how much important experience has been accrued over the years that is still of value. Also, they can underemphasize how theological beliefs and the transmission of theology inevitably become very important and need to be dealt with as the mission evolves. Evangelism alone is not enough to sustain health. We often seem to erroneously think that it is.

I would also mention three other groups: **The genuinely apathetic**, those who feel so burned that they don't care or who come from another tradition or denomination and don't even know what the issues are; **the supposedly apathetic**, those who say they don't care but who deep down just feel discouraged or resigned to nothing changing; and **the dormant**, those who would care and mobilize if someone would just call on them to mobilize.

II. Framing the Potential Dangers Ahead

Q: You have said that the Church of God pillars of holiness and unity are even more relevant in the twenty-first century, and you highlighted the way we are at a pivotal moment in our movement's future. What are the potential dangers that would cause us to miss this window of opportunity?

I think the first area we will have to struggle with is our strong propensity toward passivism. We tend to be pretty passive, and even if we are presented with a particular challenge and actually get to talking about it, we are very likely to eventually just forget about it and let nature take its course. Perhaps this is due to the fact that it's never clear what body has the authority to mobilize us (other than God) and we are very suspicious of strong leadership. Without structures or organizations that can cast a vision, as well as an ingrained hostility toward strong leaders, no group, country, or individual feels comfortable picking up the mantle. Consequently, we can easily go into our default passive and aimless mode.

Q: Do we need to have a global headquarters to serve as a unifying voice?

No. But we need to have a global gathering that brings us all together in the same room from time to time. We need more regional forums where the issues we are facing at the dawn of the twenty-first century can be discussed in a more intentional (and globally coordinated) manner and where the right hand can know what the left hand is doing. Realistically, there is some need for a particular location to serve as a hub of inter-connectivity. "Anderson" (USA) is that logical place to serve as the lodestar. This is because more than any other Church of God geographical location, the United States has built up the most relationships on six continents over time. Despite the fact that the United States is no longer living in a unipolar Church of God world (where we are the only large and influential Church of God country), it still remains the Church of God country with the most resources. In my travels, I was surprised at how often people in other countries expect and want the United States to continue serving as a center for Church of God connectivity. In the future, there may be other regions that can do it and want to do it, but for now, the United States still has the best Church of God infrastructure for Church of God interconnectivity (and English is our most widely used language).

This should not be taken as a mandate to decide issues for the whole church (like the Vatican) but rather to be the catalyst in establishing global dialogue and relationships. Ideally, many other hubs will arise in partnership alongside the United States. We are not looking for one Rome and many smaller Romes. We are talking about organic decentralized networks that share some basic uniting Church of God principles and coordinate for ministry.

Q: So we need to establish better methods of communication or we will lose connection?

With no official spokesperson and no official mouthpiece, we are a movement in which the right hand often does not know what the left hand is doing. In many cases, people wish it were not so. Many people around the Church of God are desperate to see channels of communication reopen. The vast majority still feel a strong desire to regularly meet as the global Church of God. There are some areas where communication is lost because autonomous spirits have dismissed the rest of the body as irrelevant. In other areas, that excessive autonomy has led to regions, even at times entire countries, cutting themselves off from the rest of the body in an unbiblical manner. Our inability to keep the World Conference together, as well as keep our periodicals relevant and financially supported, has taken an enormous toll on the movement's communication abilities. Conferences and camp meetings that do continue to meet are increasingly appealing to only a particular demographic group, further hindering communication. The replacement of Church of God hymns (perhaps inevitably) by more modern praise music has taken away one of our primary vehicles for learning and understanding Church of God theological heritage. Lastly, those influential people, literature, and central organizations that do still possess the influence to get the movement's ear have not always had a compelling voice or message to present to the global church. A mix of new methods and old methods will probably need to be established. It will be up to the church to decide.

Q: You mention in chapter 3 that there are three worlds of the Church of God. Is this dangerous?

There's the traditional world, the post-Christendom world, and the Book of Acts world. All of them process the faith in very different ways. The traditional world is deeply rooted in Christendom and is often in decline. This world seems conservative compared to the post-Christendom churches, but it appears liberal to the Book of Acts world. The post-Christendom world is really disconnecting from institutions and relies more on experience than propositional truths. The Book of Acts world is more community-centered, engages the supernatural, puts the Bible first minus many other trappings, and is often very dynamic and socially conservative. It often needs theological and organizational investment. I think there's a real danger that these three worlds will not be able to communicate with each other unless we create bridges of understanding now.

Q: What other dangers are we facing? You mention the generation gap in chapter 2.

In the West, it is highly probable that the post-Christendom world will grow at a more rapid pace (particularly in the United States) than the traditional world that most understands the older history, culture, and traditions of the Church of God (which, whether we like it or not, have defined us as a family). Emerging/missional churches will be prone to disconnect from the family unless it can be made clear that the movement is not about institutionalism and is relevant. So this will be one challenge.

Second, we will see more of these younger generation churches configured to deal with the postmodern mindset. They have a less dualistic worldview than the churches of the older generations and the churches in the non-Western world. The so-called emerging/missional church, will grow and this will cause friction with the traditional church and the non-Western church. They will have very different definitions of piety. Now is the time for these three different worlds to begin understanding and interacting with each other. A decision to disengage from each other and label each other as heretical could be disastrous to the Church of God movement (and all of Christianity) at this critical juncture. Although they are not dualists, neither are they pagans. They value nuance and relationship more than dogma and programs. We must keep in mind that the nature of these recent global shifts have created generational divides that are far more extreme than in previous eras. We're also dealing with very wounded young people who have grown up devoid of strong communities and healthy families.

Avoiding this division will require leaders who are willing to acknowledge that the Christian church has always been far more elastic than we often admit. Indeed, it is this elasticity in the church's structure and culture which has made Christianity the only truly global religion at the dawn of the twenty-first century. An insistence on conformity (as radical Islam tends to do) would weaken that aspect of the church that most enables it to grow from Montreal to Mozambique.

We cannot afford to cut the young people out because they don't fit our image of Christianity. Our own image of Christianity is but a snapshot in comparison to the dynamically changing panorama that global Christianity has been over two thousand years. Let us not forget, the original Church of God pioneers were young and were viewed as heretical as were Jesus and his disciples by the "God-fearing people" of his time. The church is always more flexible than we would like to admit, and the "right church" is always the one we find most comfortable to our sensibilities. In my journey around the world, I found that it is usually leaders between the ages of thirty and forty-five who do the best job of navigating the generational divides. They have been in the traditional church long enough to understand its value but have also lived in the globalized world enough to understand that younger generations have been shaped in a new way. Unfortunately, we have few leaders in this age group, and they are often not very empowered. Meanwhile older leaders are in danger of not leaving behind a legacy despite years of hard work.

Q: Are we doing enough to produce young leadership that will carry the movement forward?

For the most part, the Church of God has been too passive in identifying new leadership, creating talent pipelines, and passing the torch to younger generations. The assumption that the next generation will be Church of God because the older generation was has been proven wrong. In many cases, the young generation chooses its local church based on pragmatic reasons, not on issues of theology or out of loyalty. In some parts of the world, there is a cultural hostility toward putting a younger generation in leadership, and sometimes structures emerge that prevent it altogether. In other parts of the Church of God, leaders have simply not known how to reach out to the younger generation and perhaps this paralysis has gone on for two or three decades. Some of the countries with the largest population of young people are the worst at mentoring and producing young leadership. With the societal trends leading young people away from ministry and church altogether, a movement that hopes to survive must be extremely proactive in reaching its youth. The demographics alone suggest that as the older generation dies in many places, the Church of God (Anderson, Indiana) will die with them. The lack of a concerted effort to deal with this was startling and discouraging.

Q: How do we produce a new generation of pastors who value the Church of God in a time when so few want to go into ministry?

It appears that discipleship and mentoring need to be emphasized to a much greater degree in the future. By discipleship and mentoring, I mean a long-term investment in individuals, in ministry students, in our systems of training and ordination, and in people undergoing ordination. In many places, ordination standards have been far too lax. Too many young people are growing up devoid of a mentor (and a church) tracking them and guiding them through their lives. Then upon seeking ordination, they get a certificate without having been watched or mentored over a considerable period of time. Higher education can also lead toward a disconnection between the seminary graduate and the people in the pews. This happens in both the wealthier Western world and the non-Western world. We will need to discuss how the ordination process can focus on multiyear practical training under a mentor that is followed by multiyear educational training, which is then followed by multiyear supervised work. Pastors need academic and Bible knowledge, but they also need to be emotionally and spiritually nurtured and introduced to the day-to-day realities of ministry in their communities. Then they need to be linked to other pastors and not minister in isolation. Too often, pastors possess one thing but not the other three (academic knowledge, spiritual discipline, practical experience, and accountability to a community). This seems too often to lead to short tenures or bad experiences all around the world.

Q: Do our educational models need to be re-evaluated?

Yes. Originally, the Church of God did not believe in having institutions of higher education. In time, the benefits of higher education spread throughout the Christian world. In general, as countries modernize and people reach higher economic levels, they expect their pastors to have an equal or higher level of education. The danger has always been that education can drive a wedge between the pastor and the people. This has happened at times both in Western and non-Western nations.

The non-Western world values education as well, and many have sought education at Church of God schools. But in both the non-Western and Western worlds, more and more people are having difficulty paying for tuition. They are seeking cheaper alternatives and alternatives that do not require leaving their families behind or taking out enormous loans. Further-more, many pastors can no longer depend on the church to provide a full salary, so they are bivocational and do not have the time or money for semi-nary. These pressures will only increase in these coming decades, so schools will have to look closely at their business models. Ordination committees will have to look at their regional training programs, and more training will have to come from nontraditional methods. TEE (Theological Education by Extension) is playing an important part in educating people in the Church of God, but I ran out of both time and money to explore it further. There may be more in-house (within the church) ministry education models that emerge on a larger scale, such as those we saw in the Dominican Republic (chapter 2) or in the African-American church (chapter 4).

Q: Is there a danger that our local, regional, national, and inter-national organizations will not be able to configure themselves properly for these complexities?

Yes. As I say in the book, organization is our Achilles heel. It is vital in this new era that we have the right people, with the right skill sets, in the right job, for the right amount of time. It's not hard to fill positions with people who have a calling or a love for the church. Nobody's in it for the money. What happens too often around the world, however, is that our key organi-zations are led by people who may be great ministers or teachers but who are not great mangers, so they get into positions for which they do not possess the proper skill sets. A lack of good organizational managers is com-mon to all religious organizations, but in the case of the Church of God, we do not value organizations or leaders very much, which dilutes the talent pool. If a movement has a culture hostile toward leadership, it's not going to attract or produce strong leaders. We also have a culture that doesn't confront well. So when we get on the wrong track, few people arise to call us back to the right track. Instead, we trust that things will work out, they don't, people disconnect, and we go back into our default passive position. The end result is that we repel visionary leadership and lose many of our best people to other movements or organizations. It's a vicious cycle that you can see throughout the movement globally and across the decades.

It is always difficult for the church (of any denomination) to find the right balance of vision, management, and pastoral sensitivity in one leader, but we often don't even seem to be conscious of the need to look for these things. Key positions are filled willy-nilly, and there is an unspoken belief that God will just figure things out for us. Meanwhile, the organizations and the movement continue to weaken.

Q: What other dangers might we face on the organizational front?

Even in companies and corporations, the tendency is to make the minimal amount of deep change possible but then to make loud, showy external changes to convince people that issues are being dealt with. This is a common trap for car companies, schools, denominations, and everybody else—even in our personal spiritual lives we are like this. We are not interested in deep, internal change, which involves pain and risk, but rather we want a quick fix that gets the scrutiny off of us. In many cases, our organizations and institutions around the world need deep structural changes to avoid simply rearranging the deck chairs on the *Titanic*. The danger, however, is that there will be few people willing to make the sacrifices to create fundamental change. It is risky. It is the way of the cross instead of self-preservation. It doesn't come naturally.

At the same time that our organizations must become more adept at organizing themselves correctly for this new century, we the people need to be much more realistic about the need for organization in the church. The marginalization of administrators in the Church of God needs to stop. Had E. E. Byrum not organized the church when he did, we wouldn't be here right now. There were many other movements like ours, but an E. E. Byrum never came along to keep things running and growing. God uses human beings to help give his work direction and clarification. If our leaders take risks and deal with the deep structural issues, we need to support them, not marginalize them or be apathetic, which is our usual tendency.

Q: Will the Church of God be able to retain its unique musical heritage?

Certainly many people care about it, and the younger generation is open to it when it is presented to them in unique ways, as we saw in Vincennes, Indiana (chapter 5). Sometimes it has to be done with a few changes in presentation. The music industry (like the world of denominations) is also undergoing a period of massive decentralization, so it's not clear how a particular tradition's musical heritage would be transmitted ten years from now. What is clear is that we will probably not be able to go back to the Church of God exactly as it was at its musical pinnacle. This probably means we must use music in new and different ways to transmit our theology. I'll leave that up to people who can carry a tune.

The most important part of worship is not preserving our traditions or styles; rather it is glorifying God, and this is something that all Church of God congregations are trying to do. The consumer-oriented nature of society combined with the heretical gospels floating around have meant that many worship services are actually teaching people to view worship and church as a place to get things from God (e.g., money, fame, attention as a performing artist) instead of laying their lives down at the altar. As I mentioned previously, I believe that the Church of God emphasis on holiness can stand as a bulwark against this abuse of worship that is becoming so common throughout the entire world. We must educate the church on the meaning of worship.

Q: In the book, you make it clear that geography has affected the self-understanding of the Church of God and that it continues to be a barrier in many places.

We shouldn't expect different regions to process the faith in exactly the same way. There are a unique set of pressures on the Church of God in Siberia that differ greatly from the Church of God in West Virginia, which is nothing like the Church of God I visited in Los Angeles. Geography doesn't just affect the current religious atmosphere; it also forms invisible foundations to people's cultures. The nature of the church of Jesus Christ is that it is comfortable with these different cultural values. We tend to dismiss each other and disconnect too easily.

We also need to be careful that when we plant churches in towns or countries or continents, we do not leave them to wither in complete isolation. The Church of God in the Dominican Republic (chapter 2) does a great job of making sure that people not only remain connected but that those Church of God cultural values continue to be transmitted across the geographical regions in the country.

It is also important to make sure that our conferences are open to the widest group of people possible. If our conventions or camp meetings become something that only a small portion of people in our movement can relate to, then that creates disconnection. There is definitely a need for regional meetings and also meetings between subgroups in the Church of God. I see no problem with the Pastor's Fellowship, CMA, or West Virginia having their own conferences or camp meetings, for instance. This is needed, because they share either some cultural values or some purpose within the Church of God culture. But there also need to be conferences and get-togethers that look inviting to the widest array of people possible if we are to continue to know each other. The big ones have to be relevant to the most people.

Q: In this globalized world, the multicultural challenges seem immense. Does it look as if we are balkanizing into different Church of God cultures that don't want to relate to each other?

We are already balkanized, but it's not primarily a cultural problem. The biggest source of fragmentation is our organizational weakness and our excessive autonomy. This can be found all over the world and creates many Church of God islands.

I think our multicultural differences are less of an issue. Yes, there has been racism in our American history and in other parts of the world that also struggle with this issue. There have been regional divisions within countries because of something that happened in their county's history or something that happened in their Church of God history. There are also tribal divisions in some countries. But the future will be challenging for everyone to navigate for different reasons.

Basically, we are all missionaries now, and this is something we desperately need to internalize. Whether you live in Germany, China, or Nebraska, you are now living in a more interconnected world, and more ethnic groups are moving into your neighborhood. Globalization has ushered in a period of massive migration, which is changing the face of Ireland, Australia, and everyplace in between. All churches now have to deal with new local and global realities that were not so pressing before. Fortunately, many people, especially the younger generations, are embracing this fact and feel perfectly comfortable with it.

The bigger challenge in the future will not be race but class. From Lebanon to Los Angeles, we are seeing a significant divide between the upper class, the emerging middle class, and the poor. There's been a dramatic influx of wealth in much of the world that is creating new divisions and new cultures in places that were once more homogenous as far as class is concerned. As we saw in Torrance (chapter 7), these different economic classes can, at times, process the faith very differently. In general, there's far more religious skepticism around the world among the wealthy (and usually less dynamism).

Since the end of the cold war, globalization and urbanization have created a new, large class of urbane citizens who have upper class and middle class mentalities. This is something I have seen firsthand. So the mentality and the preconceptions of people are becoming more like the educated, skeptical Western mind as far as religion is concerned. In places of rapid modernization, religious fervor and dynamism spikes, but it eventually settles down into comfort. So this influx of wealth and global connectivity is changing countries, challenging traditions, and creating new class divides.

We need to be careful not to analyze our multicultural issues using paradigms from the previous eras. All of our countries and religious environments are changing rapidly.

Q: Despite the new wealth in the world, many churches are struggling financially. Is money a problem for the Church of God congregations, institutions, and organizations you visited?

Yes. The Church of God, like many other Christian organizations and denominations, has benefited from an era of excessive liquidity between 1991 and 2008. It has transformed our societies, but the excess cash cannot continue indefinitely. There is no doubt that globalization has raised living standards and given formerly poor countries (such as Brazil and China) the opportunity to enter a new era of economic development. However, a large part of this new wealth has been based on speculative investment. In 2008, the world entered into a global recession. While some are predicting that the recession will end, my belief is that the era of excessive liquidity is over. Money will not be as easily available for churches, missions, and Christian organizations as it was in the past. Believing that it will, could be a fatal miscalculation. While it's true that our Lord owns the cattle on a thousand hills (Ps 50:10), most places are struggling financially, and money often doesn't come in to the extent that people want. The church (around the world) has gotten used to expecting funds too easily, leading us to create ministries with high overheads. I think we continue to do this at our peril. The age of excessive liquidity was an aberration, a moment in time.

Consequently, as we go forward, we need to capture the spirit of the early pioneers and try to do high impact ministry with the lowest cost. There will be some initiatives that will be expensive and worth the expense (the World Conference comes to mind). But in general, it would be wise to be very cautious.

Tithing as a spiritual discipline needs to be emphasized so that we do not fall prey to a spirit of mammon. Whatever we do as a movement will require money, and there is probably a lot we can do if we are all willing to sacrifice. But our structures probably need to be lean and clearly dedicated to mission and healthy connectivity.

Q: If the Church of God reformation movement were able to mobilize for mission in the name of holiness and unity and connect ourselves ecclesiastically speaking, would this solve our challenges?

A stronger emphasis on our relationship to each other and a missionary emphasis based on our key strengths would be a very good start. However, if we do not add a well-articulated theology as one of our core pillars, we can easily fragment. We are entering into what many call "a post-theological age." But there's really no such thing. The traditional church in the traditional world has been good about understanding the importance of theology. However, some of the work that God is doing in the non-Western Book of Acts world and in the post-Christendom world do not neatly fit into our previous categories. The traditional church will be tempted to be inflexible (more inflexible than Christianity inherently is) as the other two worlds grow in influence. At the same time, both the non-Western world and the Emerging/missional church of the post-Christendom world can too easily deemphasize theology to the point of danger. There is a lot of theological heresy being practiced in the church today, and we need to set guards against it through coherent theological education. In the Emerging/missional church, it will increasingly become clearer that theology does matter. Theological beliefs affect our Christian core even when we are not conscious of them. The twenty-first century with its paradox of excessive pluralism and fundamentalism combined with new technological innovations will lead the church to wrestle anew with theological issues, and the Emerging/missional church needs to not underestimate this.

III. Final Questions

Q: Were there commonalities among the dynamic Church of God ministries in your journey?

Yes. In my travels, the healthiest churches, organizations, and regions have possessed the following four traits:

1. *A leader with a high intelligence and, more importantly, a high emotional quotient (EQ).* We've been skittish about leaders, but the places that seem to be succeeding have smart leadership and it is clear who the empowered leaders are. The leaders make the right decisions, and they think through issues well. But most importantly, they are intuitive people with great people skills. They know how to emotionally relate and communicate with their people. They can bring people on board by meeting them where they are and articulating what is possible.

2. *A willingness to mobilize for change.* The best leader in the world will not be able to mobilize people who are not wanting anything to change. The most successful churches and organizations that I saw are filled with people who are ready to go on a mission, and they are all planning to contribute in one way or another. This is surprisingly absent in many churches and organizations because we are drawn toward the familiar and don't like change and risk. Stagnation almost seems to be the default position of many churches and organizations. But those filled with people willing to go on an adventure seem to have a lot more dynamism.

3. *A willingness to reexamine and change structures and methods when needed.* Everything requires recalibration, and even a successful leader and a pliable people will make mistakes. Consequently, the healthiest churches and organizations that I saw have open systems. They are continually open to change, renewal, and recalibration. They are open to criticism, are not defensive, and are introspective. Criticism is not threatening, and they are not worried about saving face. There is never the assumption that "we have it all figured out" or "we "don't need to fix anything."

4. *A strong God-given vision and purpose that the church believes in.* The leader, the church, and the organization need to have a vision that is easy to articulate and understand. The healthiest ministries I found on my journey were those that really have a concrete direction. They do not just meet or have generic goals that could fit any Christian organization, but rather they are on a specific forward-looking mission that separates them from the masses.

Q: You have shared how on your journey you saw holiness and unity play important roles in the larger church. You also shared that the inherently decentralized nature of the Church of God fits this new era well. What would it look like for this to turn into a movement again?

It would require us making an effort to get to know each other again. We would have to give up being content with our passivity and isolationism. We would need to get curious about each other again. We could do this through prayer, fasting, conferences, books, cross-cultural exchanges, and theological dialogue aimed at identifying what we are doing around the globe. We would need to listen without prejudice.

Then we would need to rearticulate our message of holiness and unity framed for the twenty-first century, aware that it will be filtered through many contexts and cultures. Then we would need to intentionally remain connected and stay on our special task. Proactive connection and reflection is what would be necessary. But there's no getting around it: it requires a level of leadership and connection that has traditionally made us uncomfortable in the past.

Q: You've mentioned many different kinds of challenges, but what about the spiritual challenge?

Originally, I had planned to include that as a chapter. But as the journey went on, I began to see that everything we are talking about is a spiritual challenge. It's a spiritual challenge for an organization and its leaders to embrace risk and take chances. It's a spiritual challenge to deal with the new multicultural challenges in our neighborhoods. It's a spiritual challenge to connect ourselves to others for greater accountability, as the church in

New Zealand has done (chapter 6). The spiritual challenge begins now for the Church of God. Are we going to slumber and decline as a family in the twenty-first century, or are we going to open ourselves up to a spiritual task greater than our own local interests?

There is also not much Scripture in this book. I am not seeking to tell the Church of God what to do and back up my prescriptions with Scripture. The theological and biblical discussions come now, and I hope that we invite college students as well as respected older leaders. I hope we invite Africans as well as people from the United States. My intention has been to just create the parameters so that we do not use Scripture in a way that comes out of our local context as opposed to the global situation the entire movement finds itself in at this point and time. It's easy to revert to the provincial. And this is not only the tendency of Americans, I might add. It's a human thing.

Q: What is your hope for this book?

My hope is that it will not only generate temporary discussion among individuals but that regions and countries within the Church of God will begin dialoguing about how to create a greater interconnectivity with the purpose of fulfilling God's special task for us as a movement. I hope it is catalytic, and I hope people discuss, critique, elaborate, and expound on what I have shared. I don't aim to have the final word. Quite the opposite!

I hope that people take this discussion much farther than I ever could. That's the whole point. Perhaps that could be through forums, through conferences, through a World Conference, through seminary students writing papers and scholars writing books, or online. I don't know how this will be processed, but I hope we seize the day. Our discussions cannot be as generic or oblivious to the new complicated realities as they have been in the past. There are no easy answers or quick solutions. The way of Jesus is tough.

Q: Are there any final thoughts you have on the Church of God?

I'm tired now and need a long nap. But I will say this: I believe that God called us together for a special purpose. The fact that we are now so diverse is a testament to how many different cultures and peoples have accepted our message. It is something we should celebrate and not fear, because fear is the enemy of mission. Our forward motion as a movement is being challenged, but every day God acts through our churches, organizations, institutions, and people. We can be proud of our family even though we are not perfect. The family has grown and has become diverse and multicultural, and sub-families have arisen. Perhaps it is time for a family reunion. If we follow the ways of the world, we will disconnect. If we follow the way of the Spirit, we will seize upon these challenges and find strength out of our weakness. As Dr. Sheldon Sorge of the Louisville Institute suggested to me when I visited him in Louisville to discuss our challenge, we will need to ask ourselves, "What does it mean for us to lay down our life for the church?"

I believe if we lose our life for the church, we will find it. These are your brothers and sisters out there. Wouldn't it be great to see the Church of God mosaic for yourself with your own two eyes? It's up to you.

"Thus wisdom about our destiny is dependent upon a humble recognition of the limits of our knowledge and our power. Our most reliable understanding is the fruit of 'grace' in which faith completes our ignorance without pretending to possess its certainties as knowledge; and in which contrition mitigates our pride without destroying our hope."

—Reinhold Niebuhr[1]

1. *The Nature and Destiny of Man*, vol. 2 (New York: Scribners, 1943), 321.